WET MOON

WHERE ALL STARS FAIL TO BURN

5

ONI PRESS

AN ONI PRESS PUBLICATION

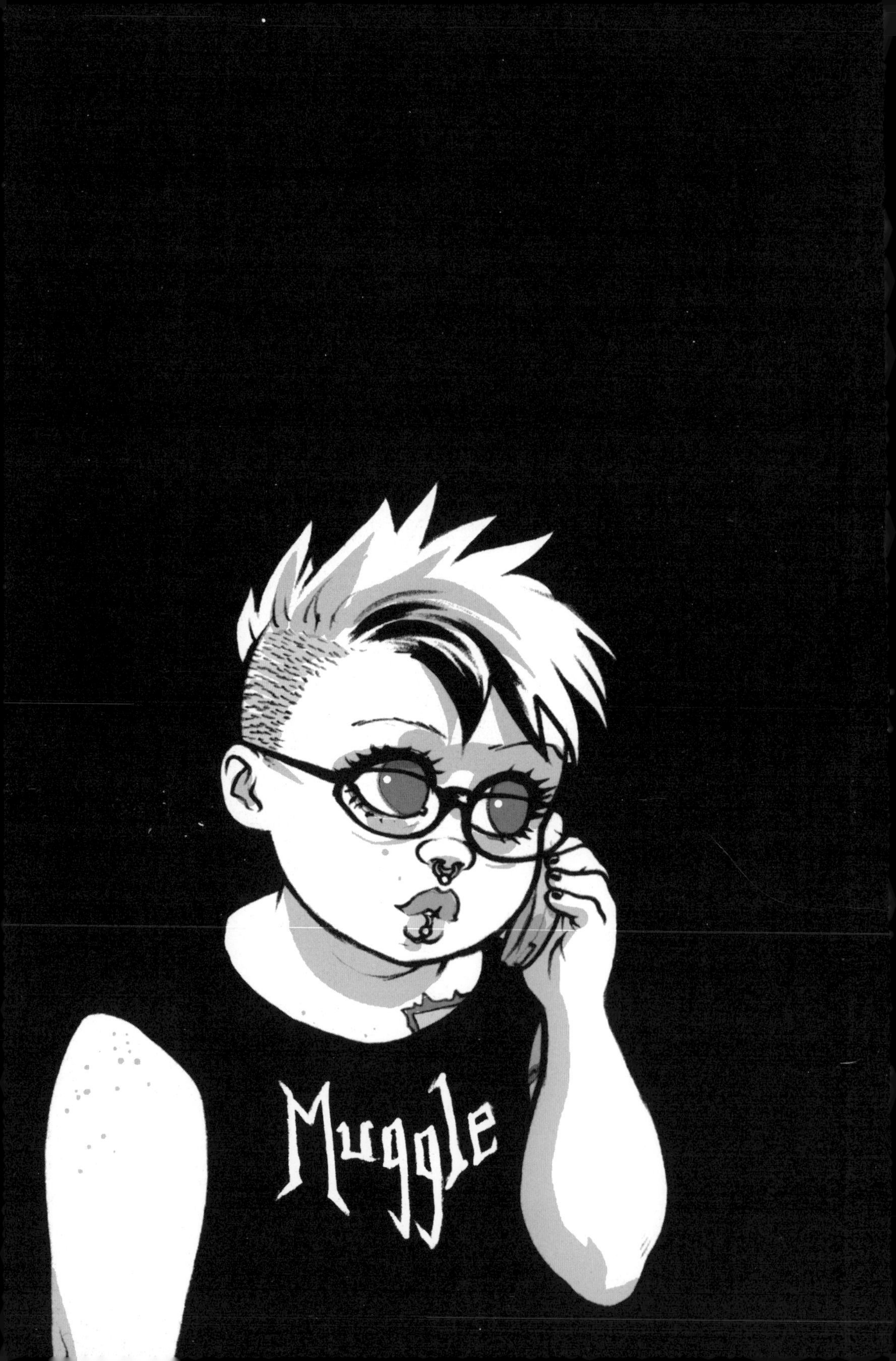
Muggle

WET MOON

WHERE ALL STARS FAIL TO BURN

5

written and illustrated by **sophie campbell**

cleo's diary pages by **jessica calderwood**

cover design by **annie mok**

book design by **hilary thompson & angie knowles**

first edition edited by **douglas sherwood & james lucas jones**

new edition edited by **robin herrera**

PUBLISHED BY ONI PRESS, INC.

Joe Nozemack, *publisher*

James Lucas Jones, *editor in chief*

Brad Rooks, *director of operations*

David Dissanayake, *director of sales*

Rachel Reed, *publicity manager*

Melissa Meszaros MacFadyen, *marketing assitant*

Troy Look, *director of design & production*

Hilary Thompson, *graphic designer*

Kate Z. Stone, *junior graphic designer*

Angie Knowles, *digital prepress technician*

Ari Yarwood, *managing editor*

Charlie Chu, *senior editor*

Robin Herrera, *editor*

Desiree Wilson, *associate editor*

Alissa Sallah, *administrative assistant*

Jung Lee, *logistics associate*

ONIPRESS.COM
FACEBOOK.COM/ONIPRESS
TWITTER.COM/ONIPRESS
ONIPRESS.TUMBLR.COM
INSTAGRAM.COM/ONIPRESS

First Edition: December 2017

ISBN 978-1-62010-331-9
eISBN 978-1-62010-367-8

Printed in China.
Library of Congress Control Number: 2017941899

1 2 3 4 5 6 7 8 9 10

1. Bowden House
2. Vance House
3. Smith House
4. Westmiller House
5. Weitz Hall
6. Polsky Hall
7. Yardley Hall
8. Joseph Hall
9. Simmons Hall
10. Page Hall
11. Meyer Hall
12. Steve Hall
13. Burial Grounds
14. Head-Butt Video
15. House of Usher
16. Denny's
17. Marco's Diner
18. Trilby's Apartment
19. Swamp Things
20. Flower Power
21. Sundae Best
22. Audrey's apartment
23. Penny's apartment
24. Glen's apartment
25. Lorelei Cemetery
26. Polly Poster
27. Zurah Cemetery
28. softball field

wet moon

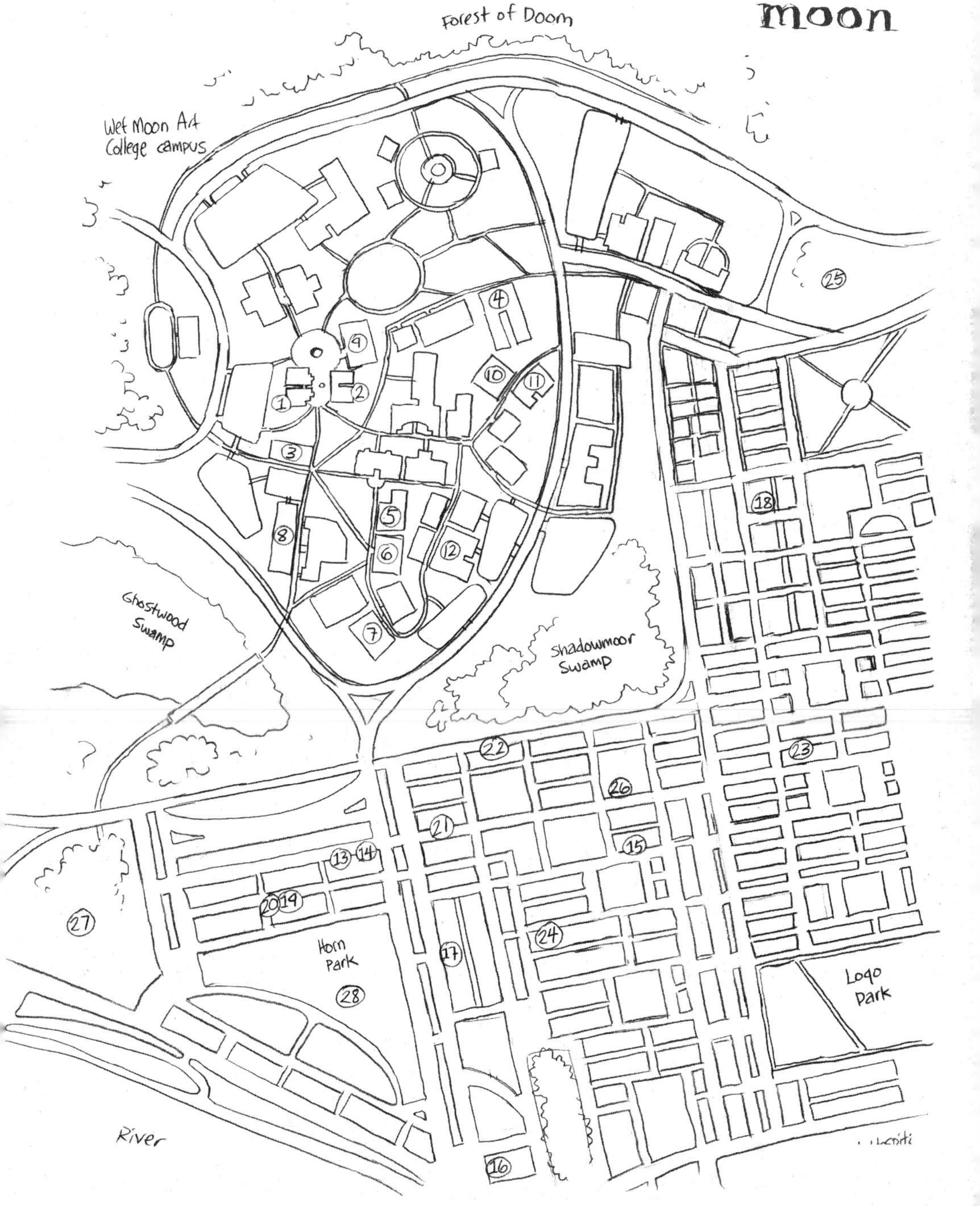

Forest of Doom
Wet Moon Art College campus
Ghostwood Swamp
Shadowmoor Swamp
Horn Park
Logo Park
River

29. The Swanhilde Residence
30. Wet Moon High School
31. The Shoe Tree
32. The Bernarde Residence
33. The Zuzanny Residence

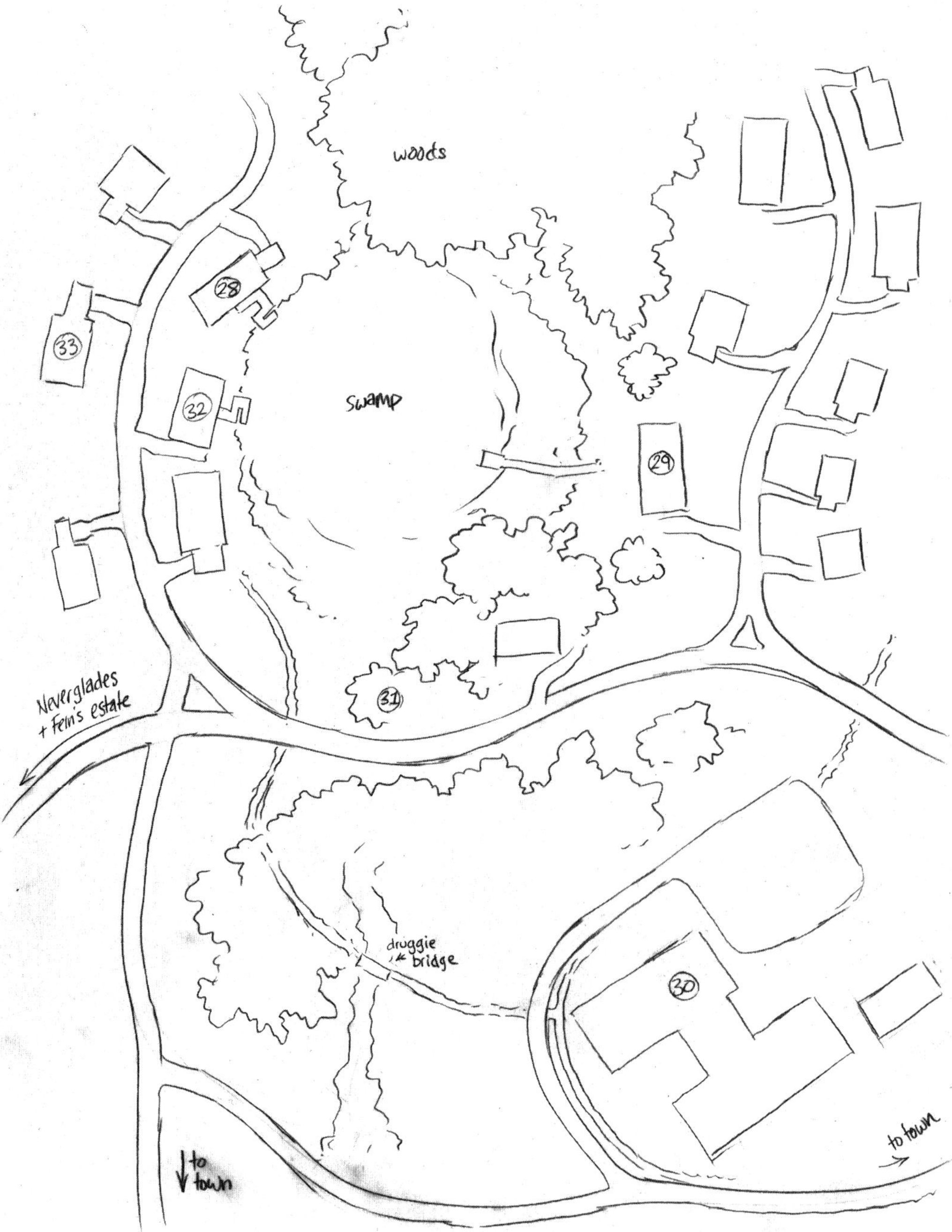
woods
swamp
28
33
32
29
31
30
Neverglades + Fein's estate
druggie bridge
to town
to town

22

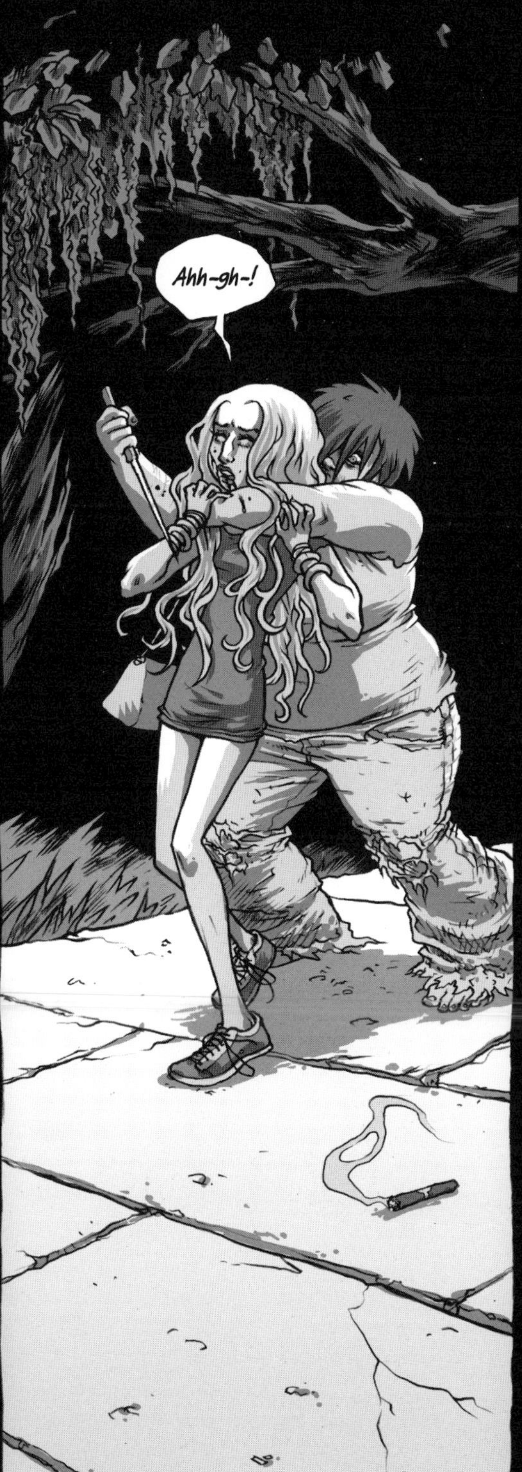
Ahh-gh-!

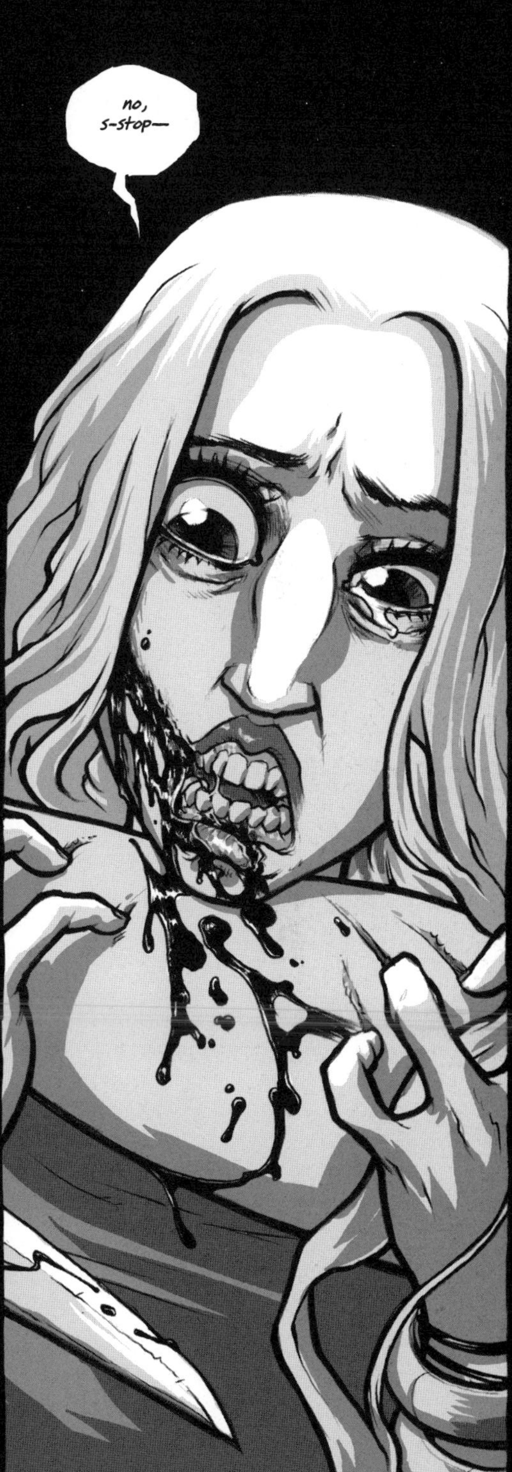
no,
s-stop—

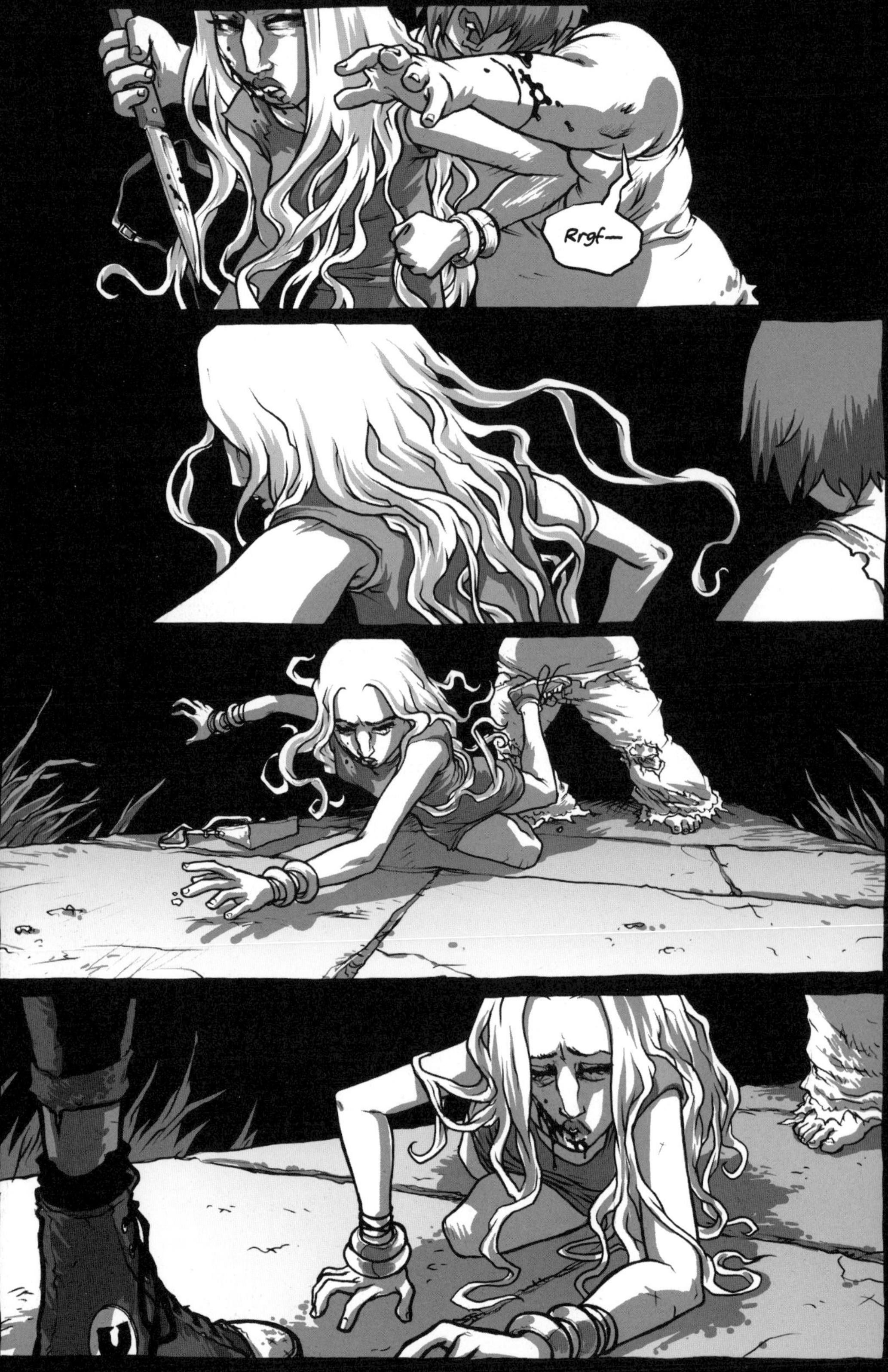
Rrgf—

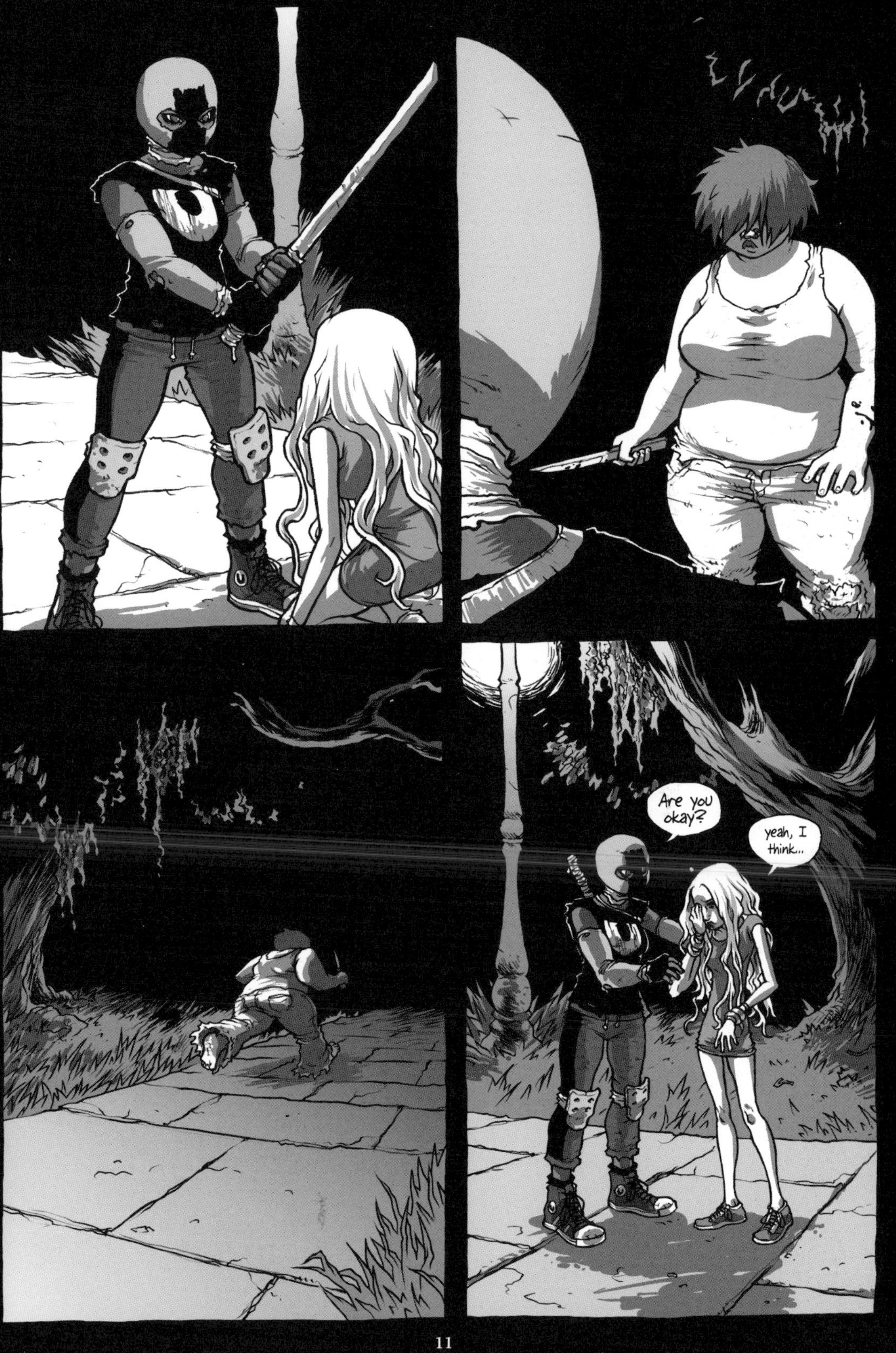
Are you okay?
yeah, I think...

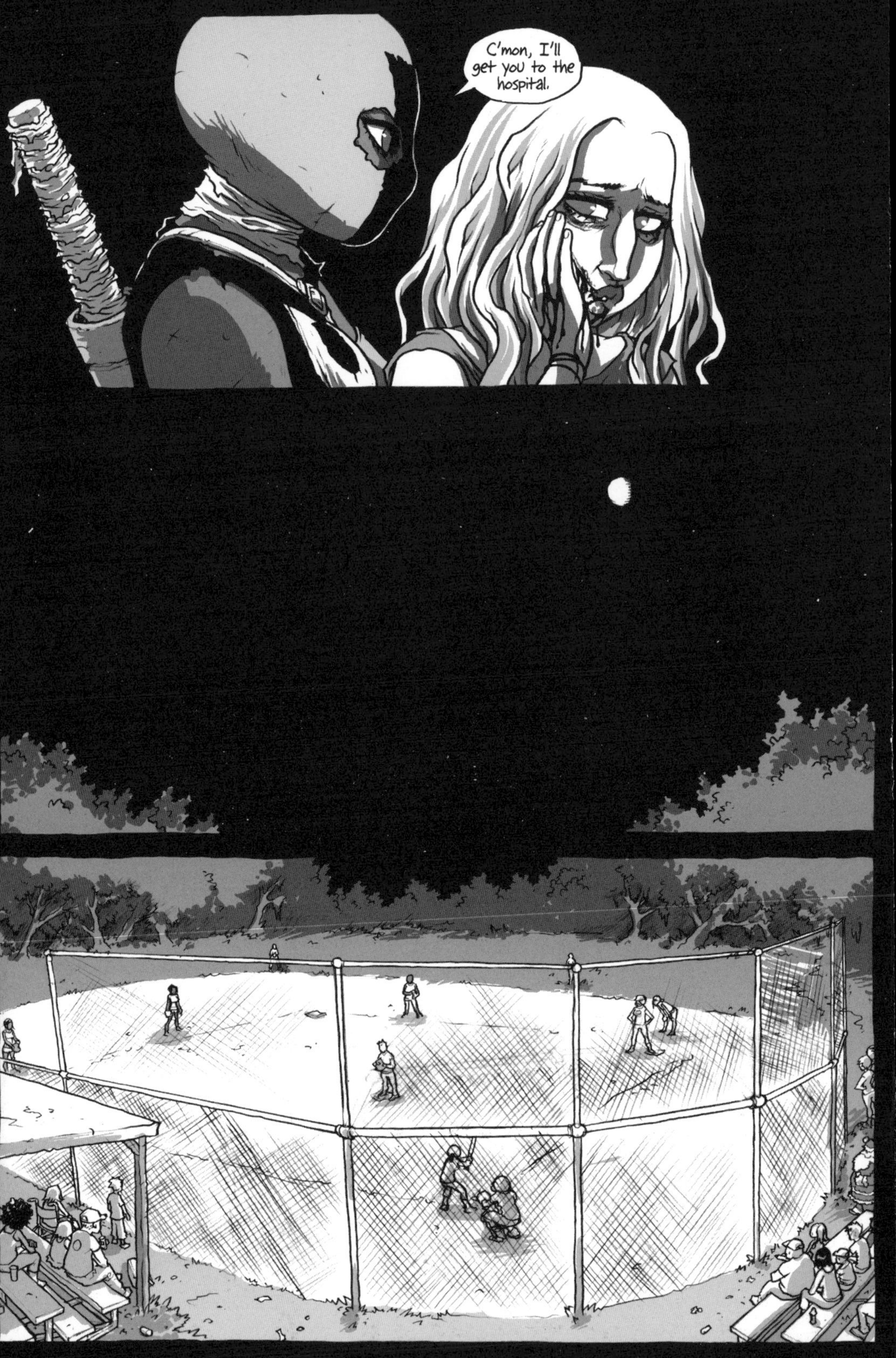
C'mon, I'll get you to the hospital.

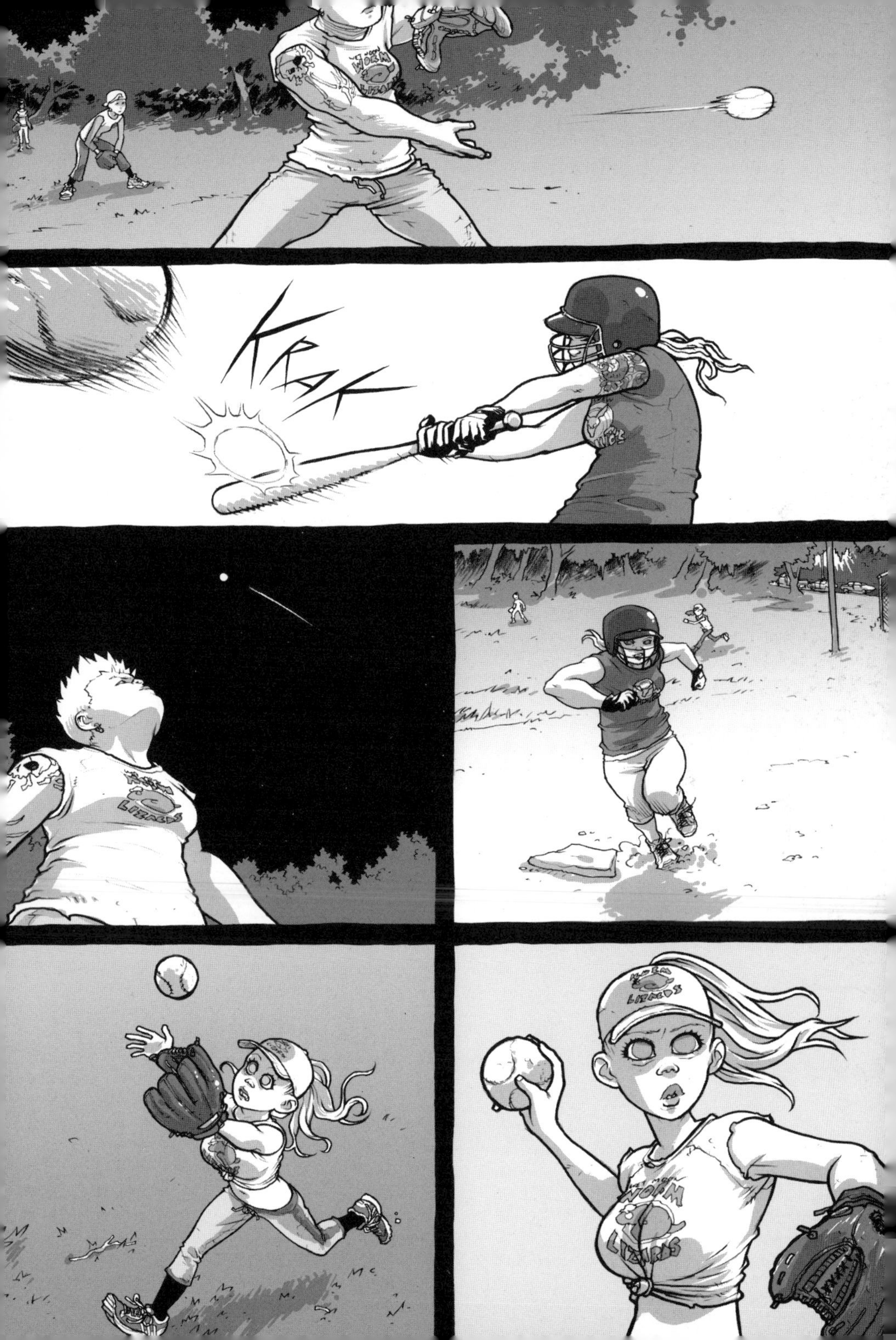
KRAK

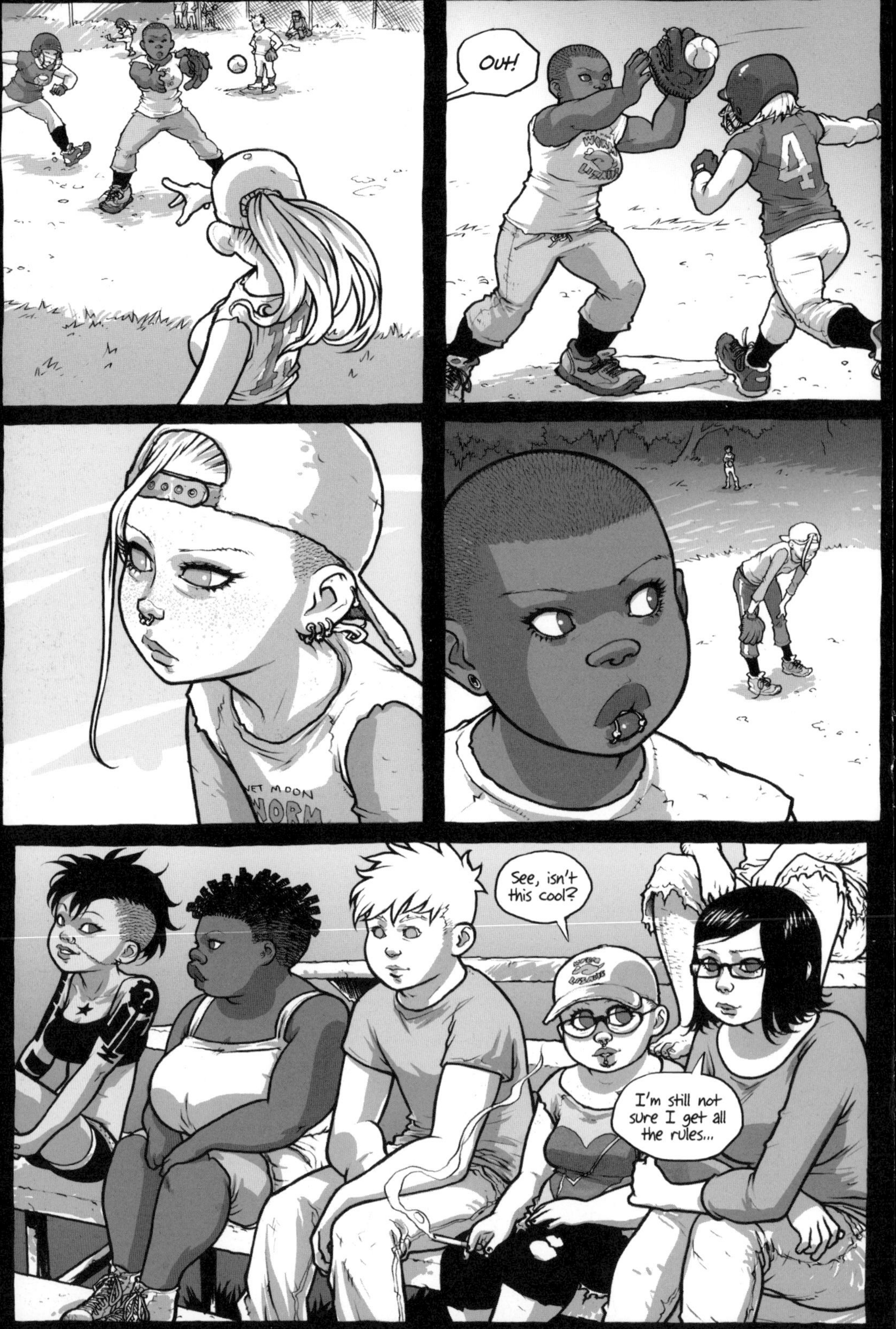
Out!
See, isn't this cool?
I'm still not sure I get all the rules...

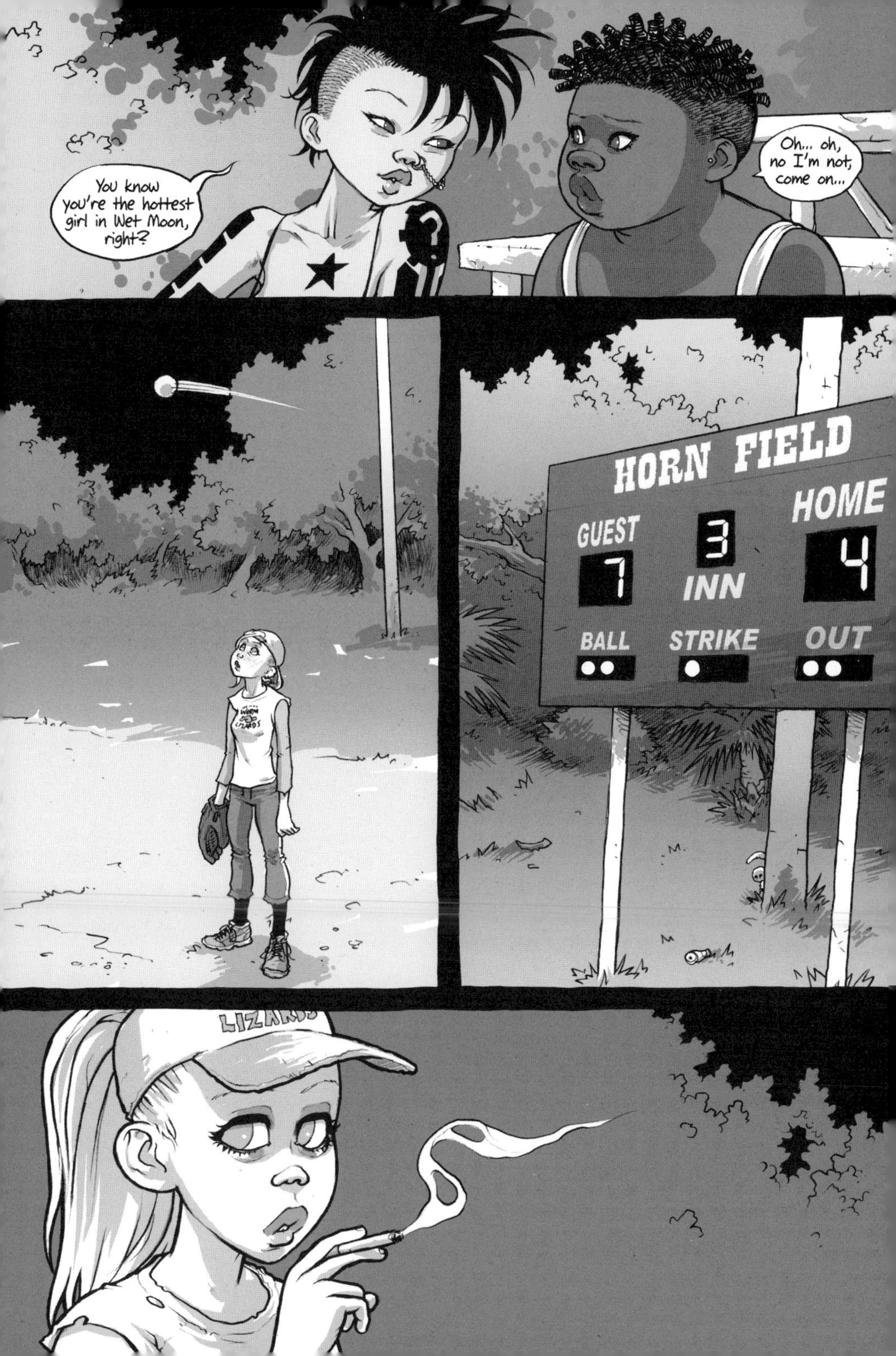
You know you're the hottest girl in Wet Moon, right?
Oh... oh, no I'm not, come on...
HORN FIELD
GUEST
7
3
INN
HOME
4
BALL
STRIKE
OUT
LIZARDS

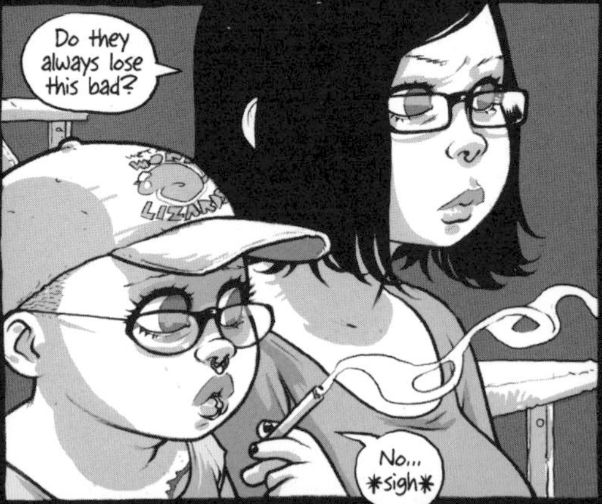
Do they always lose this bad?
No... *sigh*

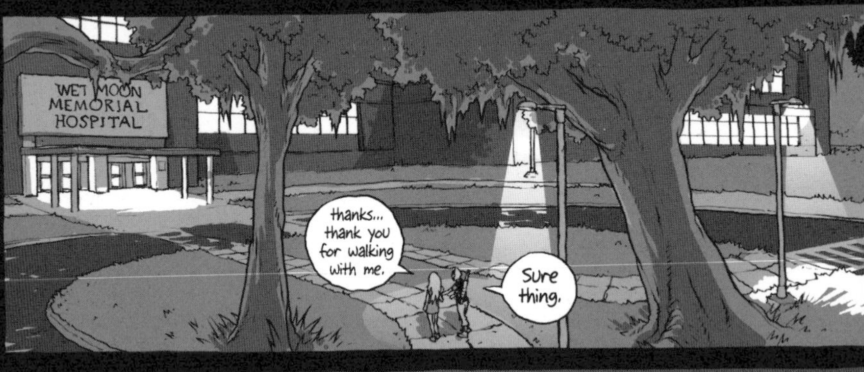
WET MOON MEMORIAL HOSPITAL
thanks... thank you for walking with me.
Sure thing.

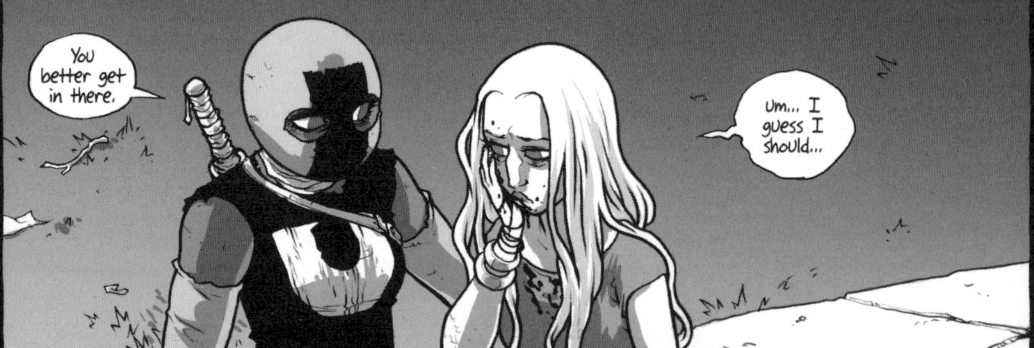
You better get in there.
Um... I guess I should...

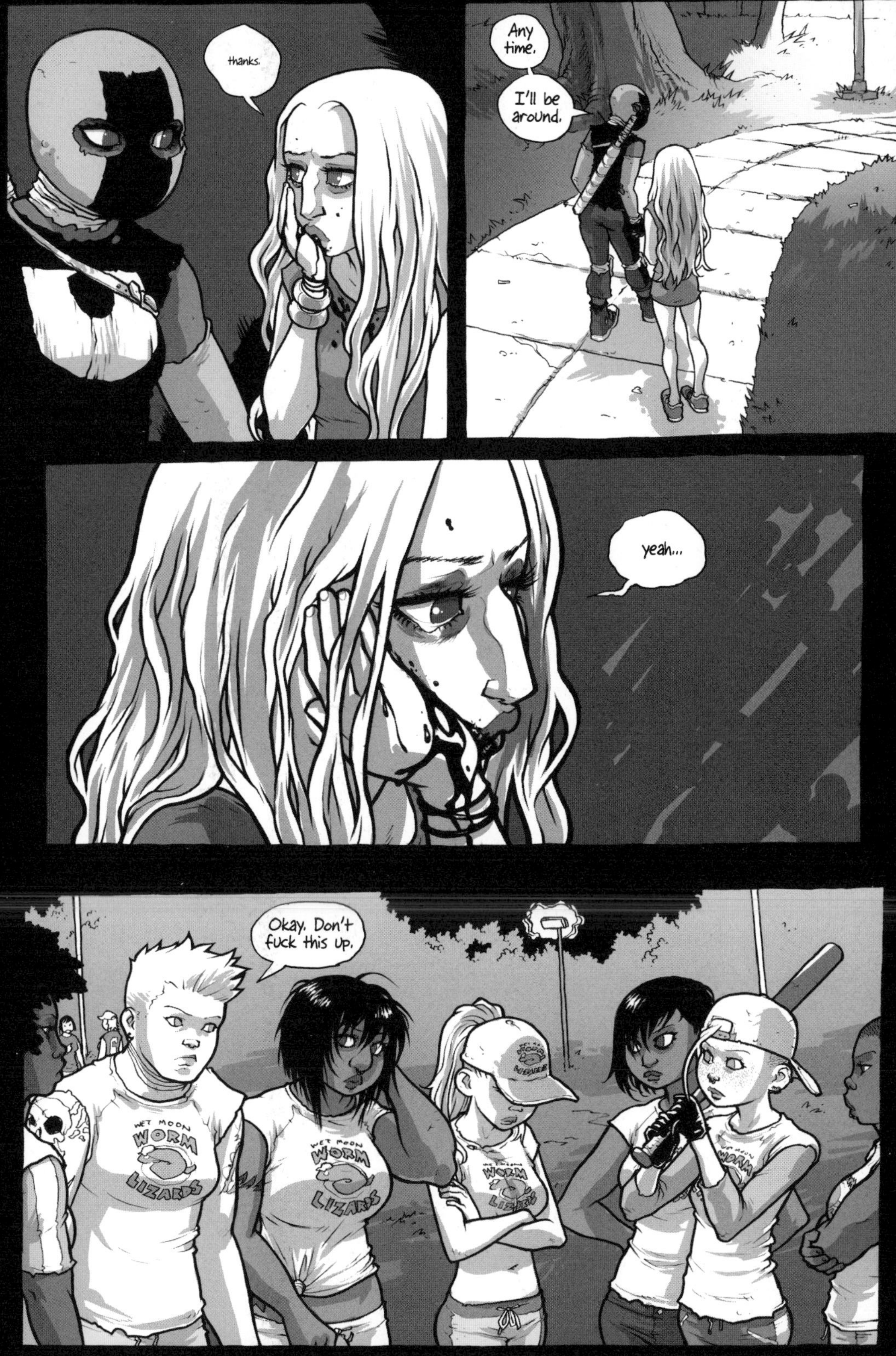
thanks.
Any time.
I'll be around.
yeah...
Okay. Don't fuck this up.
WET MOON WORM LIZARDS

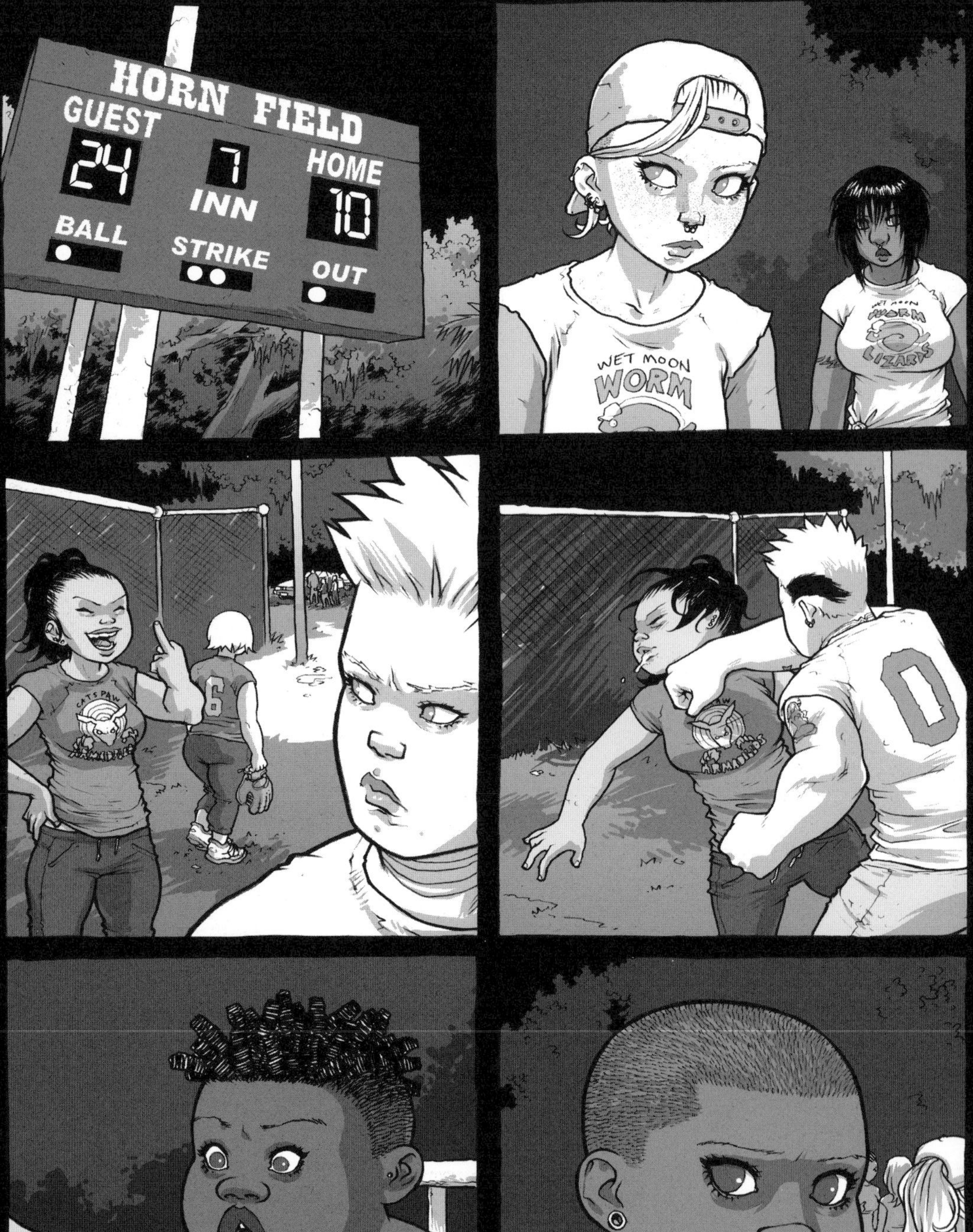
HORN FIELD
GUEST
24
7
HOME
INN
10
BALL
STRIKE
OUT
WET MOON
WORM
WET MOON
WORM
LIZARDS
6
0
13

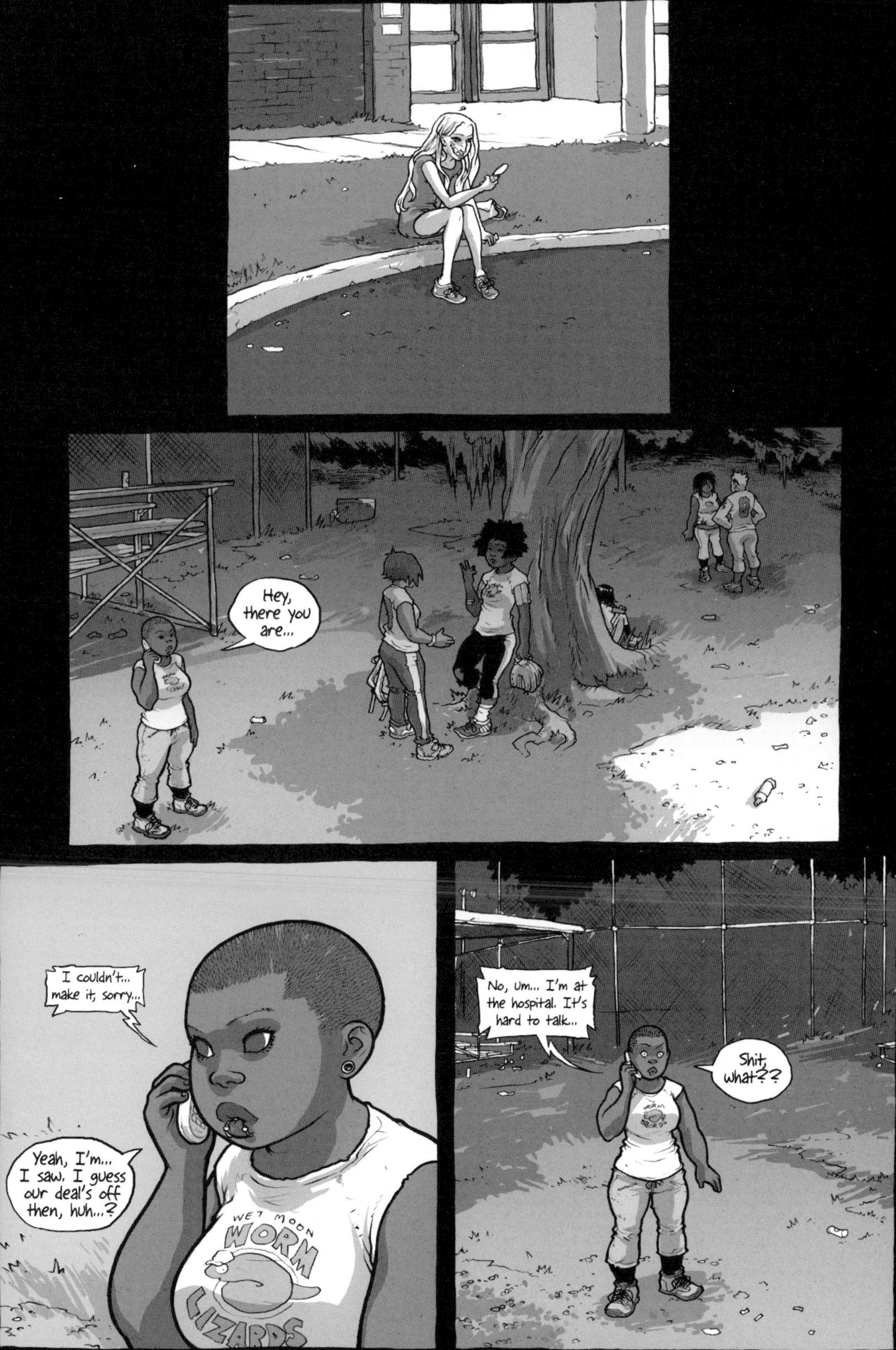
Hey, there you are...
I couldn't... make it, sorry...
Yeah, I'm... I saw. I guess our deal's off then, huh...?
WET MOON WORM LIZARDS
No, um... I'm at the hospital. It's hard to talk...
Shit, what??

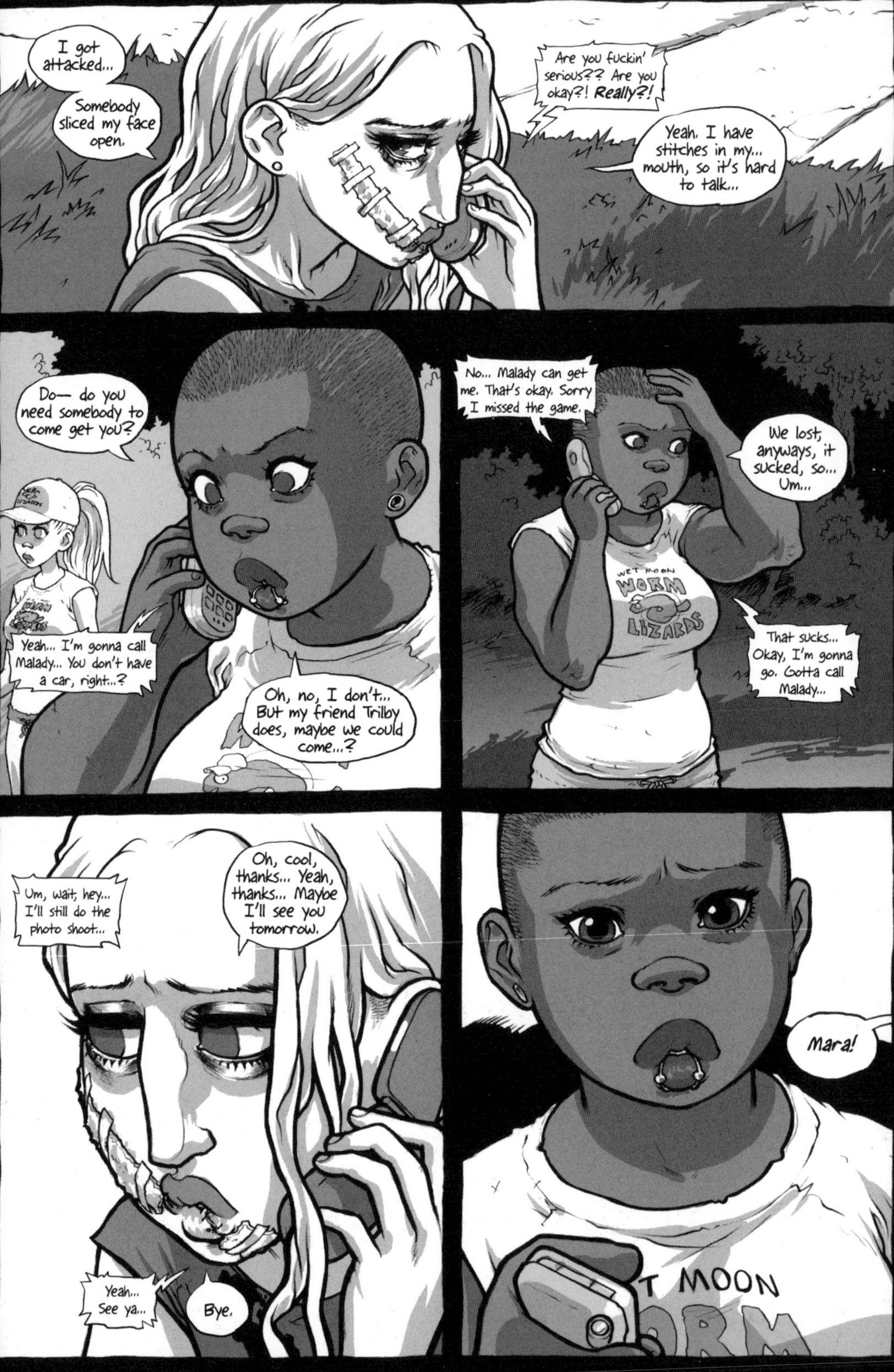

I got attacked...
Somebody sliced my face open.
Are you fuckin' serious?? Are you okay?! Really?!
Yeah. I have stitches in my... mouth, so it's hard to talk...
Do— do you need somebody to come get you?
Yeah... I'm gonna call Malady... You don't have a car, right...?
Oh, no, I don't... But my friend Trilby does, maybe we could come...?
No... Malady can get me. That's okay. Sorry I missed the game.
We lost, anyways, it sucked, so... Um...
WET MOON WORM LIZARDS
That sucks... Okay, I'm gonna go. Gotta call Malady...
Um, wait, hey... I'll still do the photo shoot...
Oh, cool, thanks... Yeah, thanks... Maybe I'll see you tomorrow.
Yeah... See ya...
Bye.
Mara!
T MOON

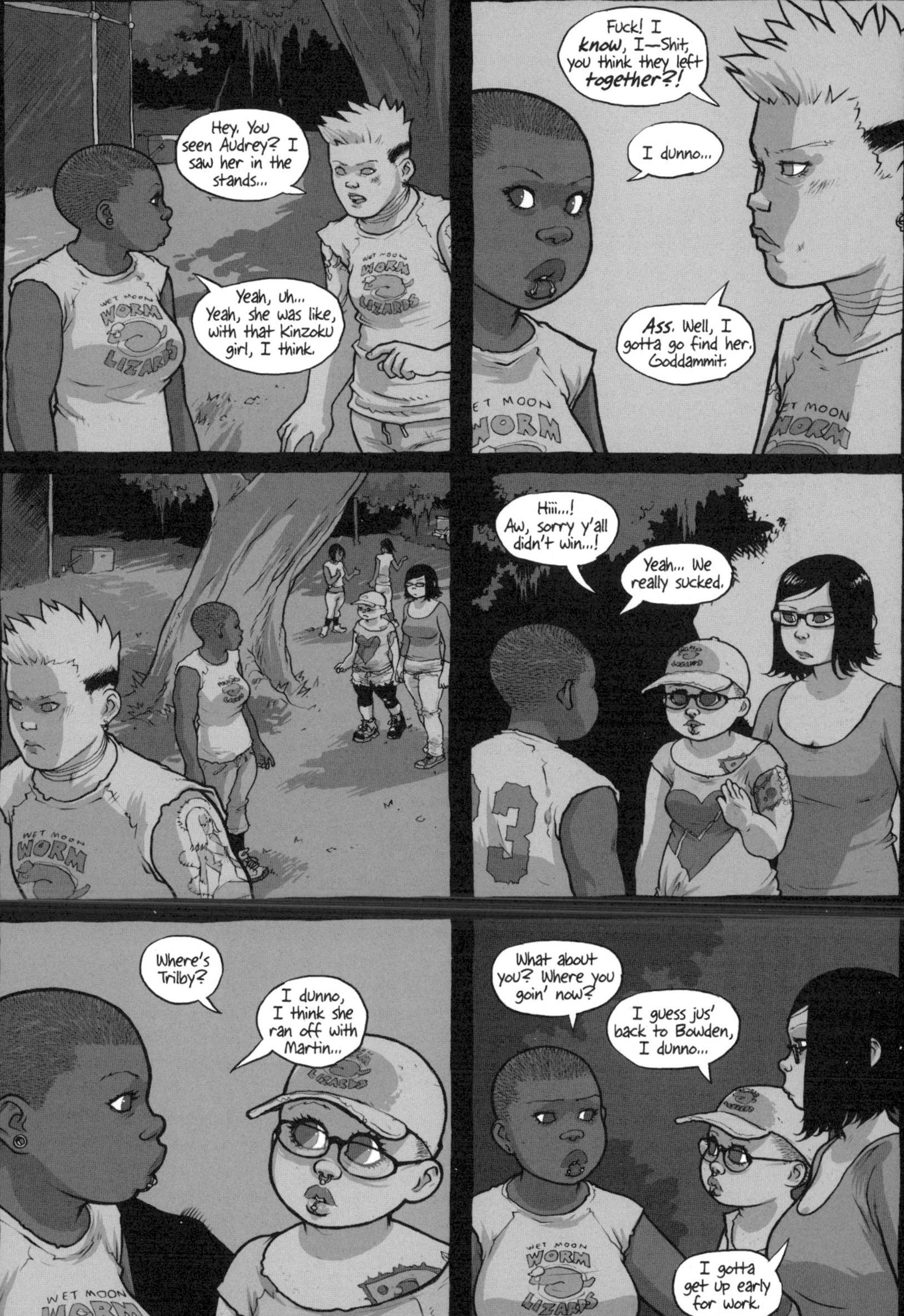
Hey. You seen Audrey? I saw her in the stands...
Yeah, uh... Yeah, she was like, with that Kinzoku girl, I think.
WET MOON WORM LIZARDS
Fuck! I know, I—Shit, you think they left together?!
I dunno...
Ass. Well, I gotta go find her. Goddammit.
WET MOON WORM
WET MOON WORM
Hiii...! Aw, sorry y'all didn't win...!
Yeah... We really sucked.
Where's Trilby?
I dunno, I think she ran off with Martin...
WET MOON WORM
What about you? Where you goin' now?
I guess jus' back to Bowden, I dunno...
WET MOON WORM LIZARDS
I gotta get up early for work.

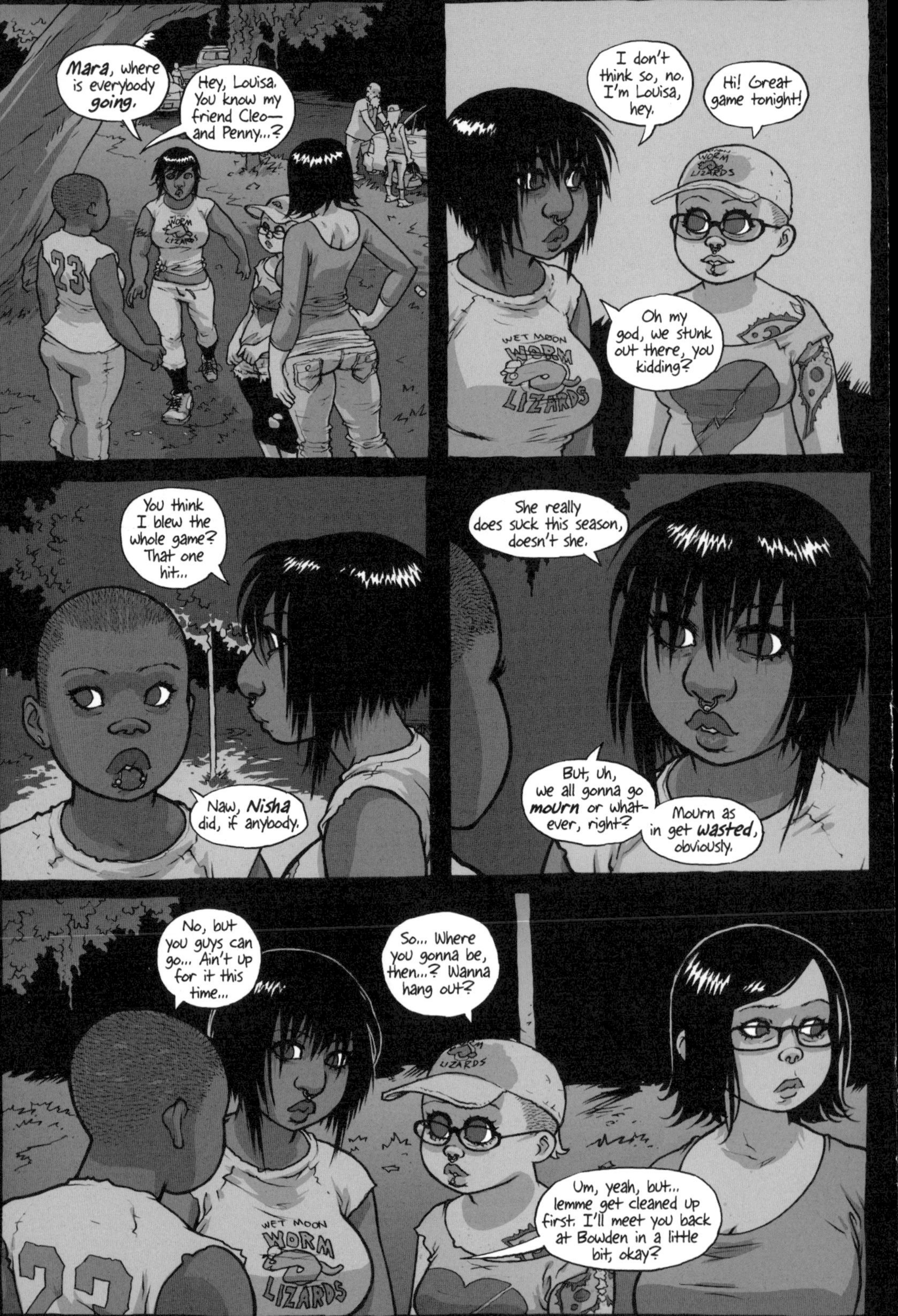
Mara, where is everybody going.
Hey, Louisa. You know my friend Cleo— and Penny...?
WORM LIZARDS
I don't think so, no. I'm Louisa, hey.
Hi! Great game tonight!
WORM LIZARDS
WET MOON WORM LIZARDS
Oh my god, we stunk out there, you kidding?
You think I blew the whole game? That one hit...
Naw, Nisha did, if anybody.
She really does suck this season, doesn't she.
But, uh, we all gonna go mourn or whatever, right?
Mourn as in get wasted, obviously.
No, but you guys can go... Ain't up for it this time...
So... Where you gonna be, then...? Wanna hang out?
LIZARDS
WET MOON WORM LIZARDS
Um, yeah, but... lemme get cleaned up first. I'll meet you back at Bowden in a little bit, okay?

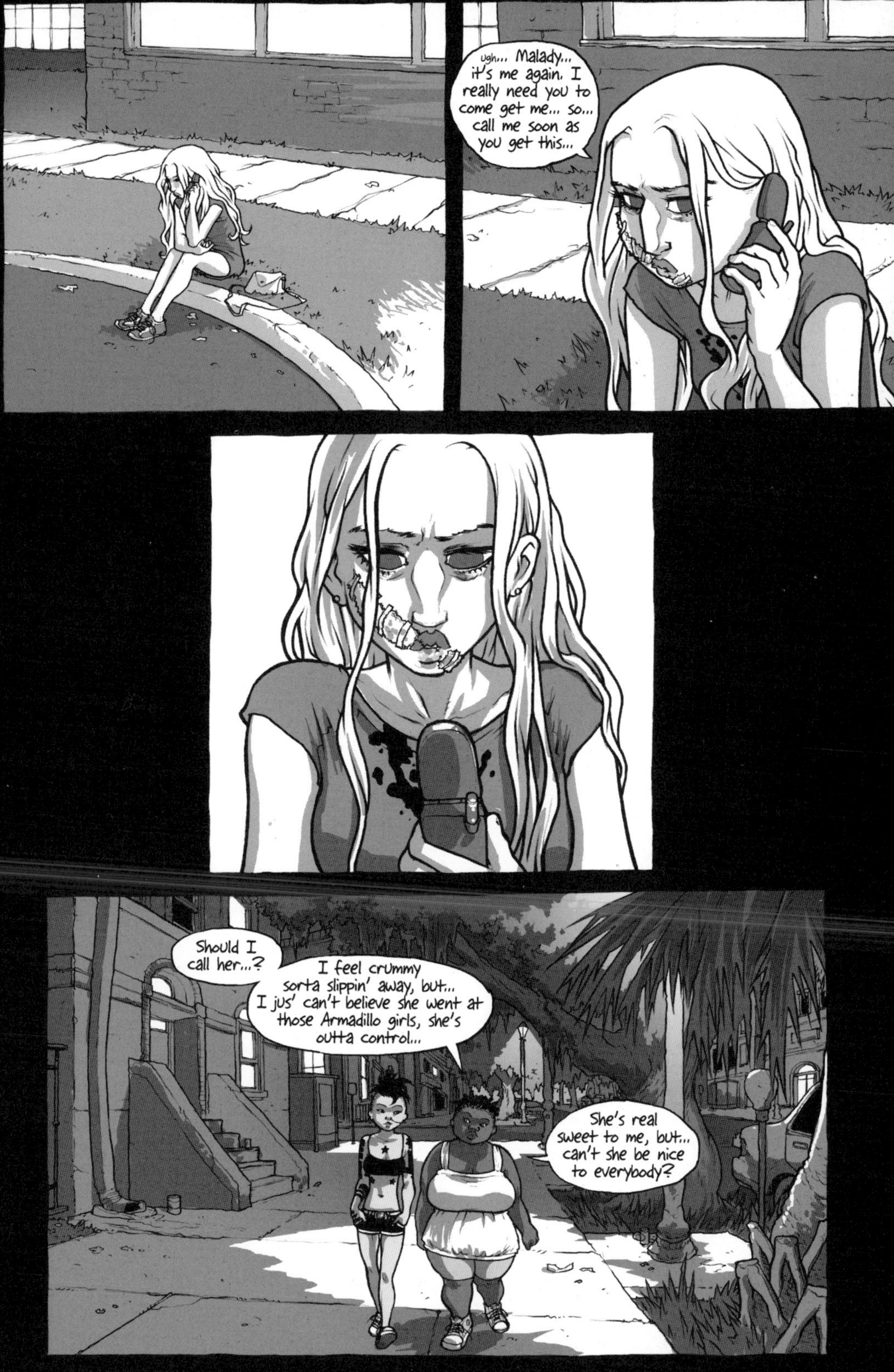
Ugh... Malady... it's me again. I really need you to come get me... so... call me soon as you get this...
Should I call her...?
I feel crummy sorta slippin' away, but... I jus' can't believe she went at those Armadillo girls, she's outta control...
She's real sweet to me, but... can't she be nice to everybody?

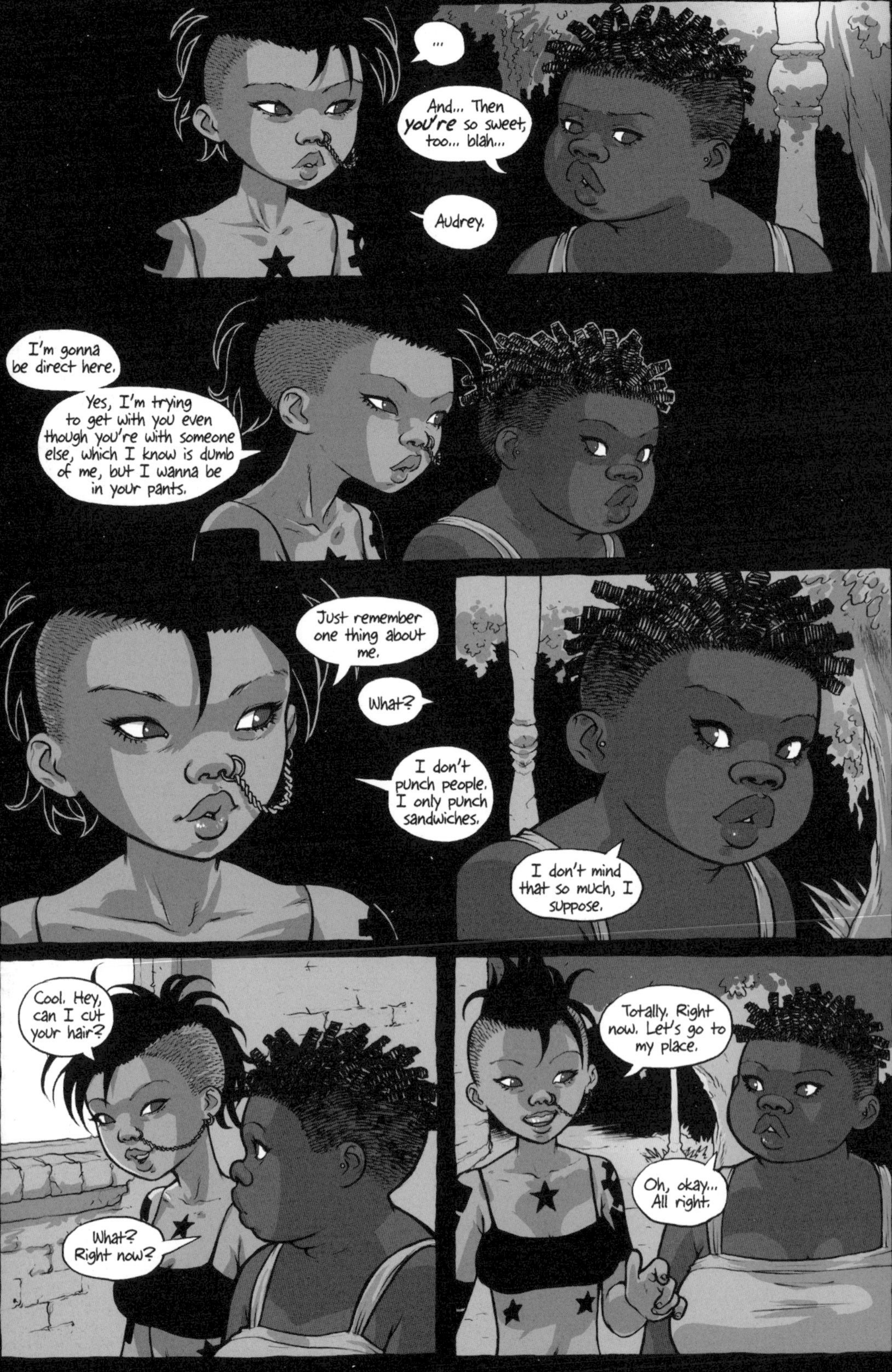
...
And... Then you're so sweet, too... blah...
Audrey.
I'm gonna be direct here.
Yes, I'm trying to get with you even though you're with someone else, which I know is dumb of me, but I wanna be in your pants.
Just remember one thing about me.
What?
I don't punch people. I only punch sandwiches.
I don't mind that so much, I suppose.
Cool. Hey, can I cut your hair?
What? Right now?
Totally. Right now. Let's go to my place.
Oh, okay... All right.

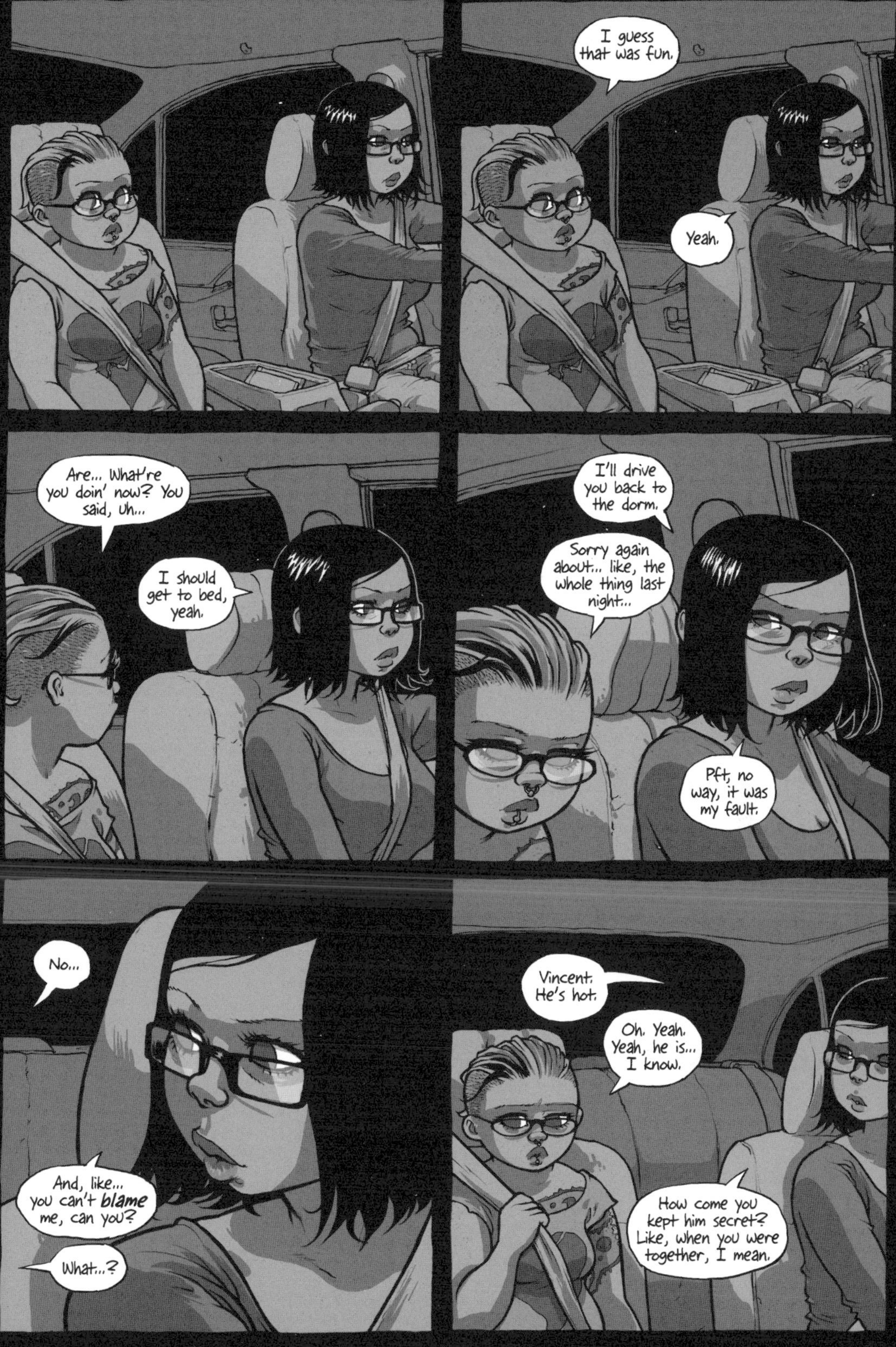
I guess that was fun.
Yeah.
Are... What're you doin' now? You said, uh...
I should get to bed, yeah.
I'll drive you back to the dorm.
Sorry again about... like, the whole thing last night...
Pft, no way, it was my fault.
No...
And, like... you can't **blame** me, can you?
What...?
Vincent. He's hot.
Oh. Yeah. Yeah, he is... I know.
How come you kept him secret? Like, when you were together, I mean.

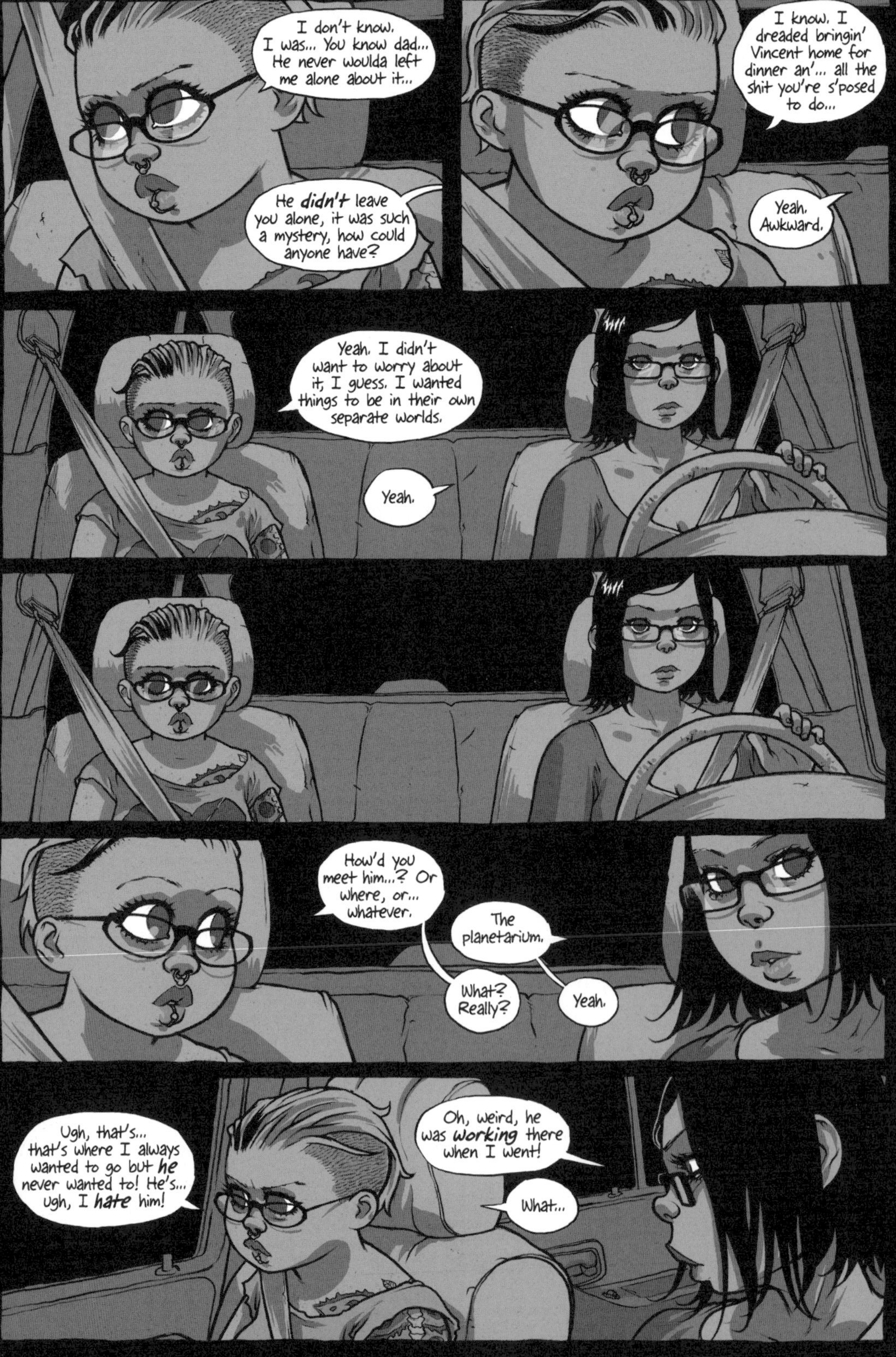
I don't know. I was... You know dad... He never woulda left me alone about it...
He **didn't** leave you alone, it was such a mystery, how could anyone have?
I know. I dreaded bringin' Vincent home for dinner an'... all the shit you're s'posed to do...
Yeah. Awkward.
Yeah. I didn't want to worry about it, I guess. I wanted things to be in their own separate worlds.
Yeah.
How'd you meet him...? Or where, or... whatever.
The planetarium.
What? Really?
Yeah.
Ugh, that's... that's where I always wanted to go but **he** never wanted to! He's... ugh, I **hate** him!
Oh, weird, he was **working** there when I went!
What...

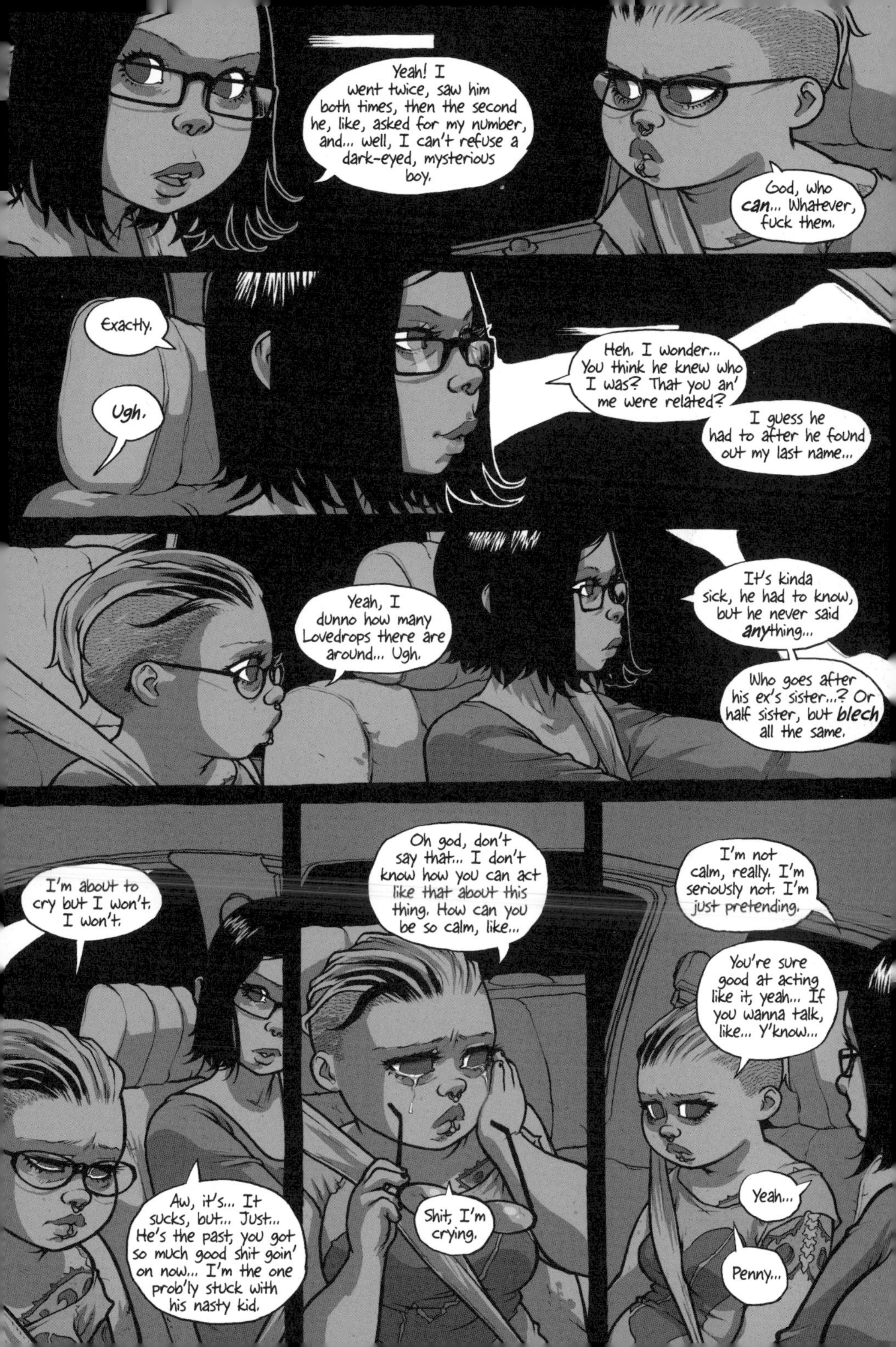
Yeah! I went twice, saw him both times, then the second he, like, asked for my number, and... well, I can't refuse a dark-eyed, mysterious boy.
God, who **can**... Whatever, fuck them.
Exactly.
Ugh.
Heh. I wonder... You think he knew who I was? That you an' me were related?
I guess he had to after he found out my last name...
Yeah, I dunno how many Lovedrops there are around... Ugh.
It's kinda sick, he had to know, but he never said **any**thing...
Who goes after his ex's sister...? Or half sister, but **blech** all the same.
I'm about to cry but I won't. I won't.
Aw, it's... It sucks, but... Just... He's the past, you got so much good shit goin' on now... I'm the one prob'ly stuck with his nasty kid.
Oh god, don't say that... I don't know how you can act like that about this thing. How can you be so calm, like...
Shit, I'm crying.
I'm not calm, really. I'm seriously not. I'm just pretending.
You're sure good at acting like it, yeah... If you wanna talk, like... Y'know...
Yeah...
Penny...

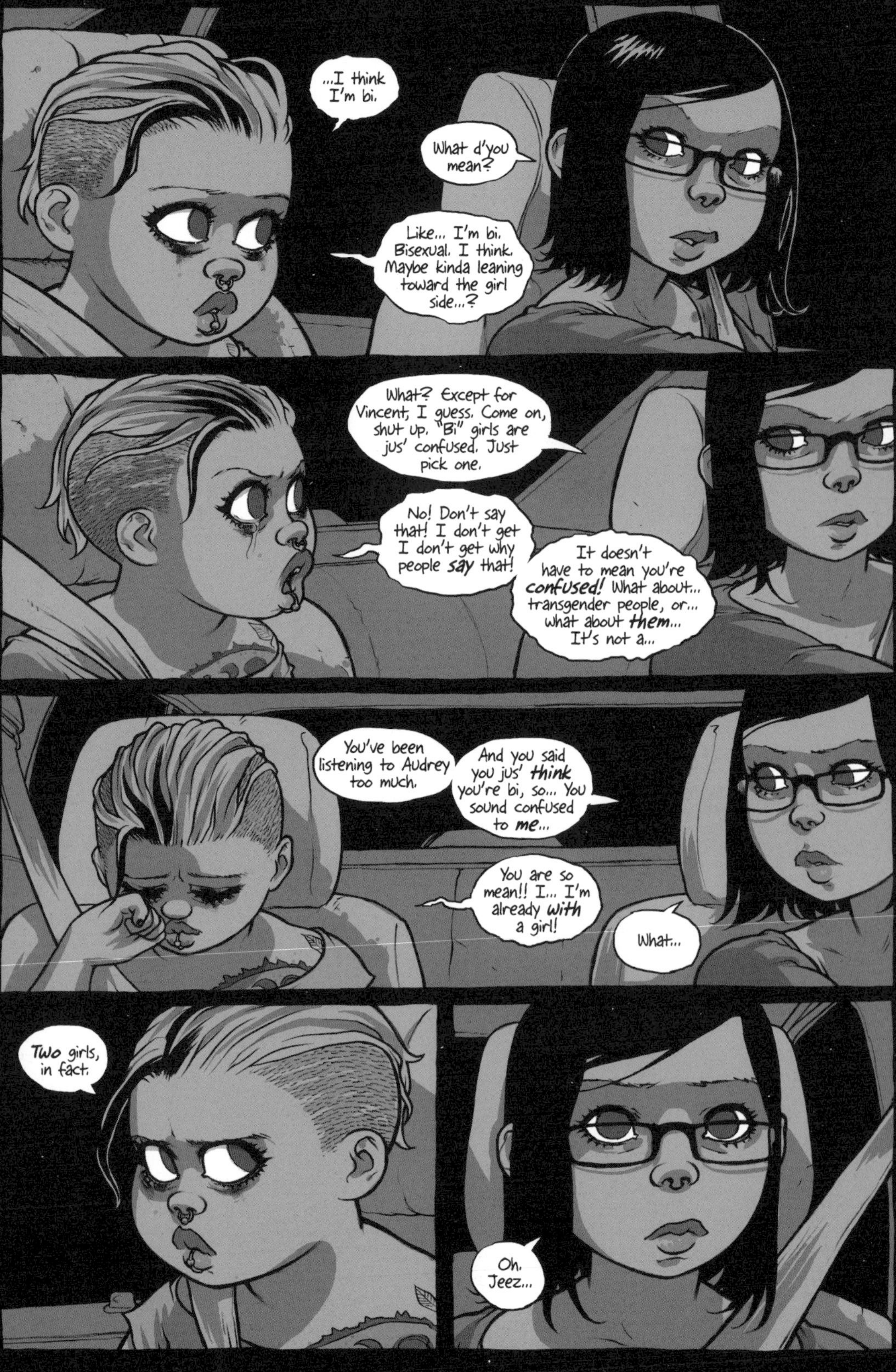
...I think I'm bi.
What d'you mean?
Like... I'm bi. Bisexual. I think. Maybe kinda leaning toward the girl side...?
What? Except for Vincent, I guess. Come on, shut up. "Bi" girls are jus' confused. Just pick one.
No! Don't say that! I don't get I don't get why people say that!
It doesn't have to mean you're confused! What about... transgender people, or... what about them... It's not a...
You've been listening to Audrey too much.
And you said you jus' think you're bi, so... You sound confused to me...
You are so mean!! I... I'm already with a girl!
What...
Two girls, in fact.
Oh. Jeez...

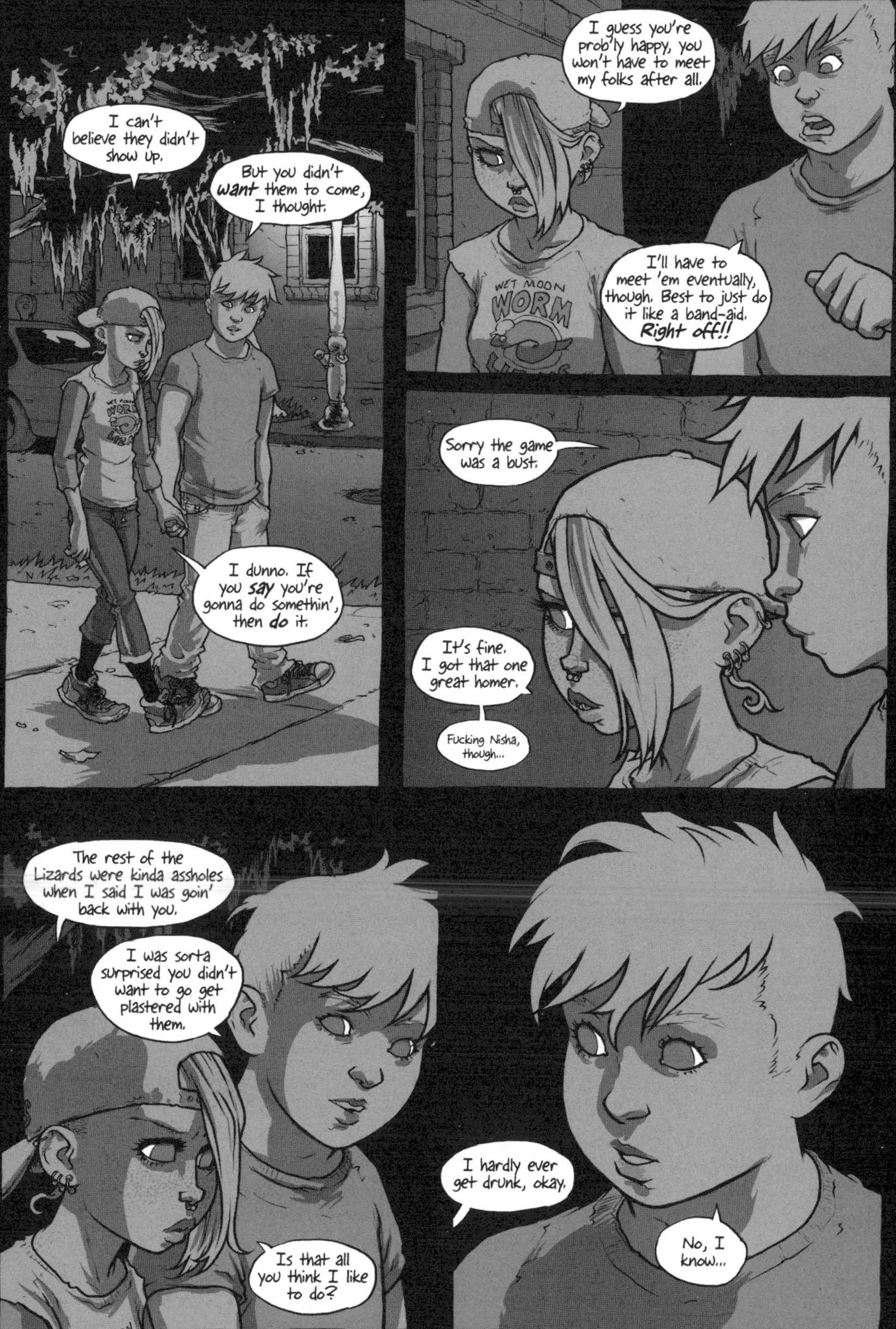
I can't believe they didn't show up.
But you didn't **want** them to come, I thought.
I dunno. If you **say** you're gonna do somethin', then **do** it.
I guess you're prob'ly happy, you won't have to meet my folks after all.
I'll have to meet 'em eventually, though. Best to just do it like a band-aid. **Right off!!**
WET MOON WORM
Sorry the game was a bust.
It's fine. I got that one great homer.
Fucking Nisha, though...
The rest of the Lizards were kinda assholes when I said I was goin' back with you.
I was sorta surprised you didn't want to go get plastered with them.
Is that all you think I like to do?
I hardly ever get drunk, okay.
No, I know...

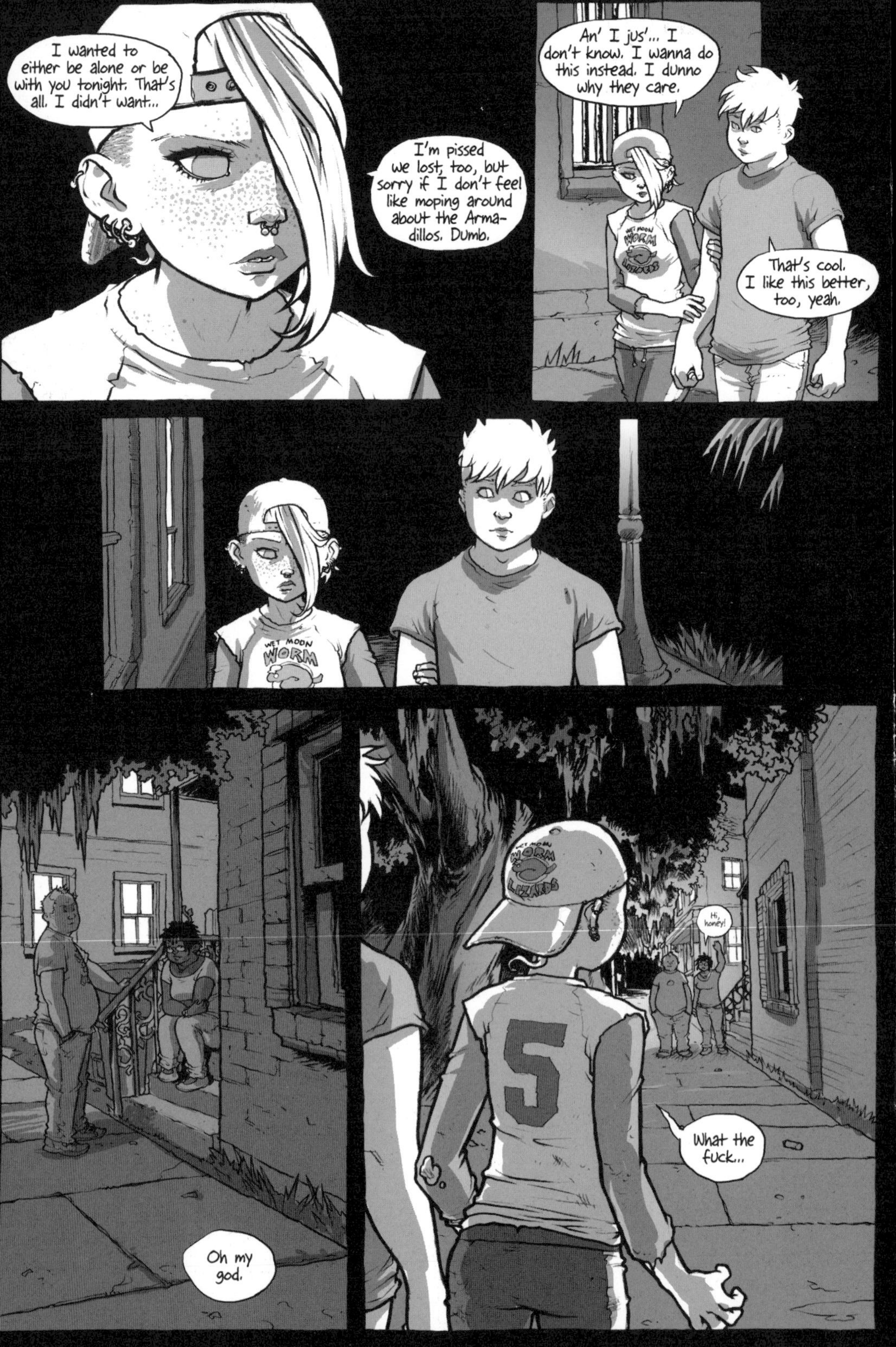
I wanted to either be alone or be with you tonight. That's all. I didn't want...
I'm pissed we lost, too, but sorry if I don't feel like moping around about the Armadillos. Dumb.
An' I jus'... I don't know. I wanna do this instead. I dunno why they care.
That's cool. I like this better, too, yeah.
Oh my god.
Hi, honey!
What the fuck...

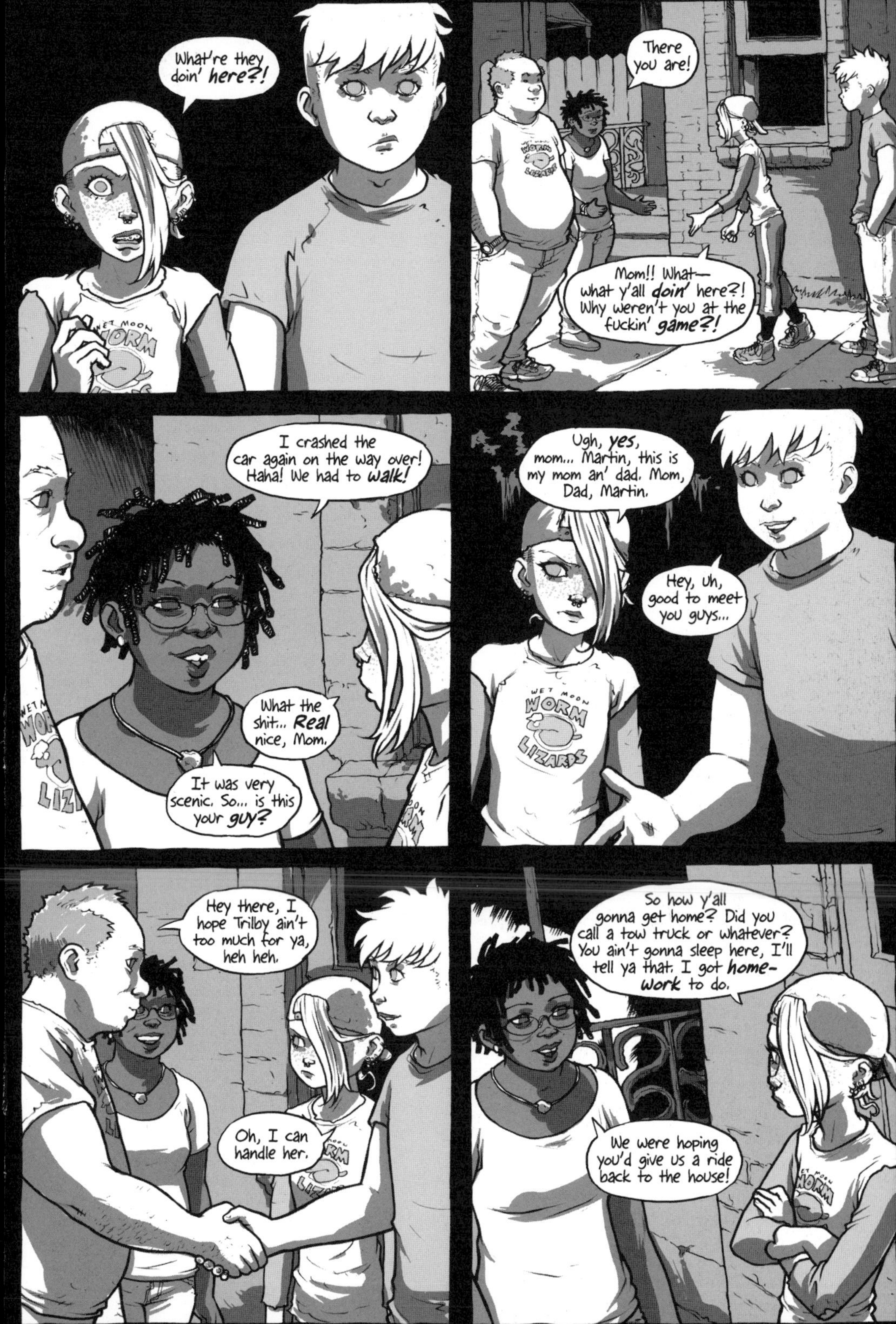
What're they doin' **here?!**
There you are!
Mom!! What— what y'all **doin'** here?! Why weren't you at the fuckin' **game?!**
I crashed the car again on the way over! Haha! We had to **walk!**
What the shit... **Real** nice, Mom.
It was very scenic. So... is this your **guy?**
Ugh, **yes**, mom... Martin, this is my mom an' dad. Mom, Dad, Martin.
Hey, uh, good to meet you guys...
Hey there, I hope Trilby ain't too much for ya, heh heh.
Oh, I can handle her.
So how y'all gonna get home? Did you call a tow truck or whatever? You ain't gonna sleep here, I'll tell ya that. I got **home-work** to do.
We were hoping you'd give us a ride back to the house!

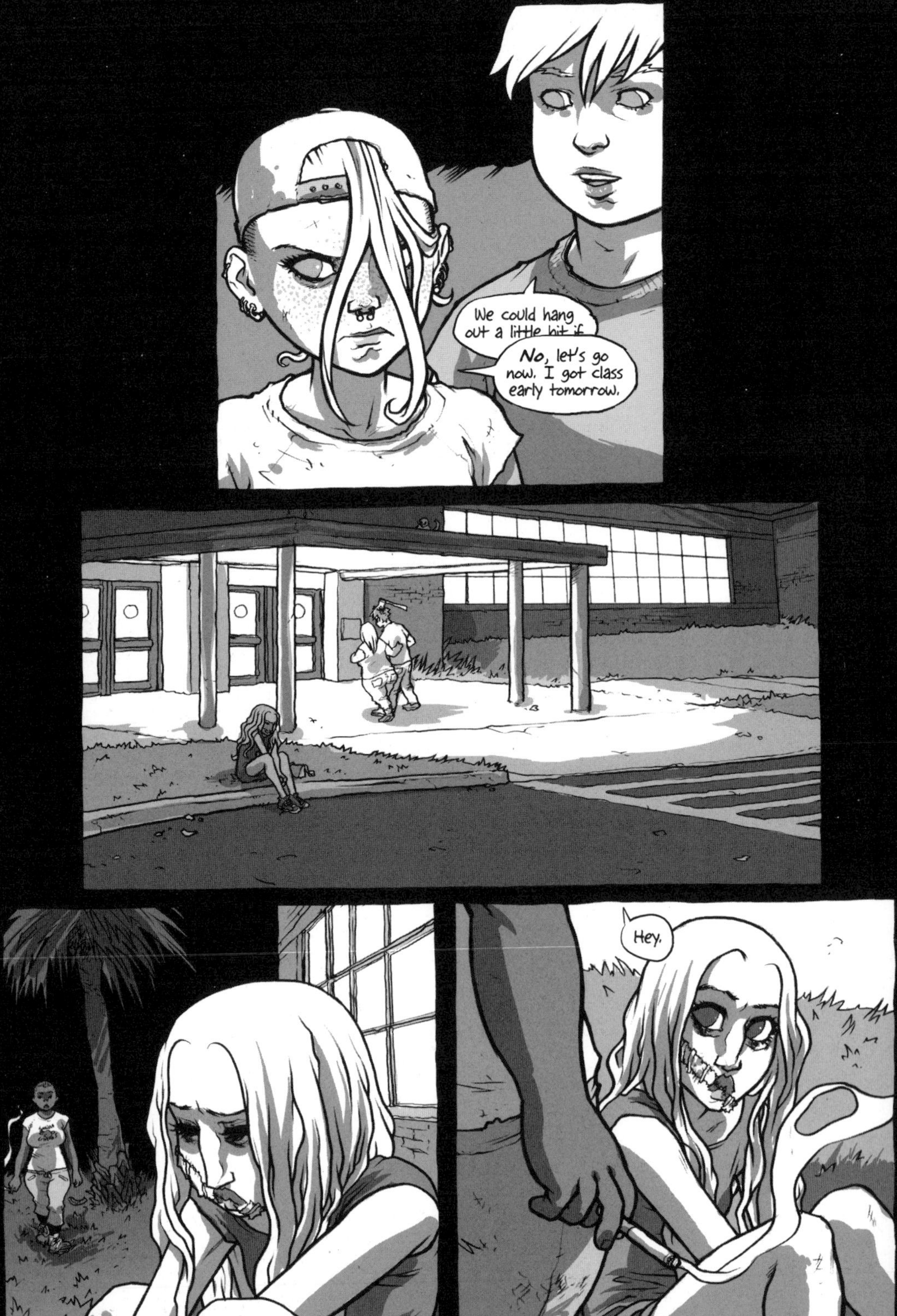
We could hang out a little bit if
No, let's go now. I got class early tomorrow.
Hey.

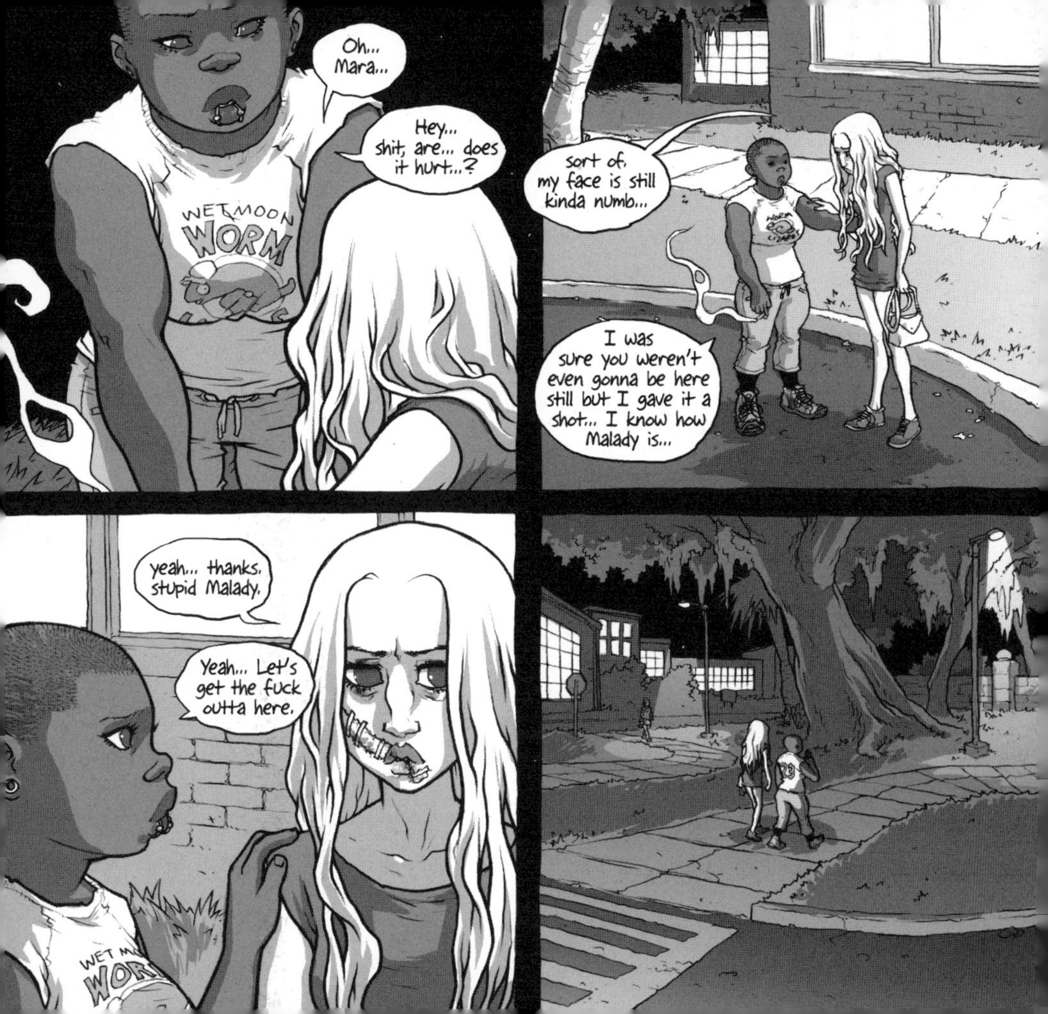
Oh... Mara...
Hey... shit, are... does it hurt...?
WET MOON WORM
sort of. my face is still kinda numb...
I was sure you weren't even gonna be here still but I gave it a shot... I know how Malady is...
yeah... thanks. stupid Malady.
Yeah... Let's get the fuck outta here.

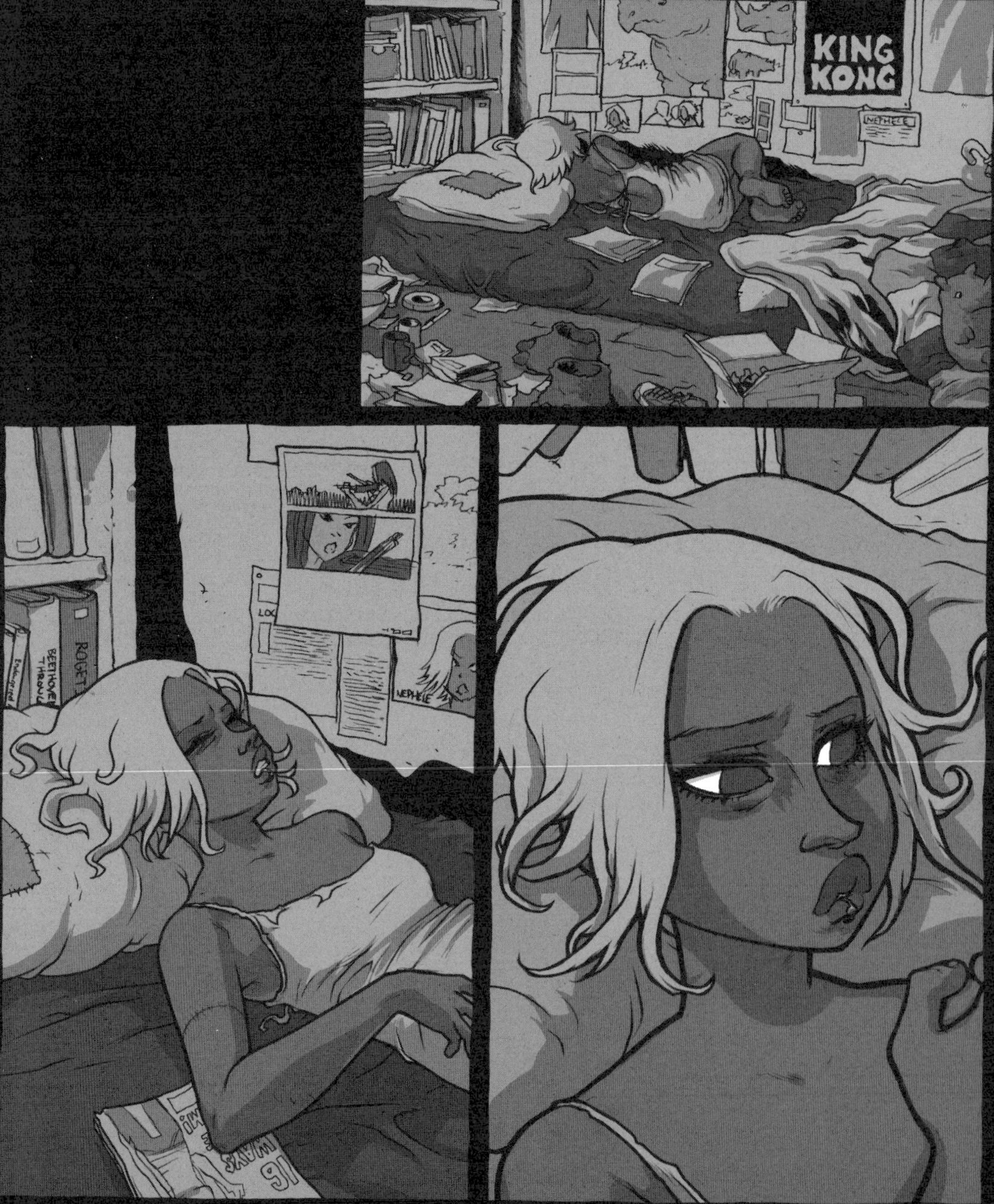
KING
KONG
NEPHELE
ROGET
NEPHELE

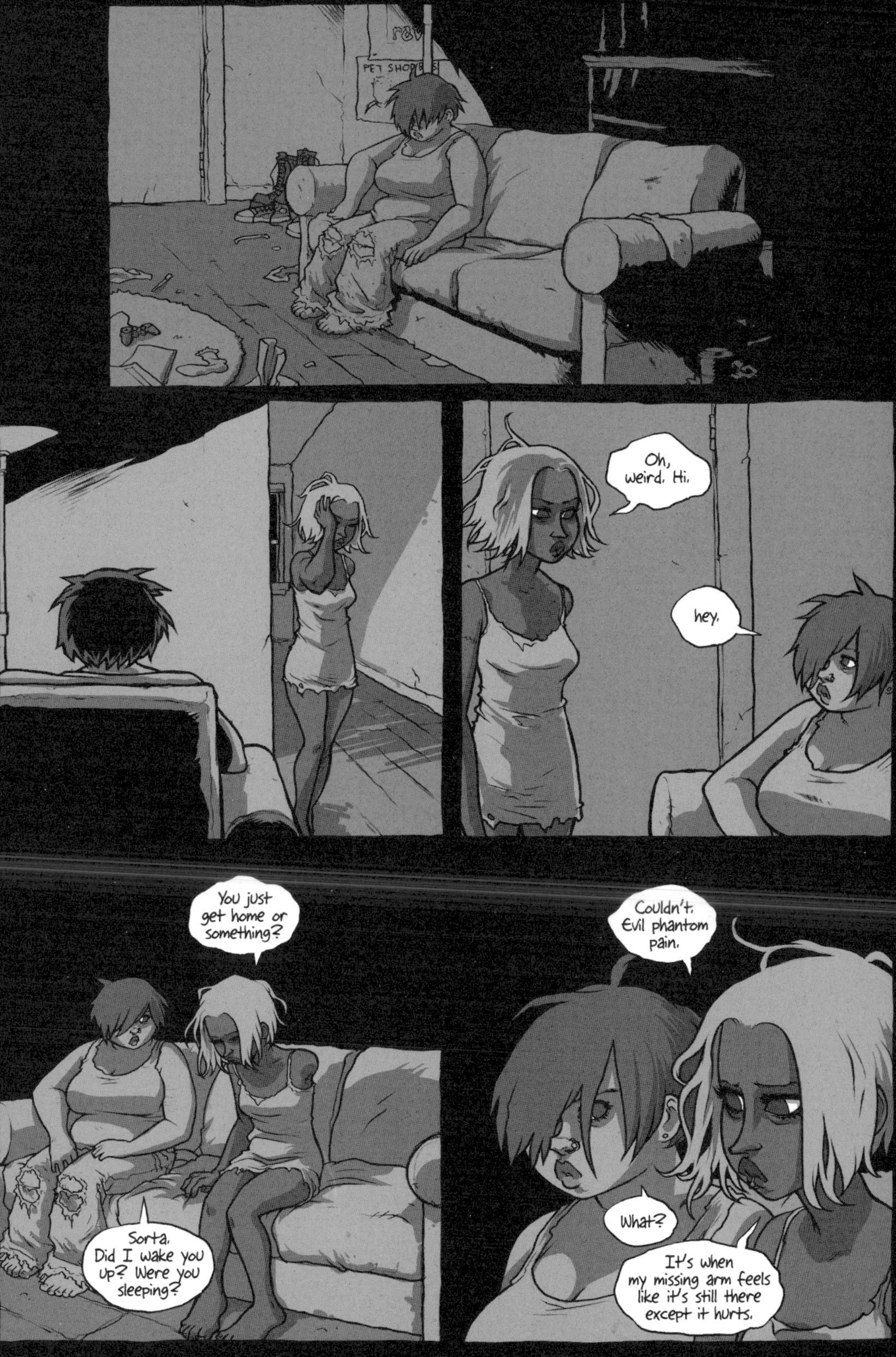
PET SHOP BOYS
Oh, weird. Hi.
hey.
You just get home or something?
Sorta. Did I wake you up? Were you sleeping?
Couldn't. Evil phantom pain.
What?
It's when my missing arm feels like it's still there except it hurts.

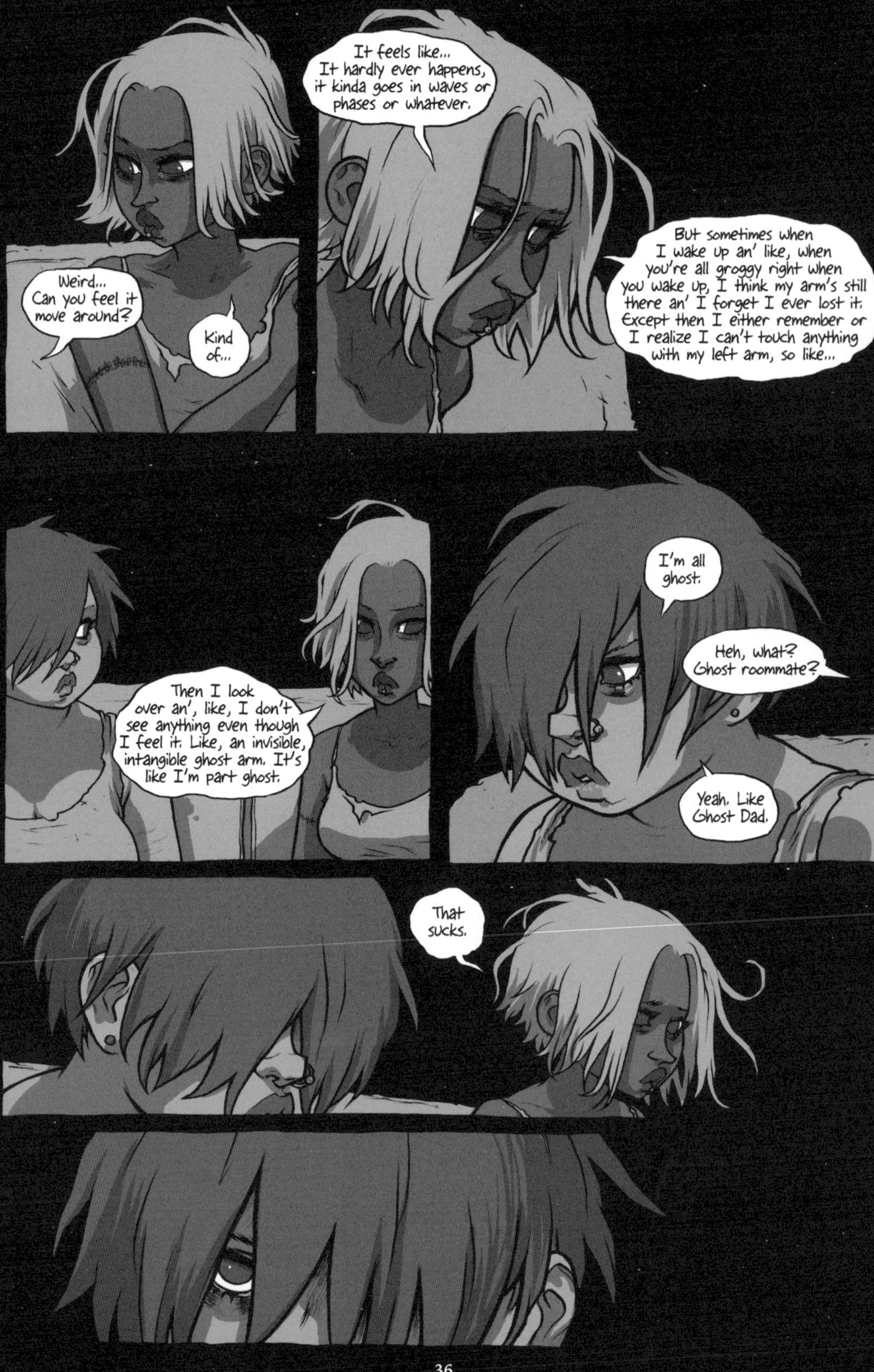
Weird... Can you feel it move around?
Kind of...
It feels like... It hardly ever happens, it kinda goes in waves or phases or whatever.
But sometimes when I wake up an' like, when you're all groggy right when you wake up, I think my arm's still there an' I forget I ever lost it. Except then I either remember or I realize I can't touch anything with my left arm, so like...
Then I look over an', like, I don't see anything even though I feel it. Like, an invisible, intangible ghost arm. It's like I'm part ghost.
I'm all ghost.
Heh, what? Ghost roommate?
Yeah. Like Ghost Dad.
That sucks.

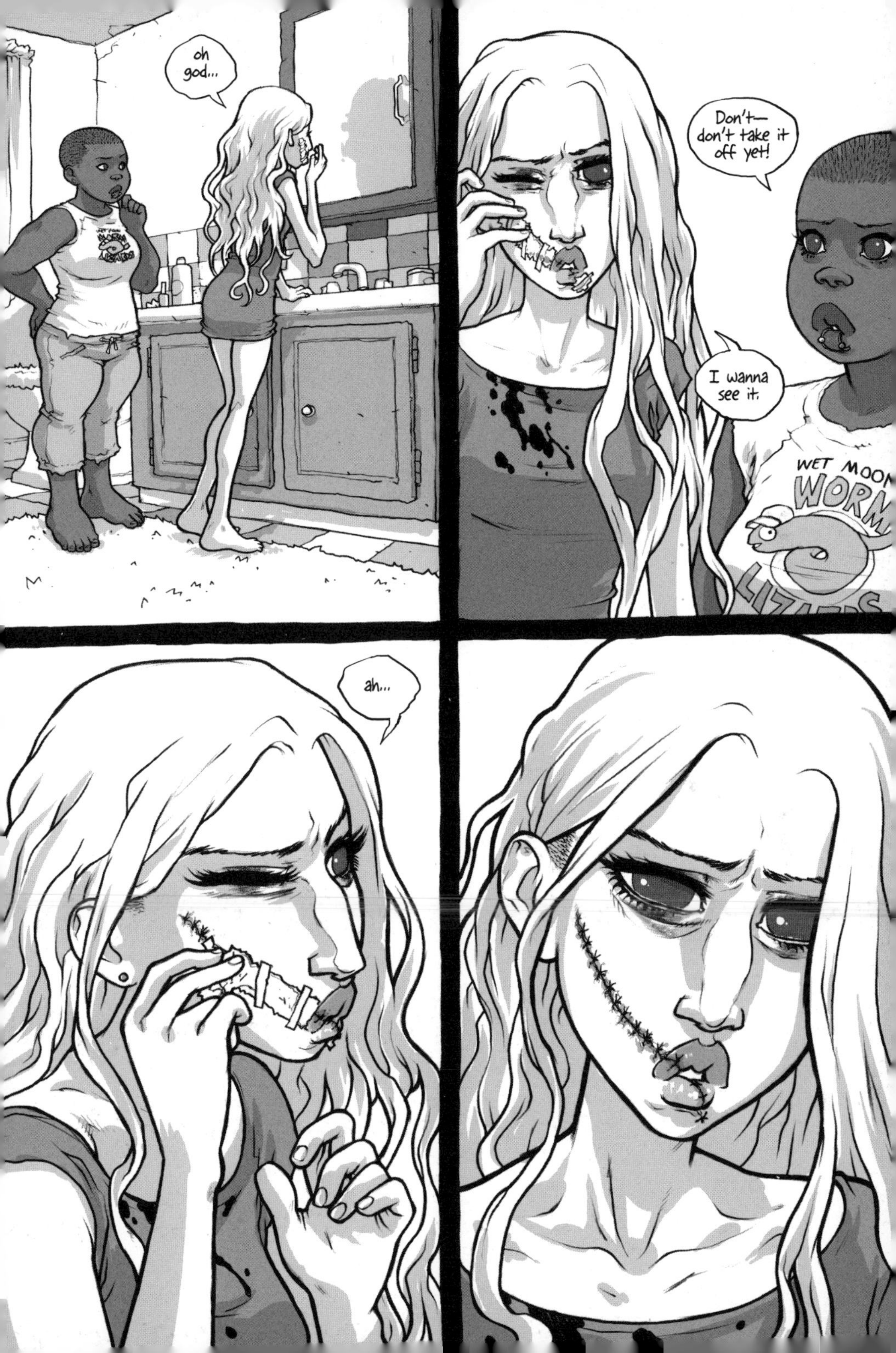

oh god...
Don't— don't take it off yet!
I wanna see it.
WET MOON
WORMS
LIZARDS
ah...

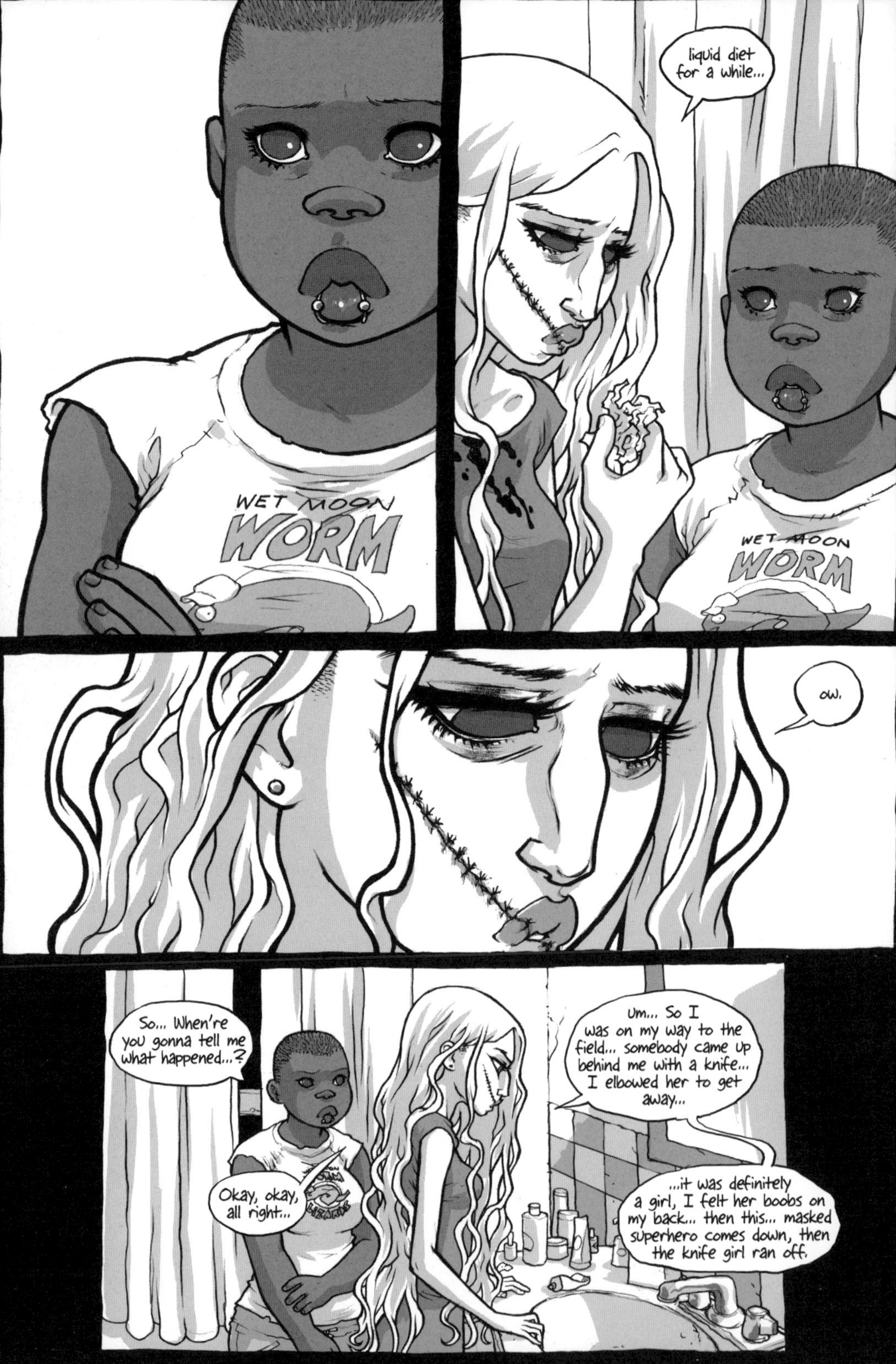
WET MOON
WORM
liquid diet for a while...
WET MOON
WORM
ow.
So... When're you gonna tell me what happened...?
Um... So I was on my way to the field... somebody came up behind me with a knife... I elbowed her to get away...
Okay, okay, all right...
...it was definitely a girl, I felt her boobs on my back... then this... masked superhero comes down, then the knife girl ran off.

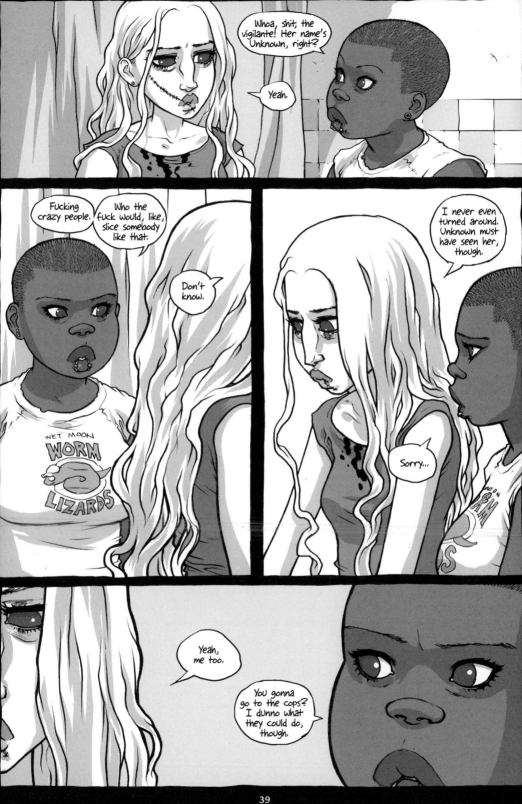

Whoa, shit, the vigilante! Her name's Unknown, right?

Yeah.

Fucking crazy people.

Who the fuck would, like, slice somebody like that.

Don't know.

I never even turned around. Unknown must have seen her, though.

WET MOON
WORM
LIZARDS

Sorry...

Yeah, me too.

You gonna go to the cops? I dunno what they could do, though.

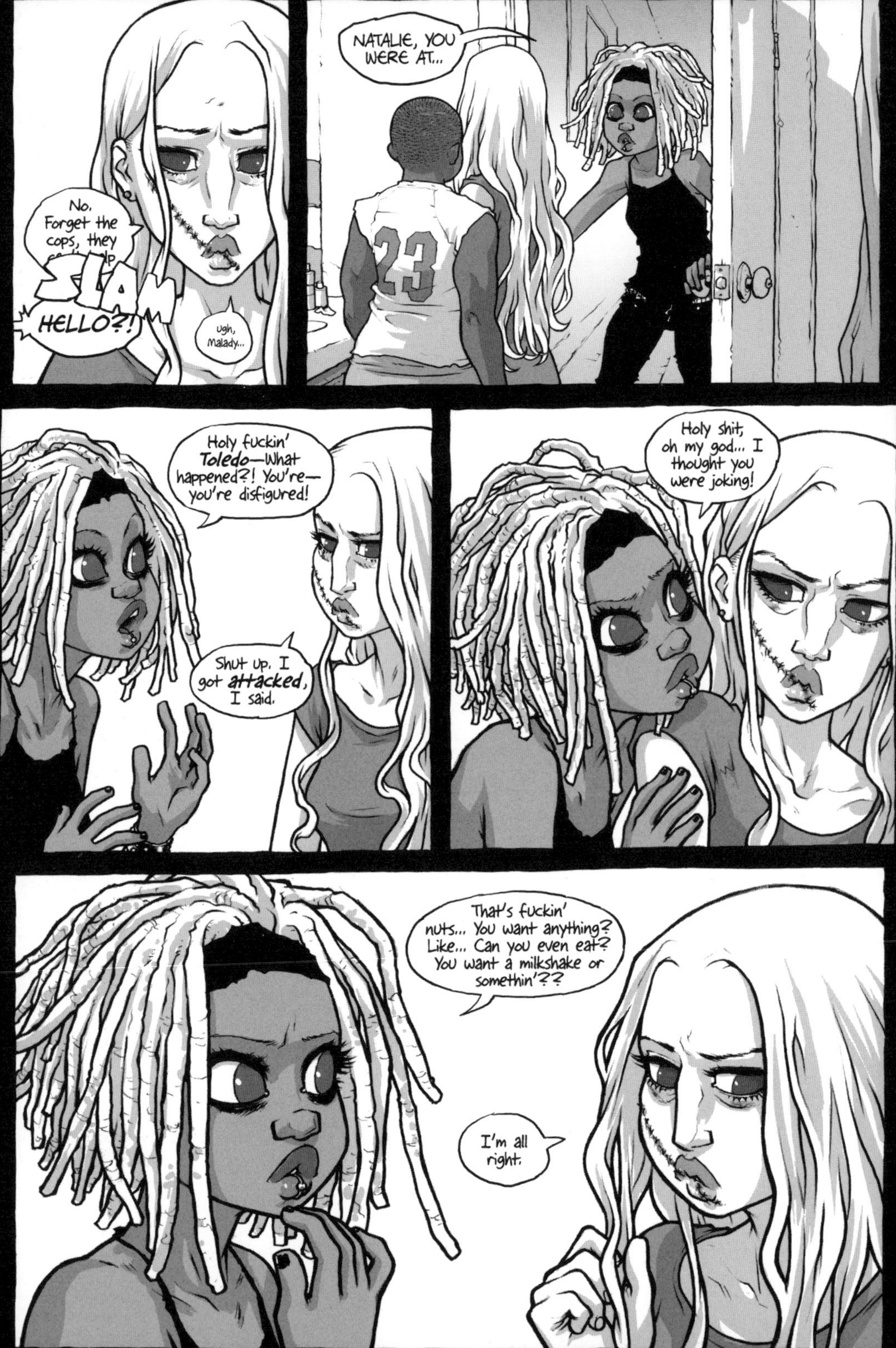
No. Forget the cops, they
SLAM
HELLO?!
Ugh, Malady...
NATALIE, YOU WERE AT...
Holy fuckin' Toledo—What happened?! You're— you're disfigured!
Shut up. I got attacked, I said.
Holy shit, oh my god... I thought you were joking!
That's fuckin' nuts... You want anything? Like... Can you even eat? You want a milkshake or somethin'??
I'm all right.

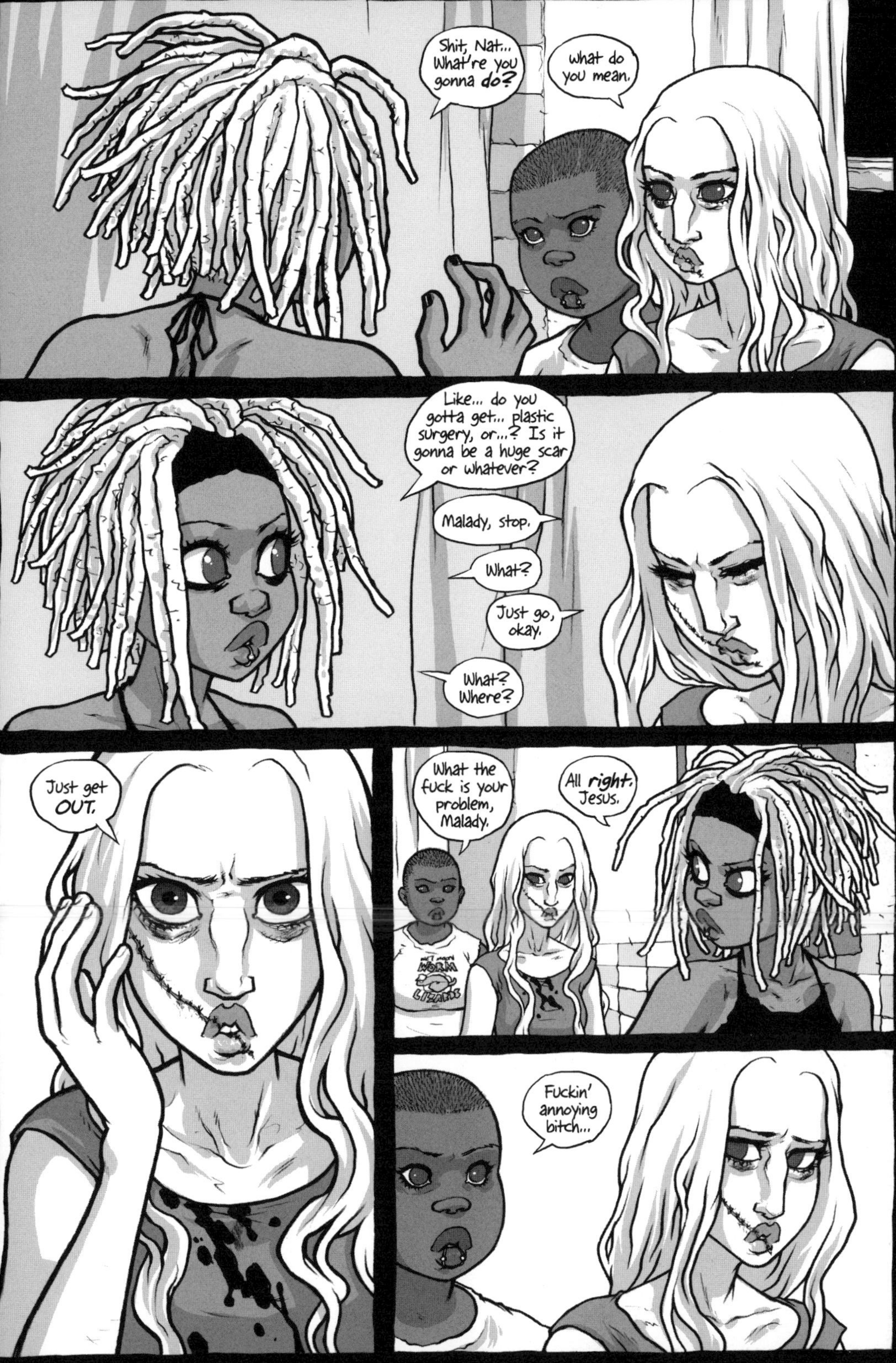
Shit, Nat... What're you gonna do?
what do you mean.
Like... do you gotta get... plastic surgery, or...? Is it gonna be a huge scar or whatever?
Malady, stop.
What?
Just go, okay.
What? Where?
Just get OUT.
What the fuck is your problem, Malady.
All right. Jesus.
Fuckin' annoying bitch...

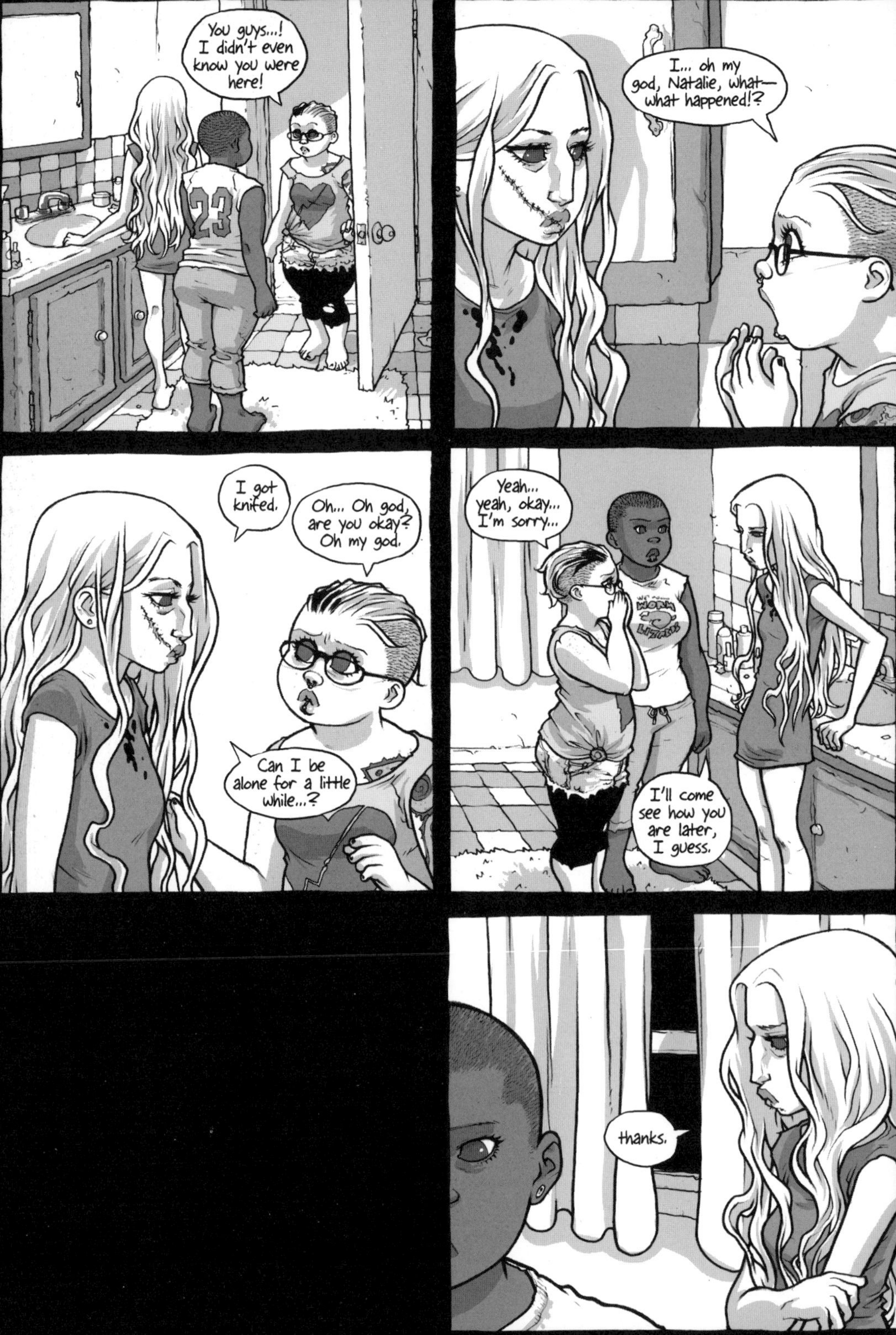
You guys...! I didn't even know you were here!
I... oh my god, Natalie, what— what happened!?
I got knifed.
Oh... Oh god, are you okay? Oh my god.
Can I be alone for a little while...?
Yeah... yeah, okay... I'm sorry...
I'll come see how you are later, I guess.
thanks.

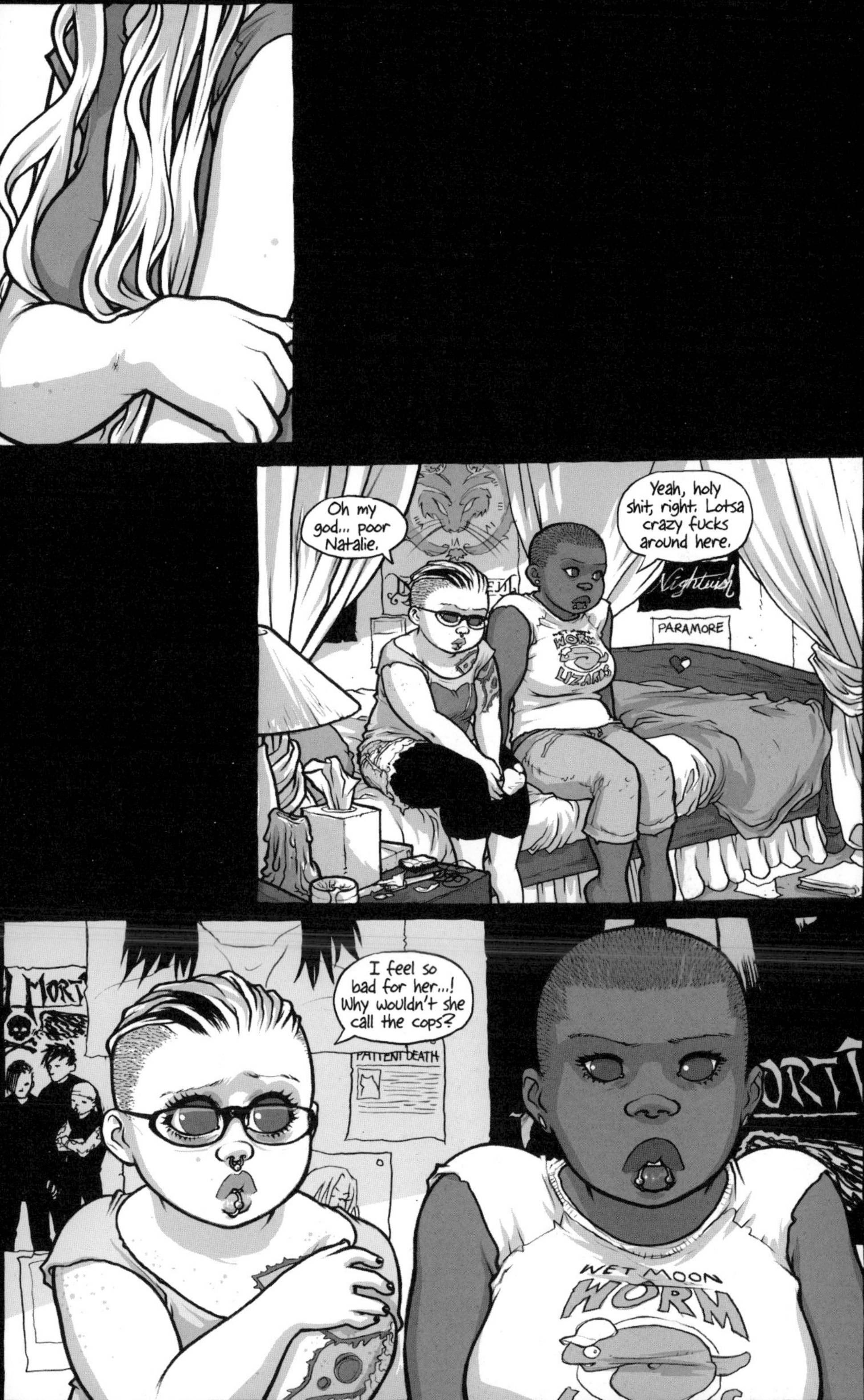
Oh my god... poor Natalie.
Yeah, holy shit, right. Lotsa crazy fucks around here.
Nightwish
PARAMORE
I feel so bad for her...! Why wouldn't she call the cops?
PATIENT DEATH
WET MOON
WORM

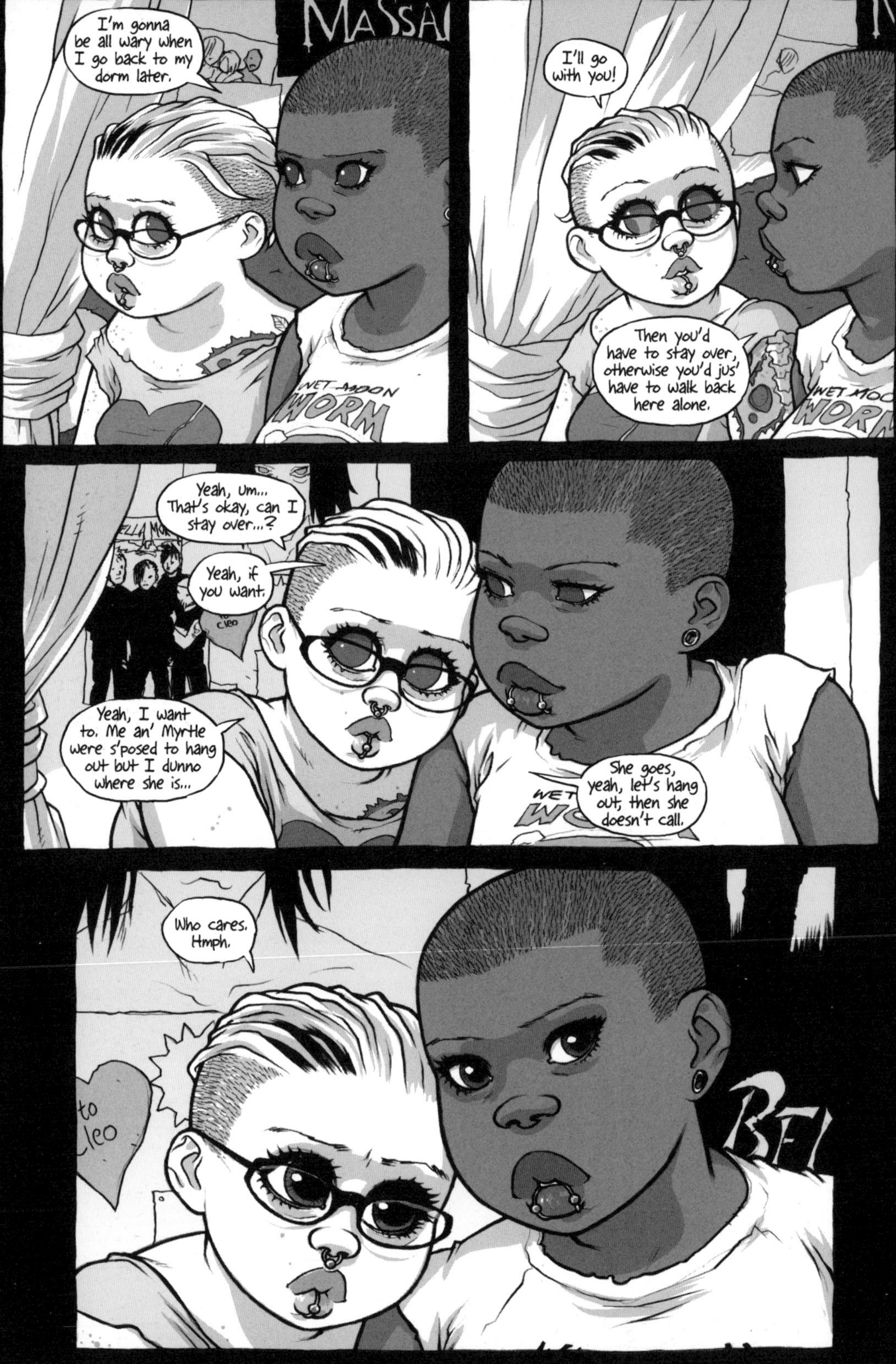
MaSSA
I'm gonna be all wary when I go back to my dorm later.
WET MOON WORM
I'll go with you!
Then you'd have to stay over, otherwise you'd jus' have to walk back here alone.
Yeah, um... That's okay, can I stay over...?
Yeah, if you want.
to cleo
Yeah, I want to. Me an' Myrtle were s'posed to hang out but I dunno where she is...
She goes, yeah, let's hang out, then she doesn't call.
Who cares. Hmph.
to cleo

The Wonders At Your Feet

[friendtoroaches@gmail.com]

Recent Entries   Archive   Friends   User Info

mara's journal

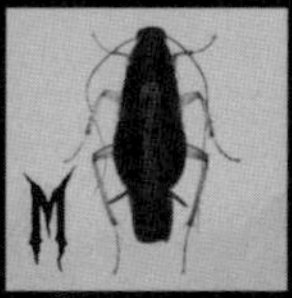

M

profile

November 5th, 2:00am

FUck.

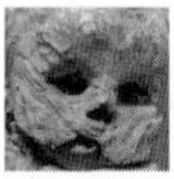

we lost the game. by a lot. we seriously tanked hard i think the hardest we ever tanked. everybody seemed out of it. Trilby, what happened? i know you erad this, you can't escape. oh well. actually she wasn't even the most off, because she did hit a home run so that was cool, but Nisha. she failed. maybe this entry should be custom. whatever. i'm sorry Nisha. i don't care. i don't know if i even care that much that we lost the game. somehow it doesnt seem that importnt. like we'll just play the NEXT game, there will always be another one, so what.

a friend of mine got mugged and got slashed in her face right across it. it's gruesome. i feel like it is partly my fault because it happend when she was on the way to see the game, which i concinved her to go to. shit. she'll never come to another one, that's for sure. i feel sick thinking about it. like a bumpy ball in my stomach. i know it isn't REALLY my fault, how could i of known but i don't know. i should have walked with her to the game but she was busy, she had to come later. fuck. Wet Moon is so fucking not safe, so many women get fucking raped and people get mugged or killed or wahtever left and fucking right. anyway i don't realy know what to do, like how to "be there" for my friend or what you'res suposed to do in siaution like this. i guess it'll be a permanent scar. she'll still be just as pretty as she was though, but i know most other people won't think so which fucking sucks. sad sacks of shit. all the crime and shit always felt really distant, but this hits pretty close to home. i've only known this girl for a short time, so it makes me keep wondering when like something will happen to me or my family or friends. it has to, right? i don't know what the statistics are. actually my mom's been mugged a couple times but nothing happened and the second time she fought the guy off with a stick. go mom.

still gross from the game, gotta shower. another friend who i'll keep secret is sleeping over right now. my roommate is over at her boyfriend's place where she pretty much stays all the time so i have the room to myself. or my friend and i have the room to ourselves. i think i busted one of my toenails off. should i grow my hair out? i don't know. hair is such a hassle. and everybody always seems scared off by kinky nappy hair like mine. when i used go to get it cut or whatever the stylists always go "you should straighten it!" or like... whatever. people want me to "tame" my hair or whatever but tame THIS motherfucker. okay i'm going, i gotta tend to my cute guest and have a smoke. i know, i swear i'm quitting i haven't forgotten!! that's probably why the Armadillos killed us. MY LUNGS FAULT

mood: horny
current music: flatlinerz - run

[0 comments | leave a comment]

November 4th, 11:35am

PRINCESS OF SLAUGHTER.

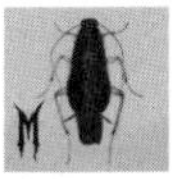

M

i'm at home real quick before i go to the field for practice. we're doing one last serious long practice before the game at 8. i think i wrote before about how Shoshana quit, and now we have this new girl Galaxy (crazy name) who is cool but i feel really uncertain about her. whether she can perform out there. Nisha is pretty flakey recently, i don't know what the hell is up with her. Paquita is good, we can count on her. and Fall, she is an awesome player but she's the biggest flake of all, you can never count on her to do anything and i always expect she won't even show up. she's really into boxing, i guess, i think she spends more of her time focusing on that. whatever.

yestrday i dumped a ton of my old clothes off at goodwill. all the goth shit i was into for those three or four years or whatever. i kept some of it, i still like some of the cool pants i

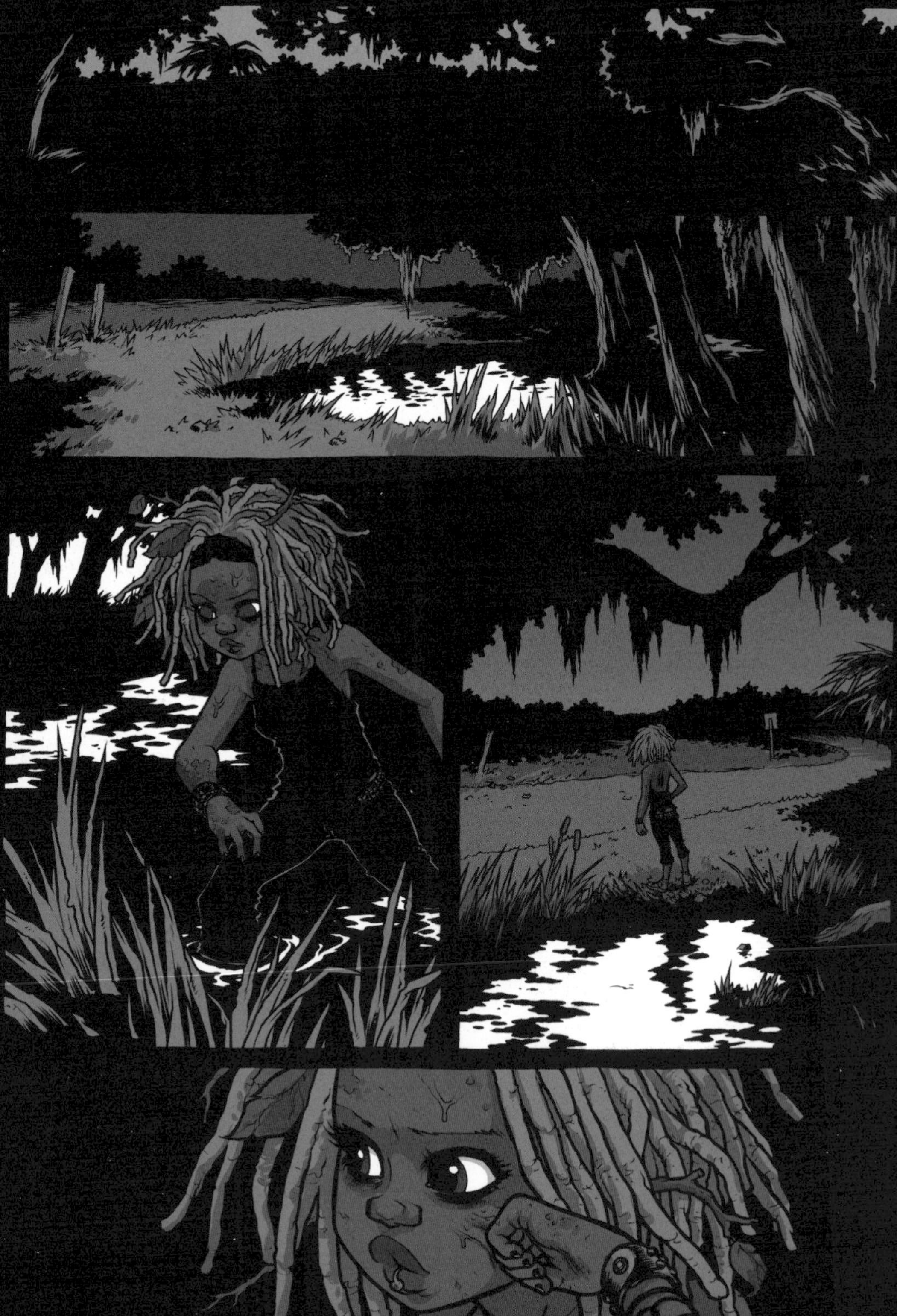

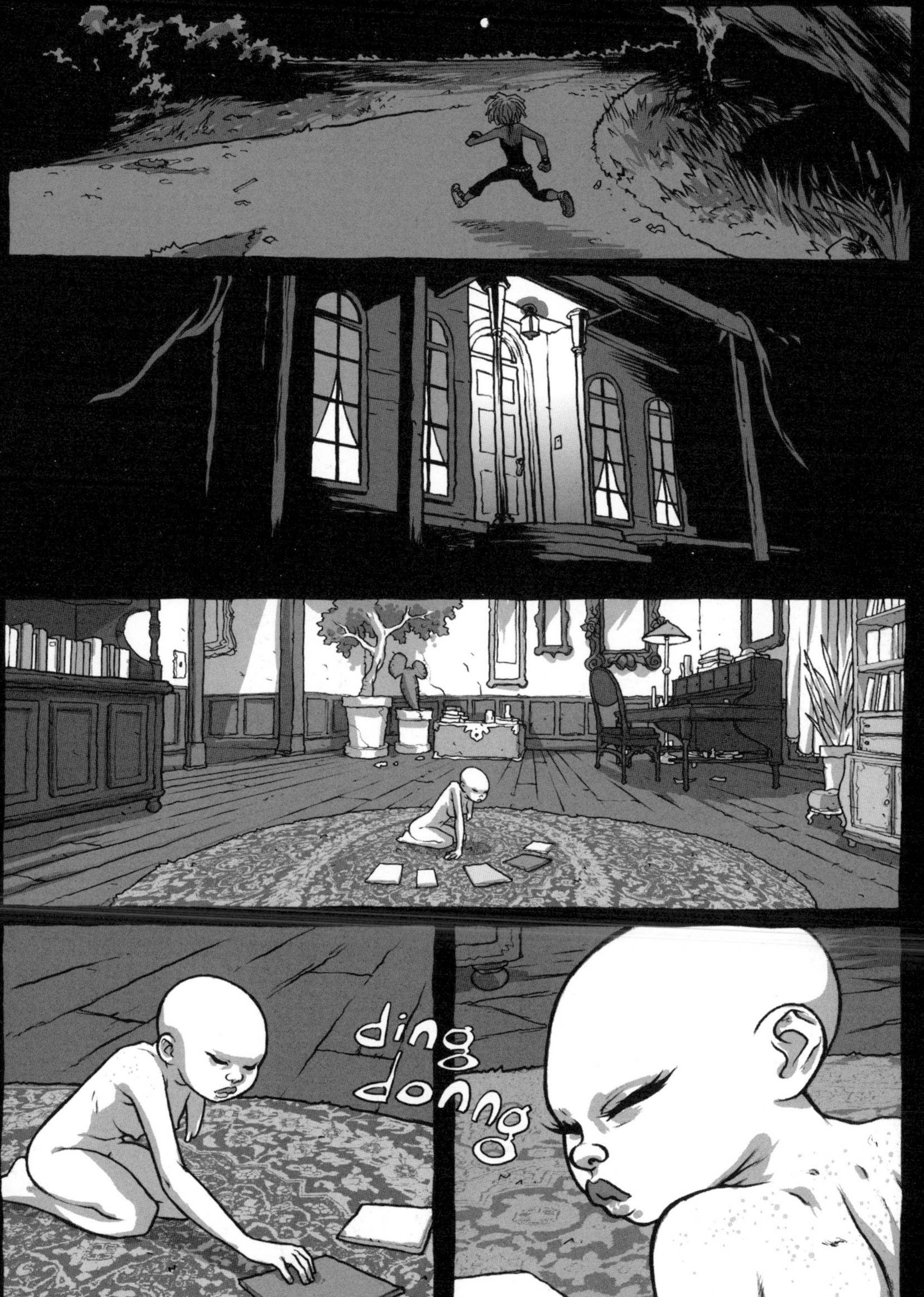
ding donng

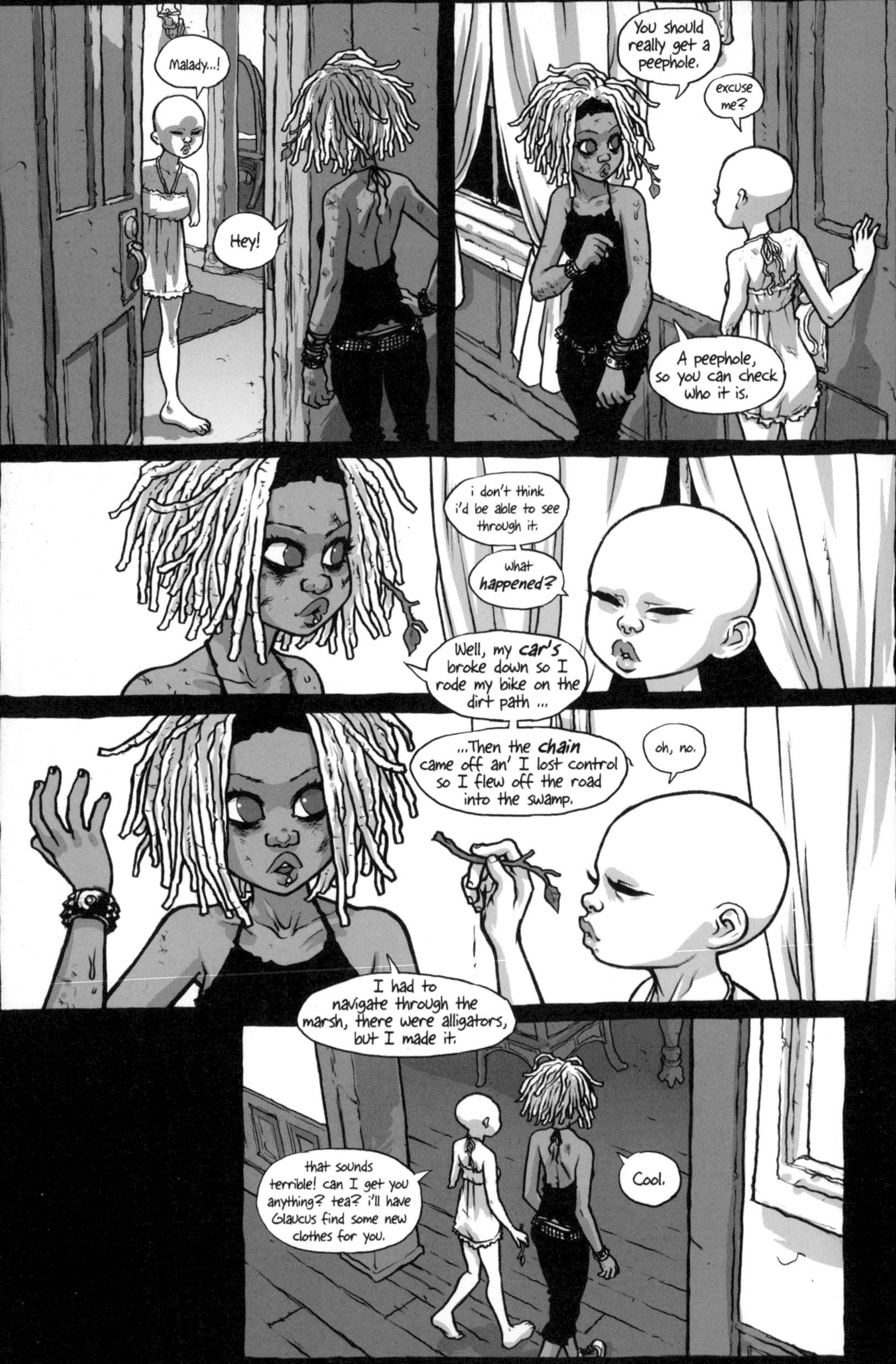
Malady...!
Hey!
You should really get a peephole.
excuse me?
A peephole, so you can check who it is.
i don't think i'd be able to see through it.
what happened?
Well, my car's broke down so I rode my bike on the dirt path ...
...Then the chain came off an' I lost control so I flew off the road into the swamp.
oh, no.
I had to navigate through the marsh, there were alligators, but I made it.
that sounds terrible! can I get you anything? tea? i'll have Glaucus find some new clothes for you.
Cool.

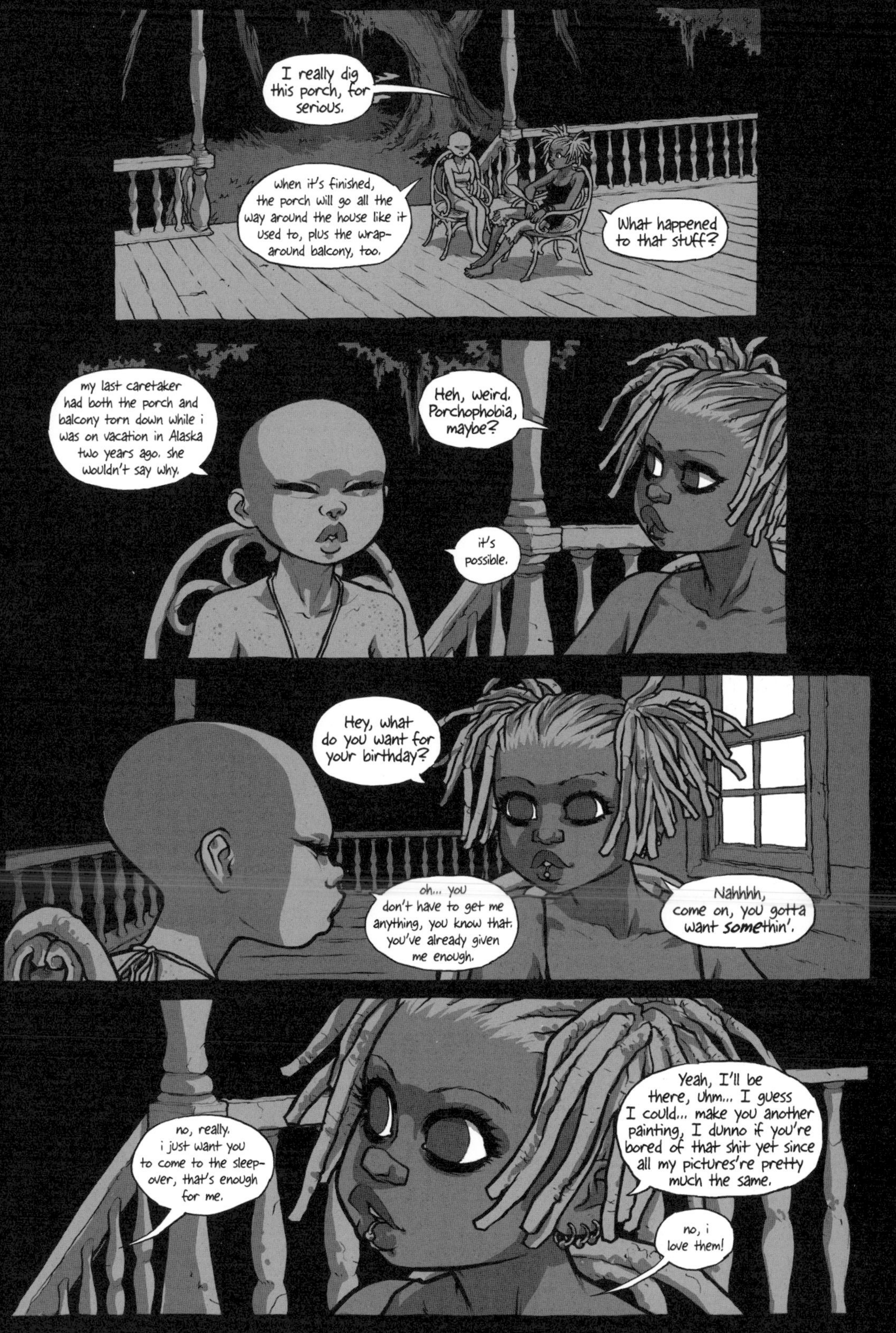
I really dig this porch, for serious.
when it's finished, the porch will go all the way around the house like it used to, plus the wrap-around balcony, too.
What happened to that stuff?
my last caretaker had both the porch and balcony torn down while i was on vacation in Alaska two years ago. she wouldn't say why.
Heh, weird. Porchophobia, maybe?
it's possible.
Hey, what do you want for your birthday?
oh... you don't have to get me anything, you know that. you've already given me enough.
Nahhhh, come on, you gotta want *some*thin'.
no, really. i just want you to come to the sleep-over, that's enough for me.
Yeah, I'll be there, uhm... I guess I could... make you another painting, I dunno if you're bored of that shit yet since all my pictures're pretty much the same.
no, i love them!

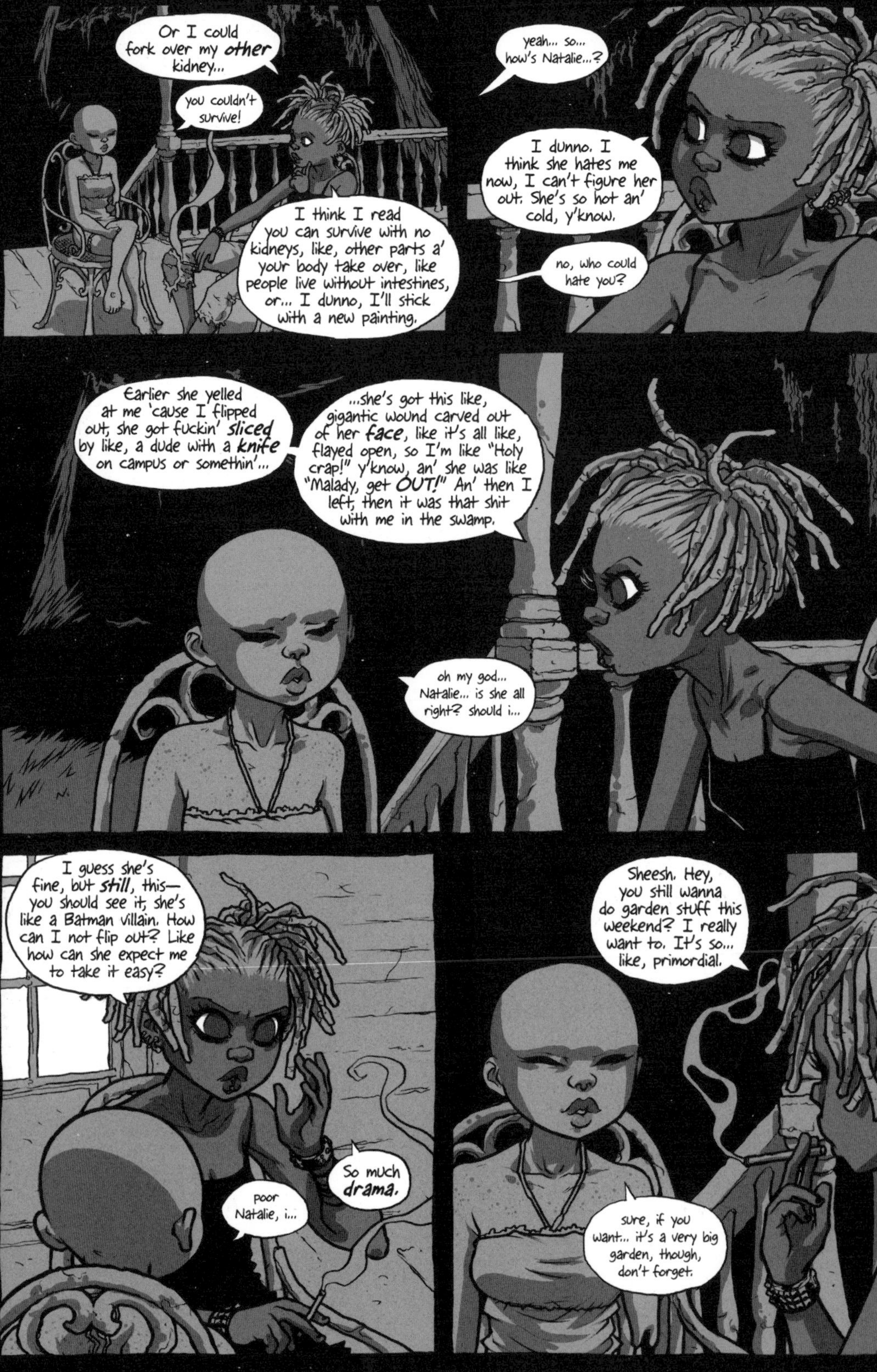
Or I could fork over my other kidney...
you couldn't survive!
I think I read you can survive with no kidneys, like, other parts a' your body take over, like people live without intestines, or... I dunno, I'll stick with a new painting.
yeah... so... how's Natalie...?
I dunno. I think she hates me now, I can't figure her out. She's so hot an' cold, y'know.
no, who could hate you?
Earlier she yelled at me 'cause I flipped out, she got fuckin' sliced by like, a dude with a knife on campus or somethin'...
...she's got this like, gigantic wound carved out of her face, like it's all like, flayed open, so I'm like "Holy crap!" y'know, an' she was like "Malady, get OUT!" An' then I left, then it was that shit with me in the swamp.
oh my god... Natalie... is she all right? should i...
I guess she's fine, but still, this— you should see it, she's like a Batman villain. How can I not flip out? Like how can she expect me to take it easy?
poor Natalie, i...
So much drama.
Sheesh. Hey, you still wanna do garden stuff this weekend? I really want to. It's so... like, primordial.
sure, if you want... it's a very big garden, though, don't forget.

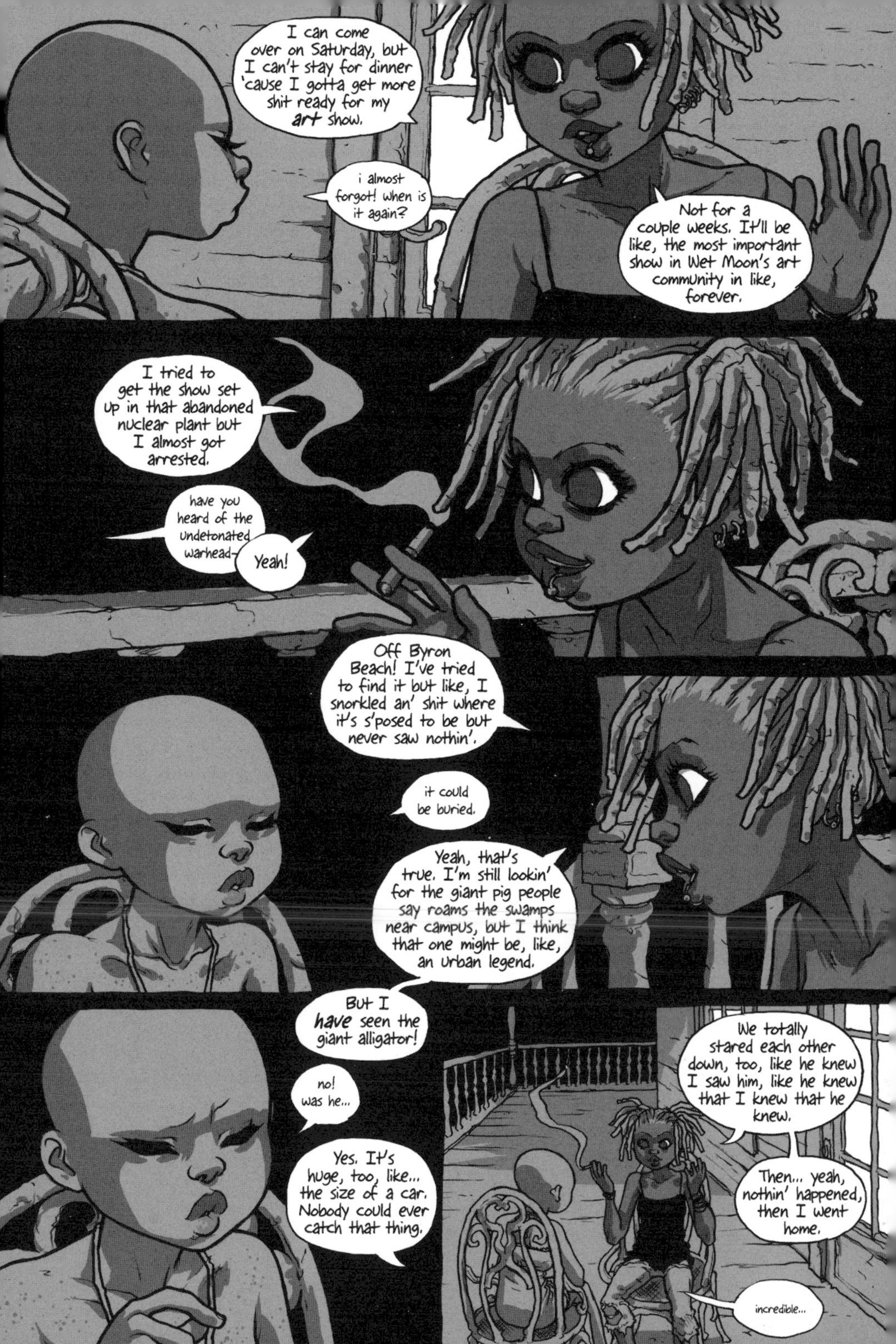
I can come over on Saturday, but I can't stay for dinner 'cause I gotta get more shit ready for my **art** show.
i almost forgot! when is it again?
Not for a couple weeks. It'll be like, the most important show in Wet Moon's art community in like, forever.
I tried to get the show set up in that abandoned nuclear plant but I almost got arrested.
have you heard of the undetonated warhead-
Yeah!
Off Byron Beach! I've tried to find it but like, I snorkled an' shit where it's s'posed to be but never saw nothin'.
it could be buried.
Yeah, that's true. I'm still lookin' for the giant pig people say roams the swamps near campus, but I think that one might be, like, an urban legend.
But I **have** seen the giant alligator!
no! was he...
Yes. It's huge, too, like... the size of a car. Nobody could ever catch that thing.
We totally stared each other down, too, like he knew I saw him, like he knew that I knew that he knew.
Then... yeah, nothin' happened, then I went home.
incredible...

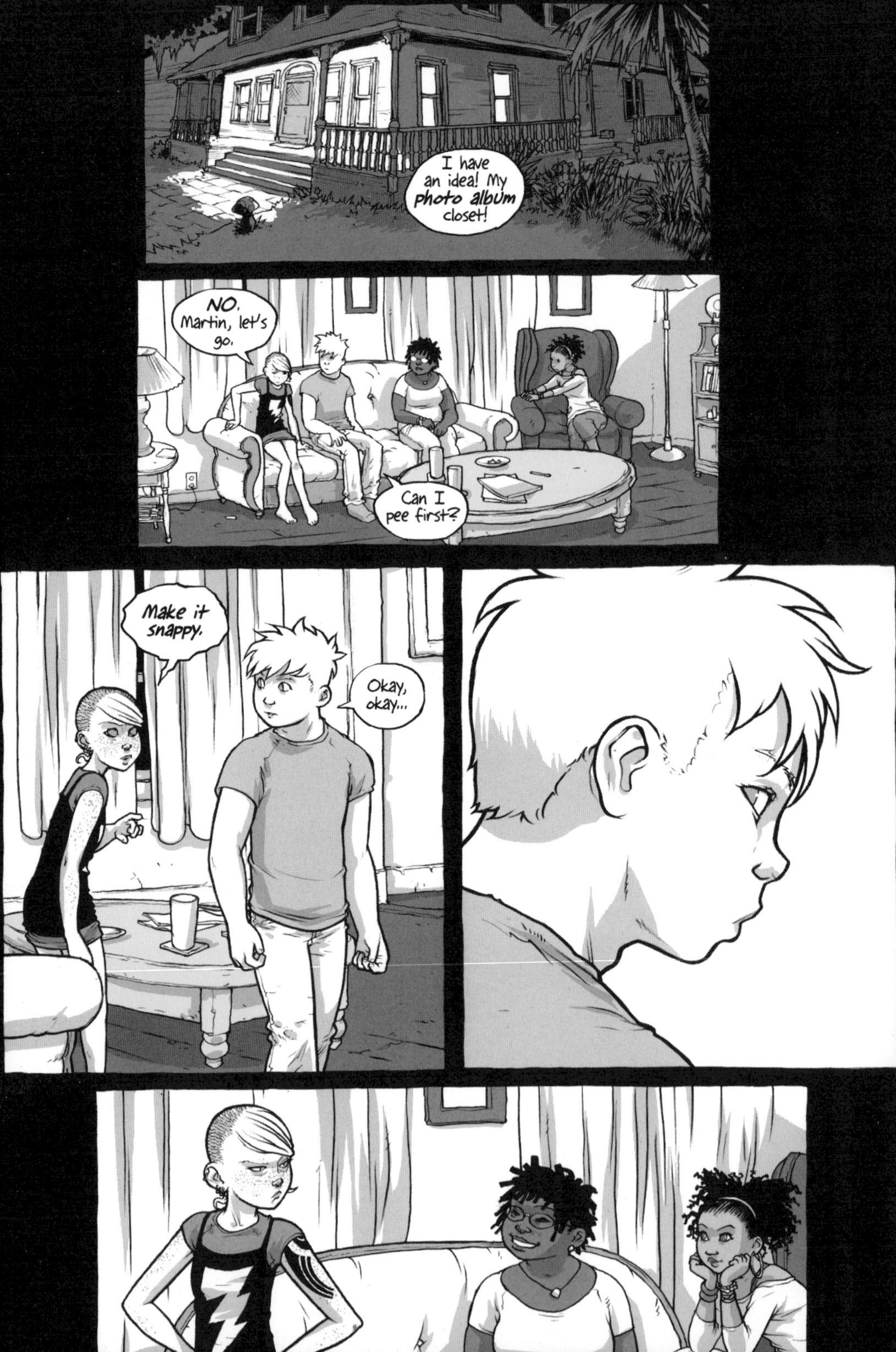
I have an idea! My photo album closet!
NO. Martin, let's go.
Can I pee first?
Make it snappy.
Okay, okay...

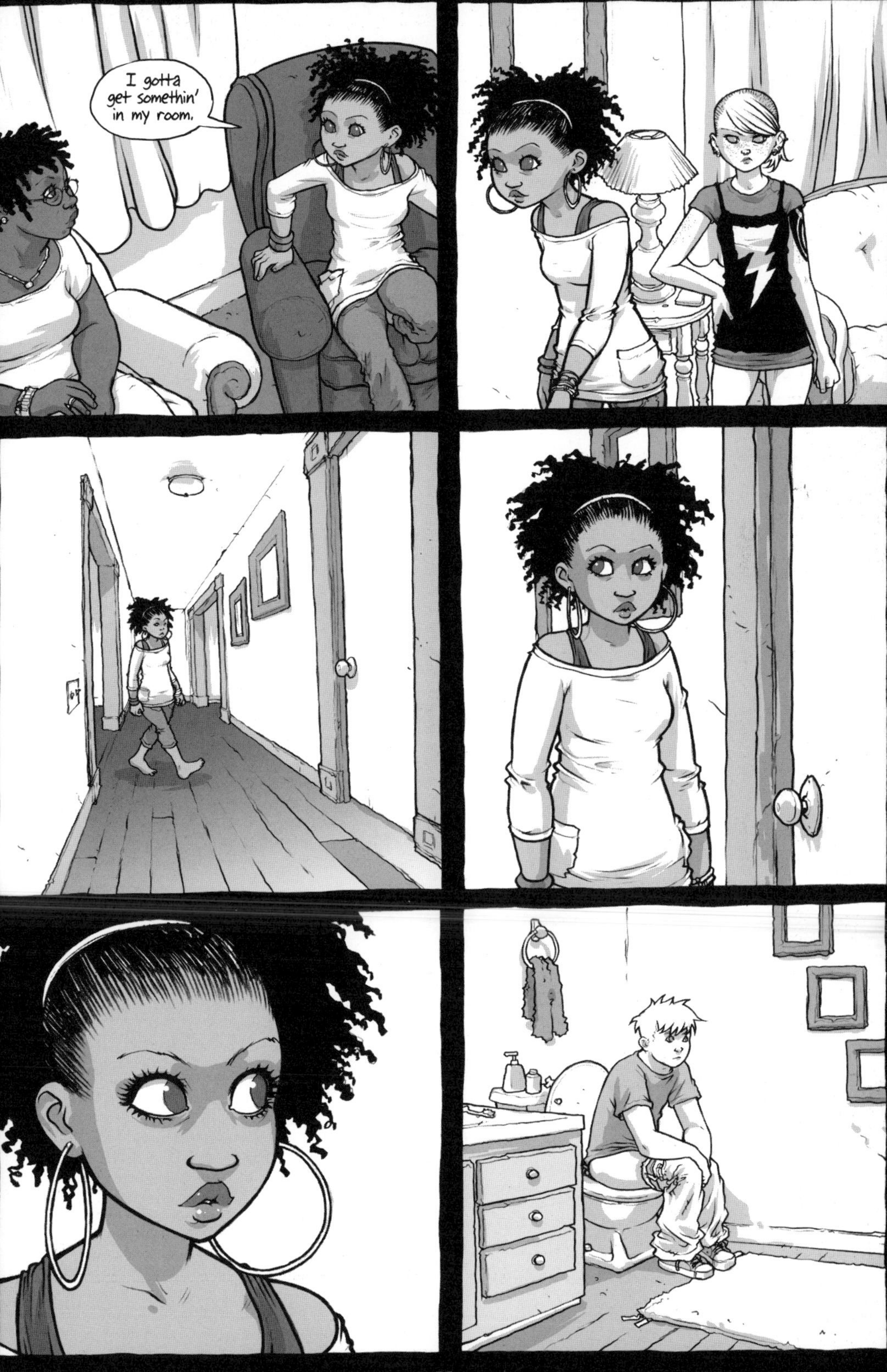
I gotta get somethin' in my room.

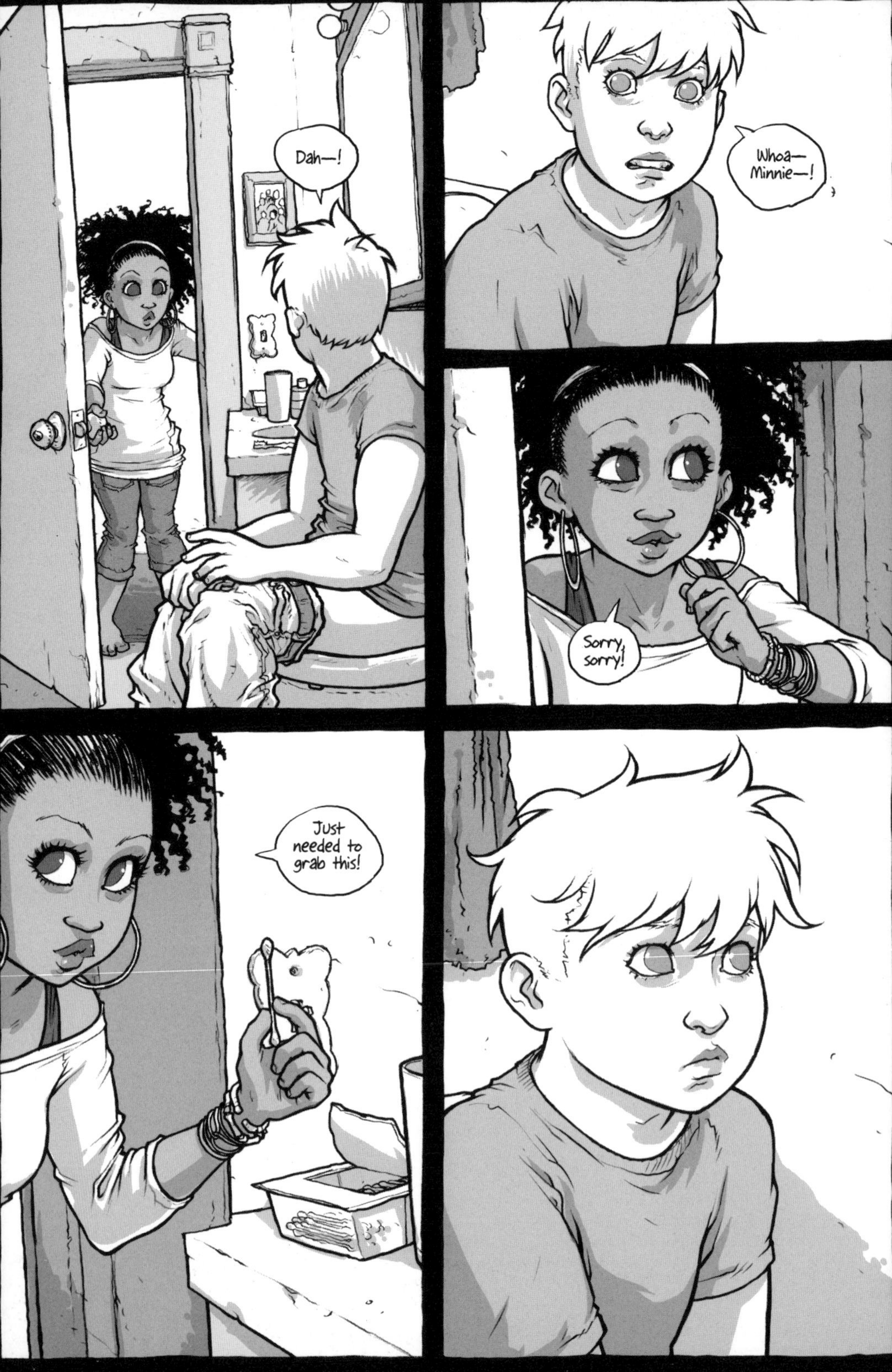
Dah—!
Whoa— Minnie—!
Sorry, sorry!
Just needed to grab this!

New diary, my old one finally ended. Trilby gave me this sketchbook a while ago so I could doodle in it, but I never did, so I'm using it as a new diary. I'm really not an artist so whatever.

I can't find Myrtle. She won't answer her phone and the times I went by her room she wasn't there. I stopped going over there because every time Zia is there instead and I end up talking to her ~~she~~ for hours. I guess Myrtle must be avoiding me, and I can't blame her. I'd avoid me, too. I don't know what happened, the last time we hung out was so great, I just don't know. I wonder if she's ditching me completely, like I'll never see her again and this is it... I know I've been cheating on her and she's a little weird sometimes but but I really like her a lot and I don't even know what to do, where is she??!

I told Penny I'm bi and she was so dumb about it, she said "pick one!" or something like that, but it doesn't work that way! It doesn't mean you're confused or greedy! She is so narrow-minded and homophobic sometimes, I hate it. I wanted to try and make her see where I'm coming from, but I caved and didn't really even bother, and I tried not to but I cried, it was stupid. I think maybe it wasn't a good idea to tell her, but I don't even know, I even said I was with two girls so now she must be thinking I'm a total slut and screwing around with every girl in wet moon or something. I don't know. I think I could've reacted better if penny wasn't pregnant, that's all I keep thinking about and I feel like I want to be extra nice to her because I know she's going through a really tough thing but at the same time I really want to just lay into her for being such a cunt.

where the fuck is myrtle. I'm calling her again.

FUCK

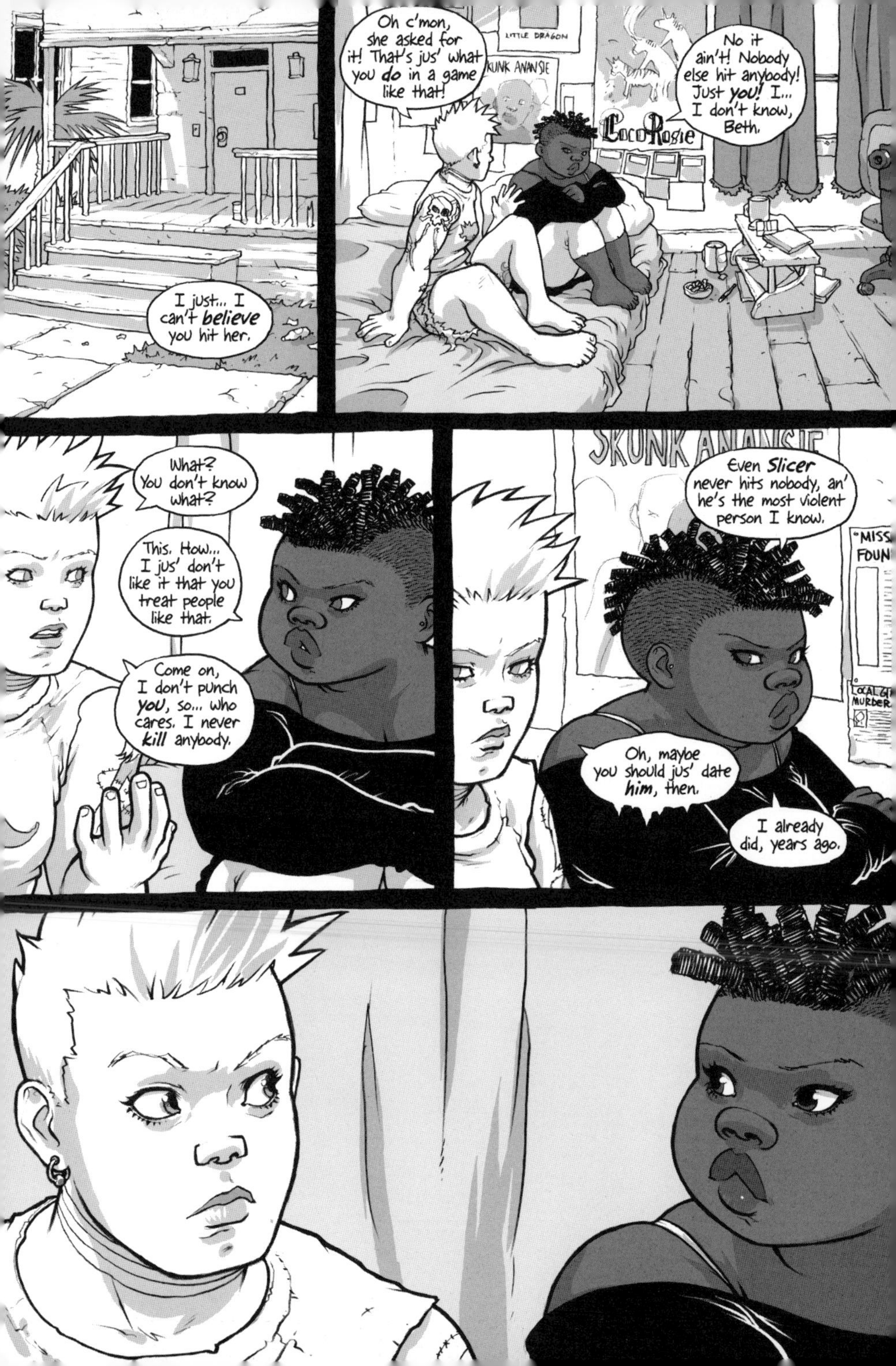
I just... I can't believe you hit her.
Oh c'mon, she asked for it! That's jus' what you do in a game like that!
LITTLE DRAGON
SKUNK ANANSIE
CocoRosie
No it ain't! Nobody else hit anybody! Just you! I... I don't know, Beth.
What? You don't know what?
This. How... I jus' don't like it that you treat people like that.
Come on, I don't punch you, so... who cares. I never kill anybody.
Even Slicer never hits nobody, an' he's the most violent person I know.
Oh, maybe you should jus' date him, then.
I already did, years ago.

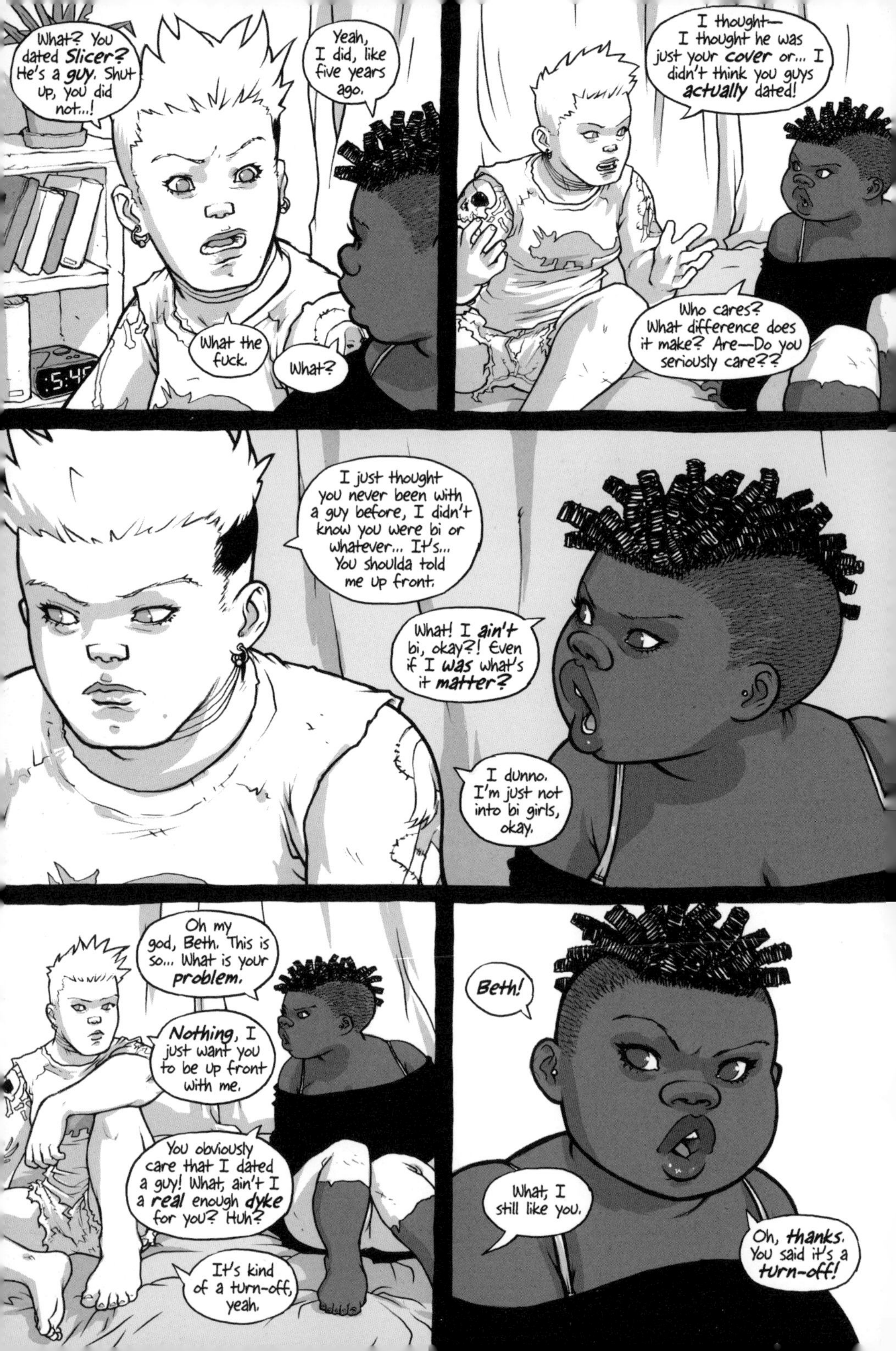
What? You dated Slicer? He's a guy. Shut up, you did not...!
Yeah, I did, like five years ago.
What the fuck.
What?
I thought— I thought he was just your cover or... I didn't think you guys actually dated!
Who cares? What difference does it make? Are—Do you seriously care??
I just thought you never been with a guy before, I didn't know you were bi or whatever... It's... You shoulda told me up front.
What! I ain't bi, okay?! Even if I was what's it matter?
I dunno. I'm just not into bi girls, okay.
Oh my god, Beth. This is so... What is your problem.
Nothing, I just want you to be up front with me.
You obviously care that I dated a guy! What, ain't I a real enough dyke for you? Huh?
It's kind of a turn-off, yeah.
Beth!
What, I still like you.
Oh, thanks. You said it's a turn-off!

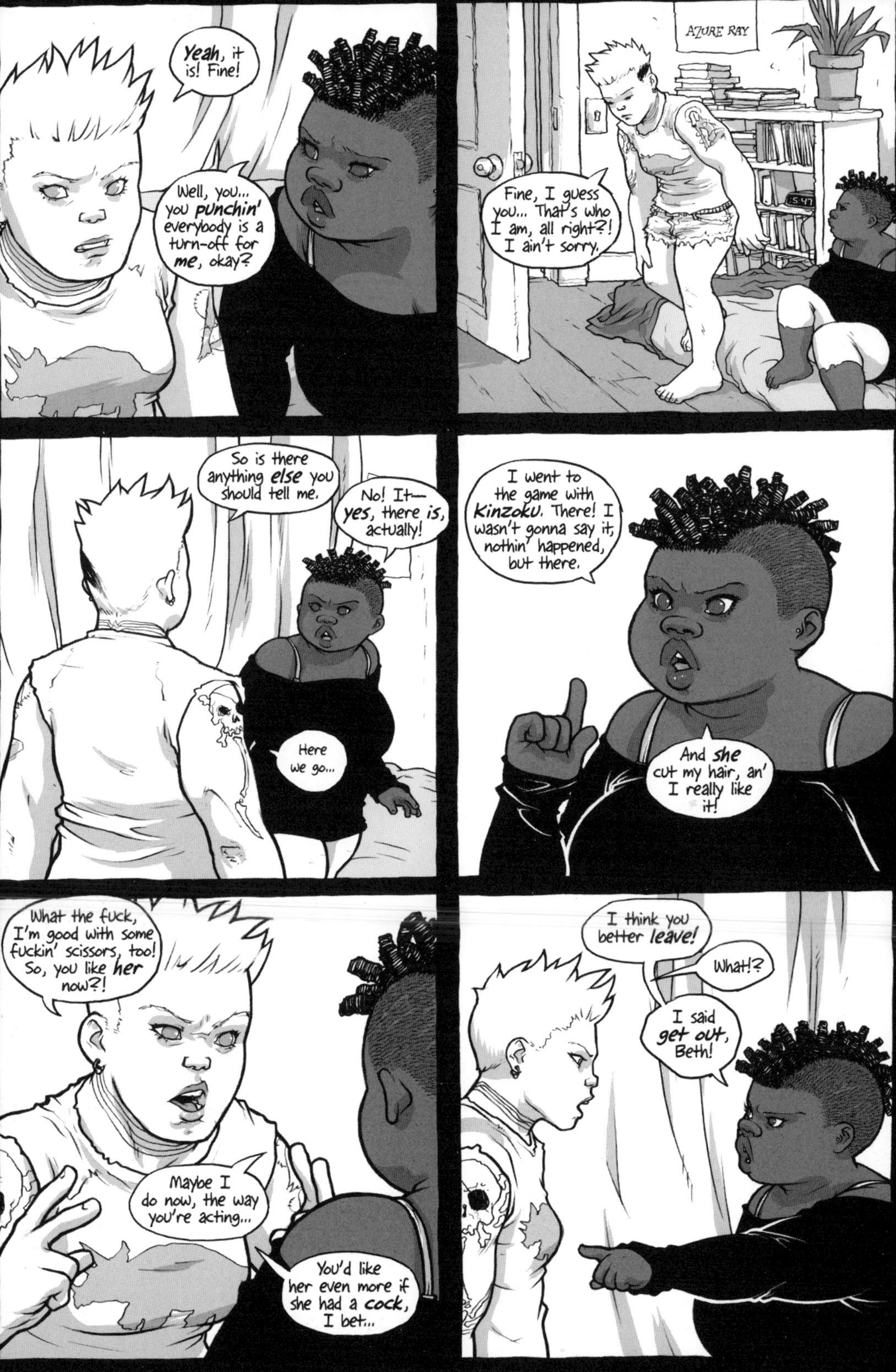

Yeah, it is! Fine!
Well, you... you punchin' everybody is a turn-off for me, okay?
AZURE RAY
Fine, I guess you... That's who I am, all right?! I ain't sorry.
So is there anything else you should tell me.
No! It— yes, there is, actually!
Here we go...
I went to the game with Kinzoku. There! I wasn't gonna say it, nothin' happened, but there.
And she cut my hair, an' I really like it!
What the fuck, I'm good with some fuckin' scissors, too! So, you like her now?!
Maybe I do now, the way you're acting...
You'd like her even more if she had a cock, I bet...
I think you better leave!
What!?
I said get out, Beth!

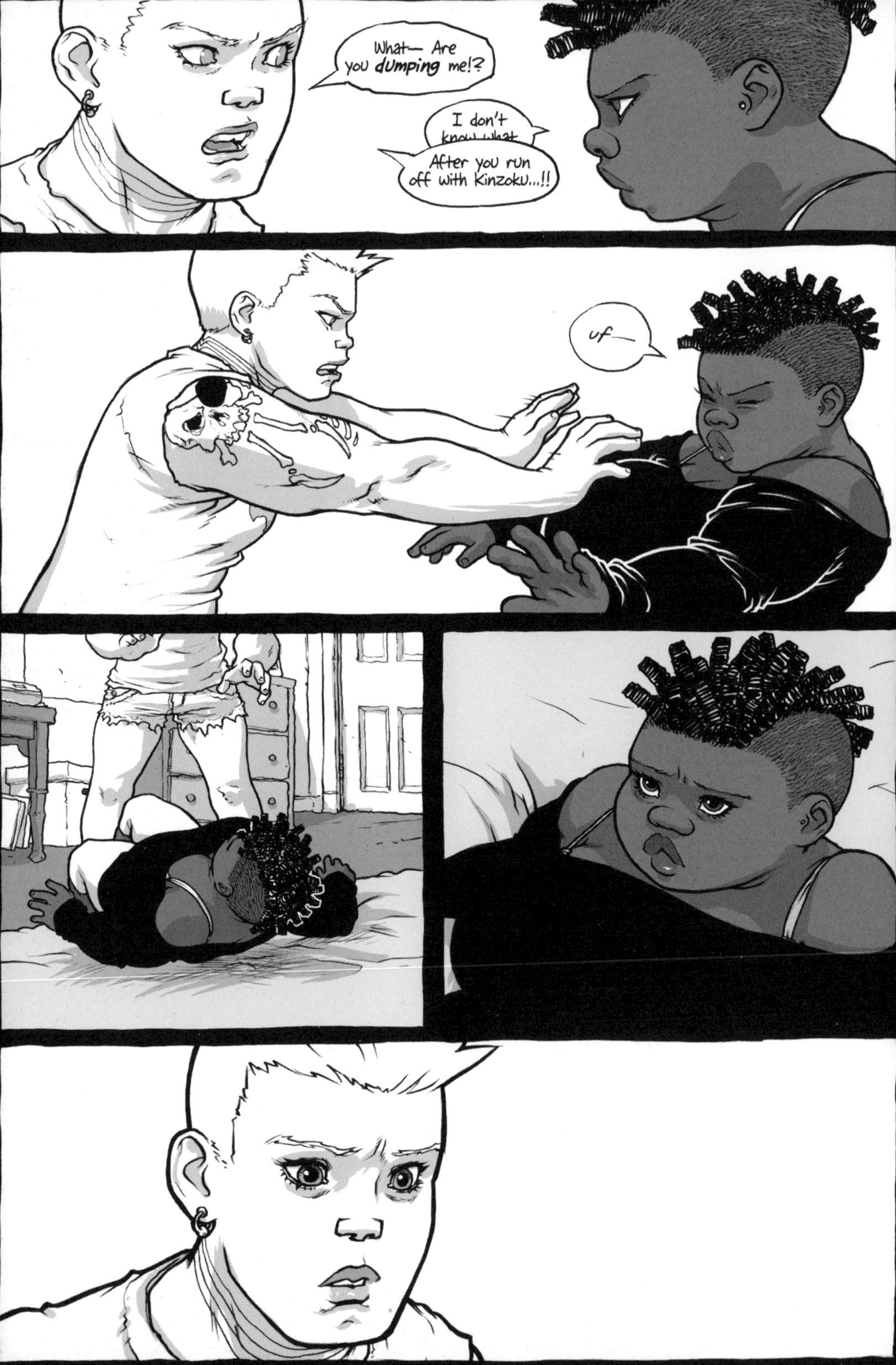
What— Are you dumping me!?
I don't
After you run off with Kinzoku...!!
uf—

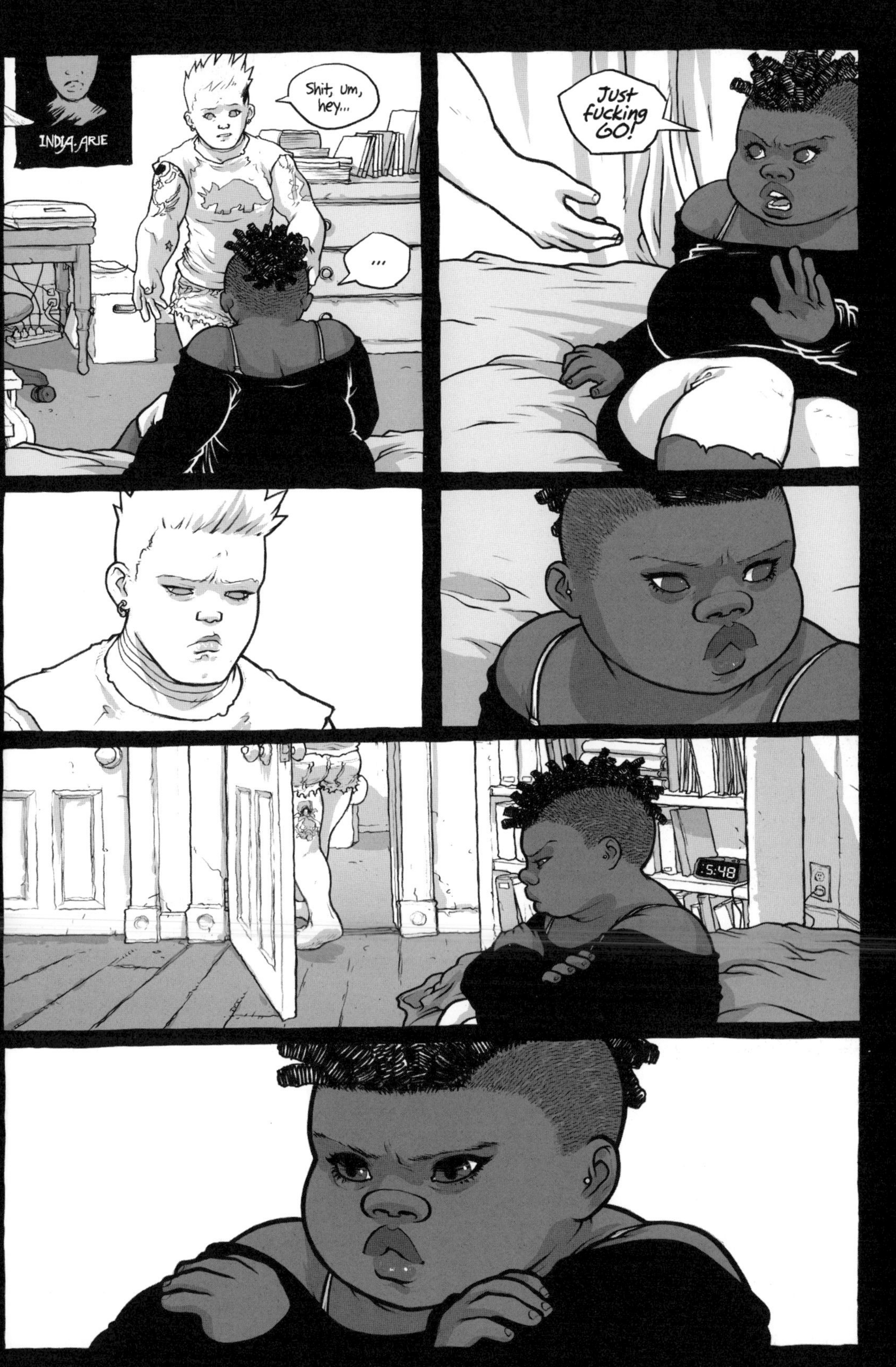
INDIA.ARIE
Shit, um, hey...
...
Just fucking GO!
5:48

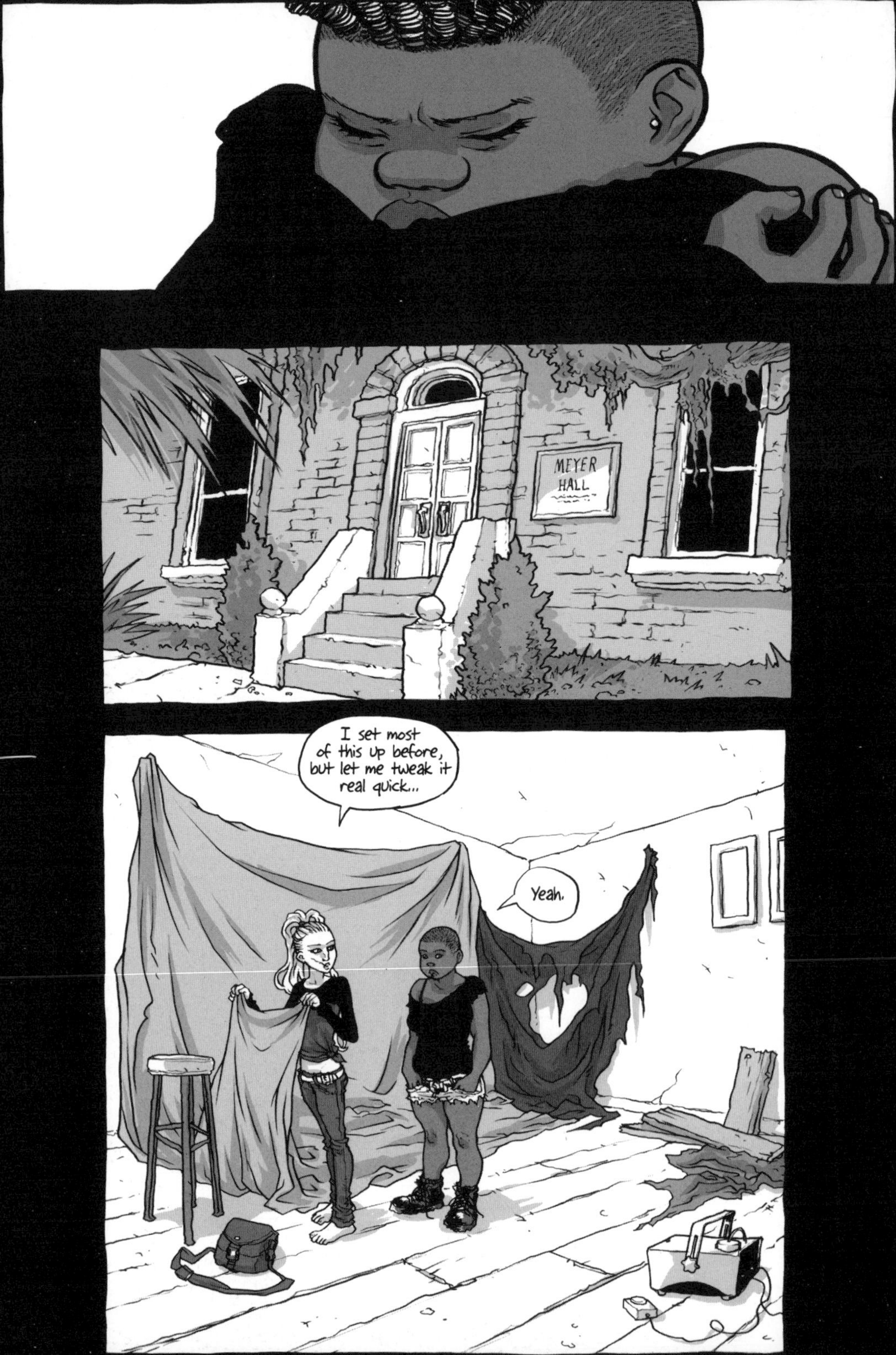
MEYER HALL
I set most of this up before, but let me tweak it real quick...
Yeah.

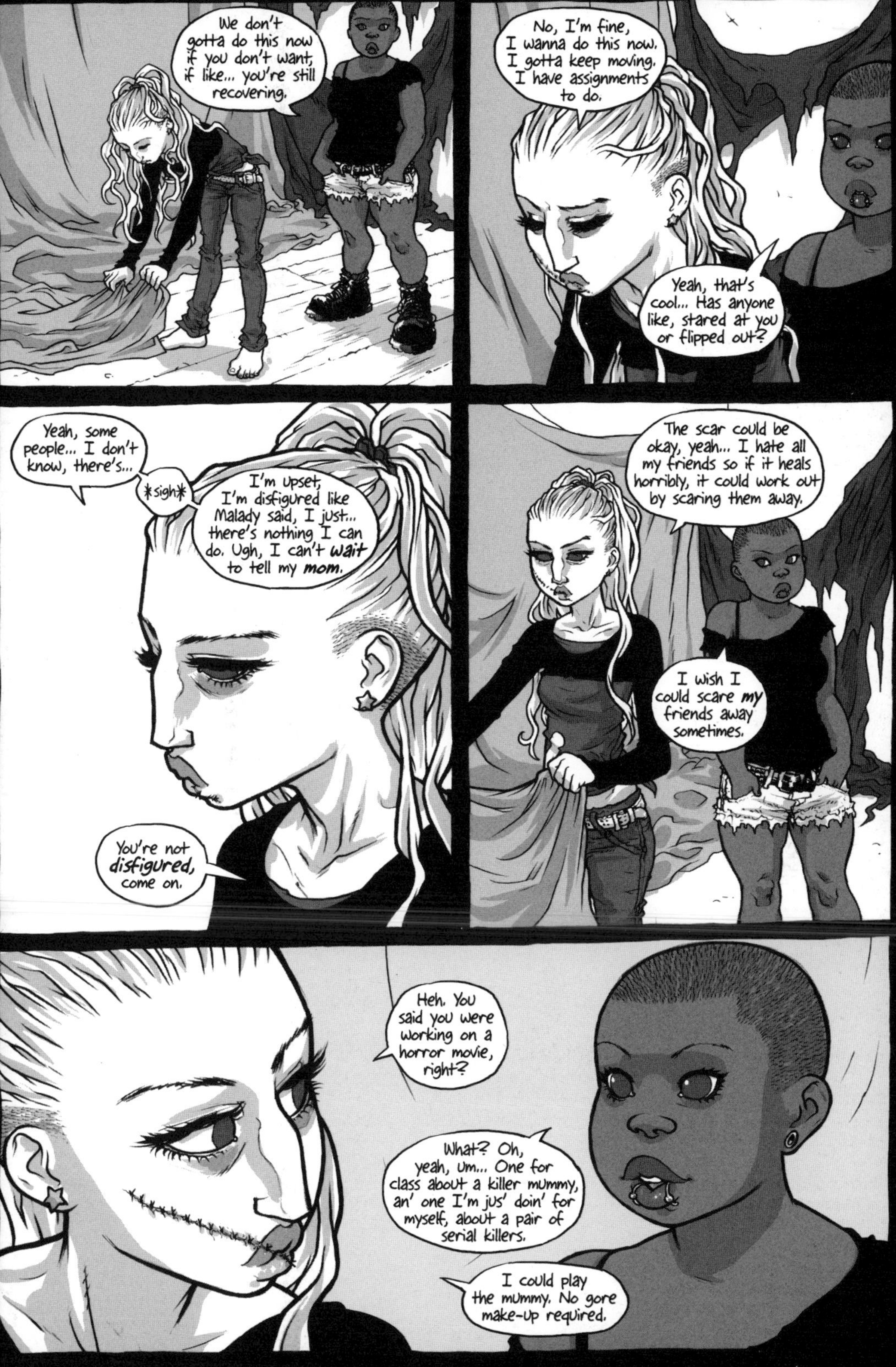
We don't gotta do this now if you don't want, if like... you're still recovering.
No, I'm fine, I wanna do this now. I gotta keep moving. I have assignments to do.
Yeah, that's cool... Has anyone like, stared at you or flipped out?
Yeah, some people... I don't know, there's...
sigh
I'm upset, I'm disfigured like Malady said, I just... there's nothing I can do. Ugh, I can't **wait** to tell my **mom**.
You're not **disfigured,** come on.
The scar could be okay, yeah... I hate all my friends so if it heals horribly, it could work out by scaring them away.
I wish I could scare **my** friends away sometimes.
Heh. You said you were working on a horror movie, right?
What? Oh, yeah, um... One for class about a killer mummy, an' one I'm jus' doin' for myself, about a pair of serial killers.
I could play the mummy. No gore make-up required.

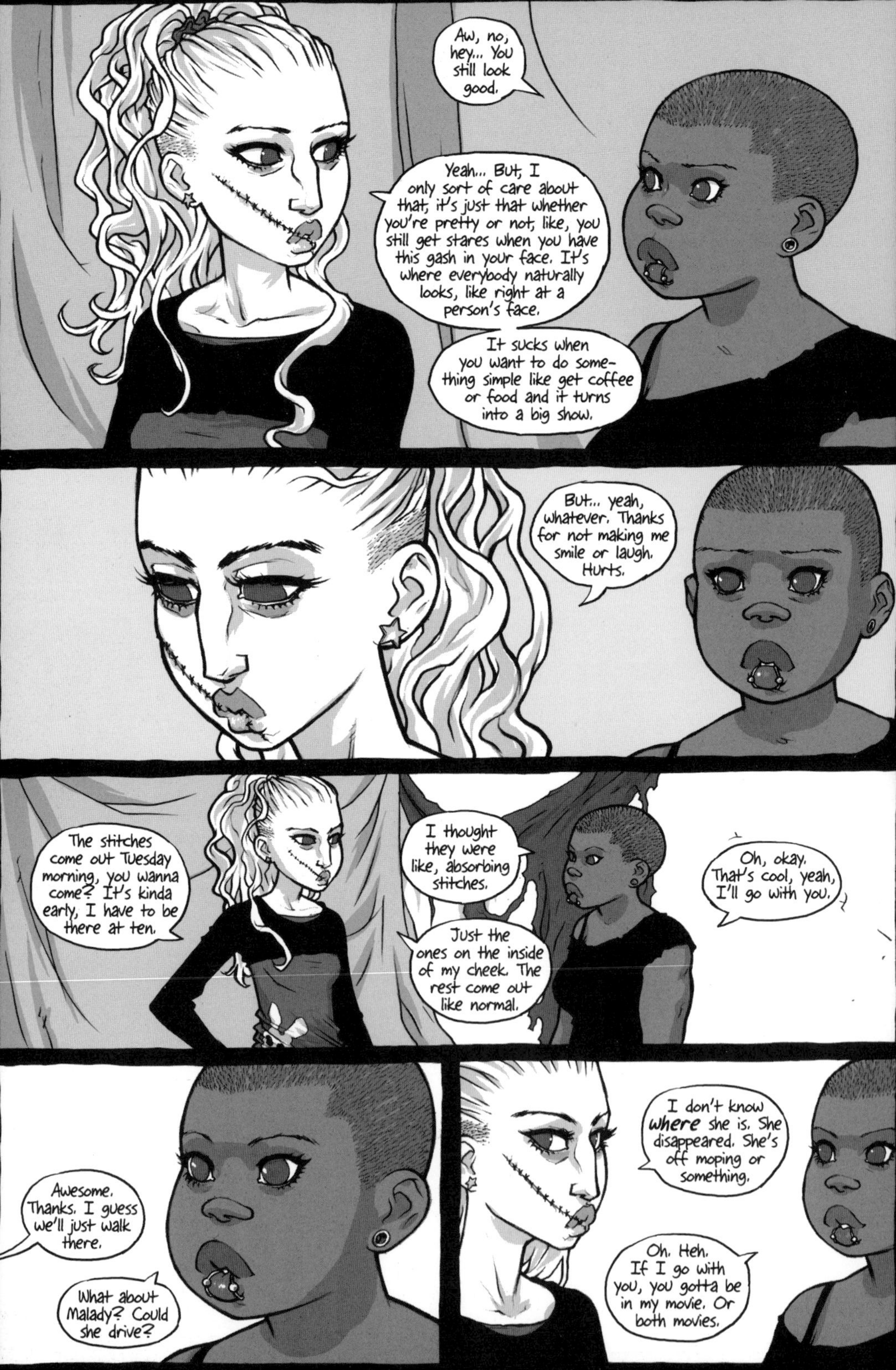

Aw, no, hey... You still look good.
Yeah... But, I only sort of care about that, it's just that whether you're pretty or not, like, you still get stares when you have this gash in your face. It's where everybody naturally looks, like right at a person's face.
It sucks when you want to do something simple like get coffee or food and it turns into a big show.
But... yeah, whatever. Thanks for not making me smile or laugh. Hurts.
The stitches come out Tuesday morning, you wanna come? It's kinda early, I have to be there at ten.
I thought they were like, absorbing stitches.
Just the ones on the inside of my cheek. The rest come out like normal.
Oh, okay. That's cool, yeah, I'll go with you.
Awesome. Thanks. I guess we'll just walk there.
What about Malady? Could she drive?
I don't know *where* she is. She disappeared. She's off moping or something.
Oh. Heh. If I go with you, you gotta be in my movie. Or both movies.

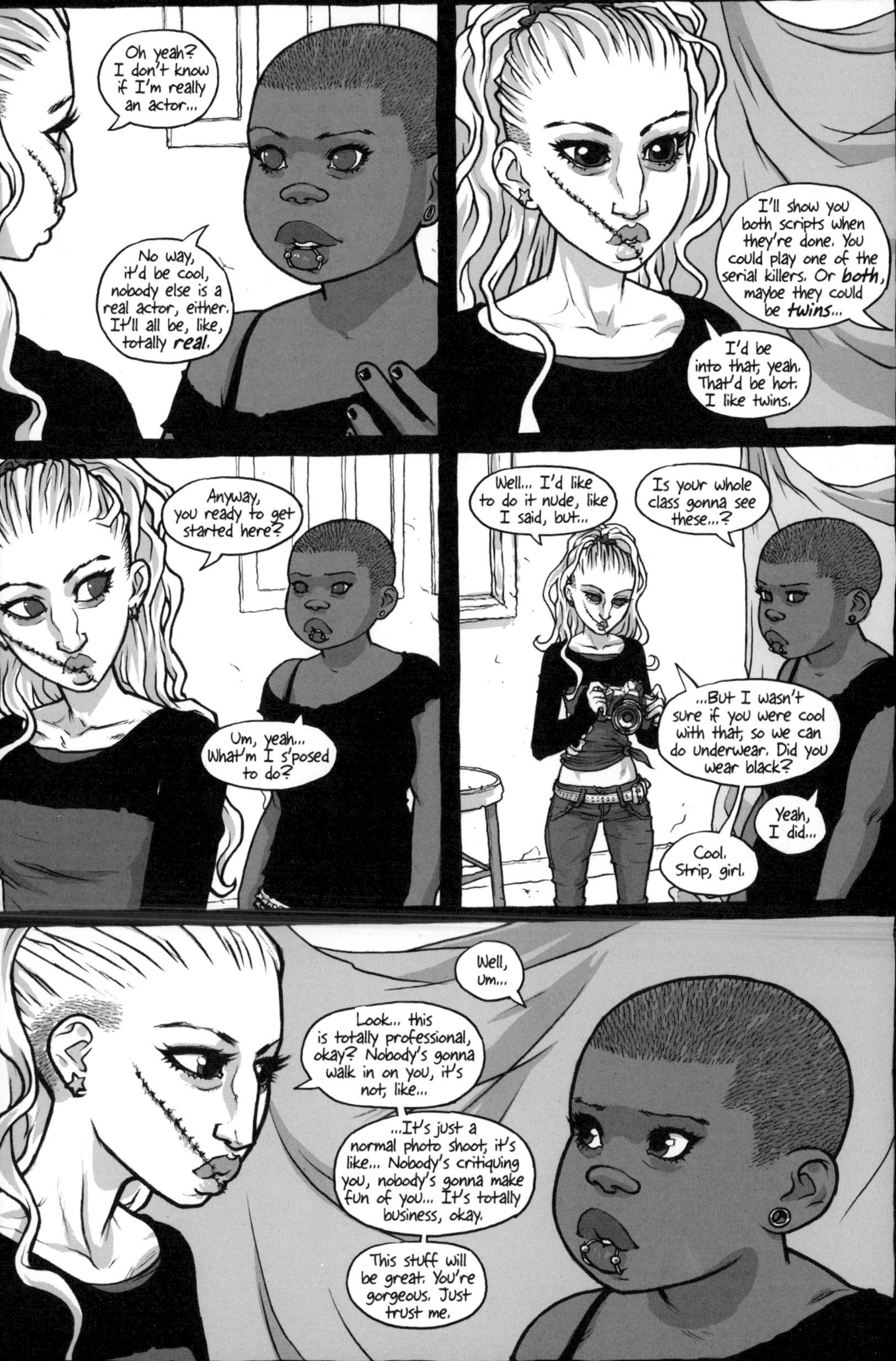
Oh yeah? I don't know if I'm really an actor...
No way, it'd be cool, nobody else is a real actor, either. It'll all be, like, totally *real*.
I'll show you both scripts when they're done. You could play one of the serial killers. Or *both*, maybe they could be *twins*...
I'd be into that, yeah. That'd be hot. I like twins.
Anyway, you ready to get started here?
Um, yeah... What'm I s'posed to do?
Well... I'd like to do it nude, like I said, but...
Is your whole class gonna see these...?
...But I wasn't sure if you were cool with that, so we can do underwear. Did you wear black?
Yeah, I did...
Cool. Strip, girl.
Well, um...
Look... this is totally professional, okay? Nobody's gonna walk in on you, it's not, like...
...It's just a normal photo shoot, it's like... Nobody's critiquing you, nobody's gonna make fun of you... It's totally business, okay.
This stuff will be great. You're gorgeous. Just trust me.

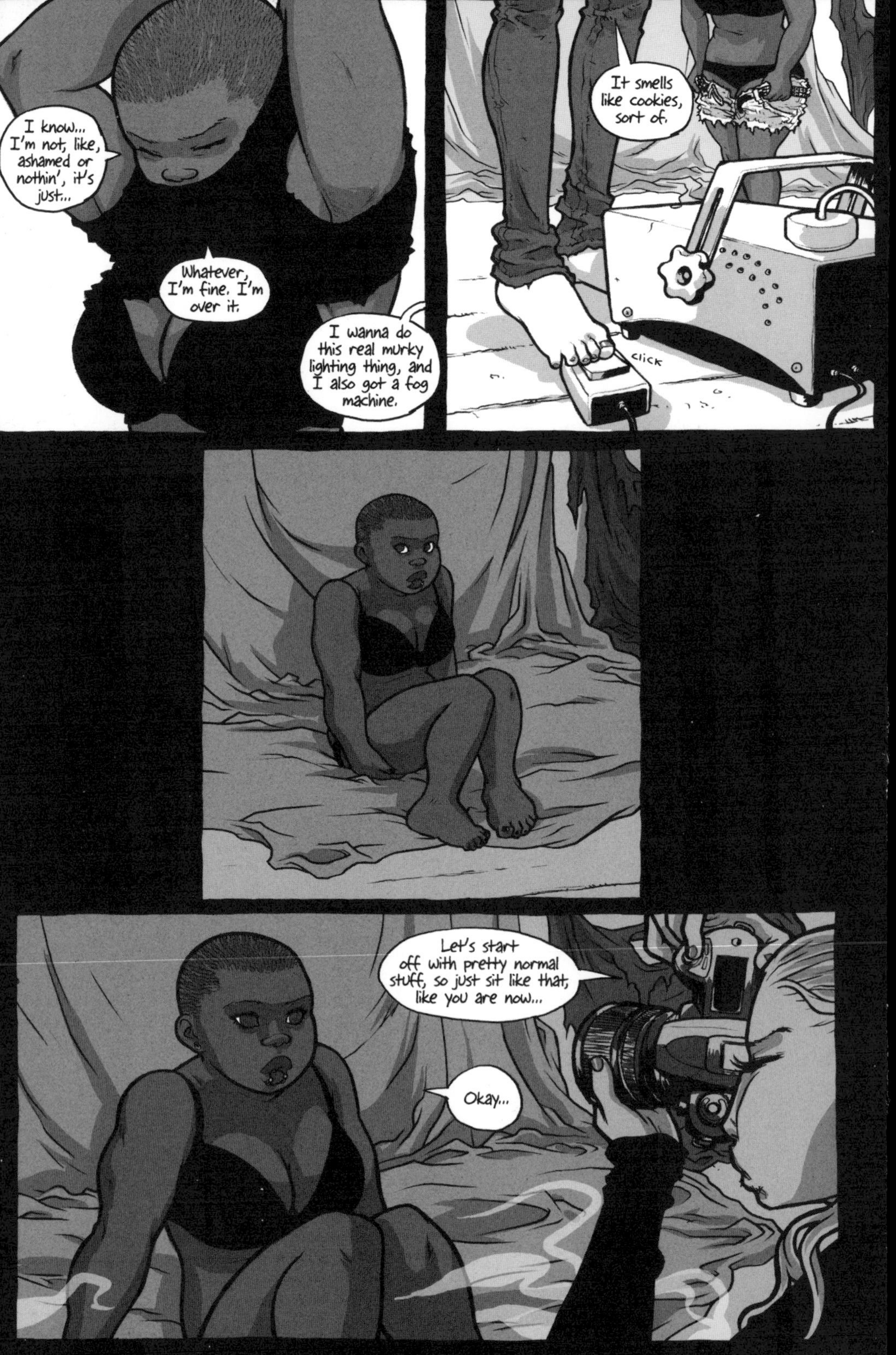

I know... I'm not, like, ashamed or nothin', it's just...
Whatever, I'm fine. I'm over it.
I wanna do this real murky lighting thing, and I also got a fog machine.
It smells like cookies, sort of.
click
Let's start off with pretty normal stuff, so just sit like that, like you are now...
Okay...

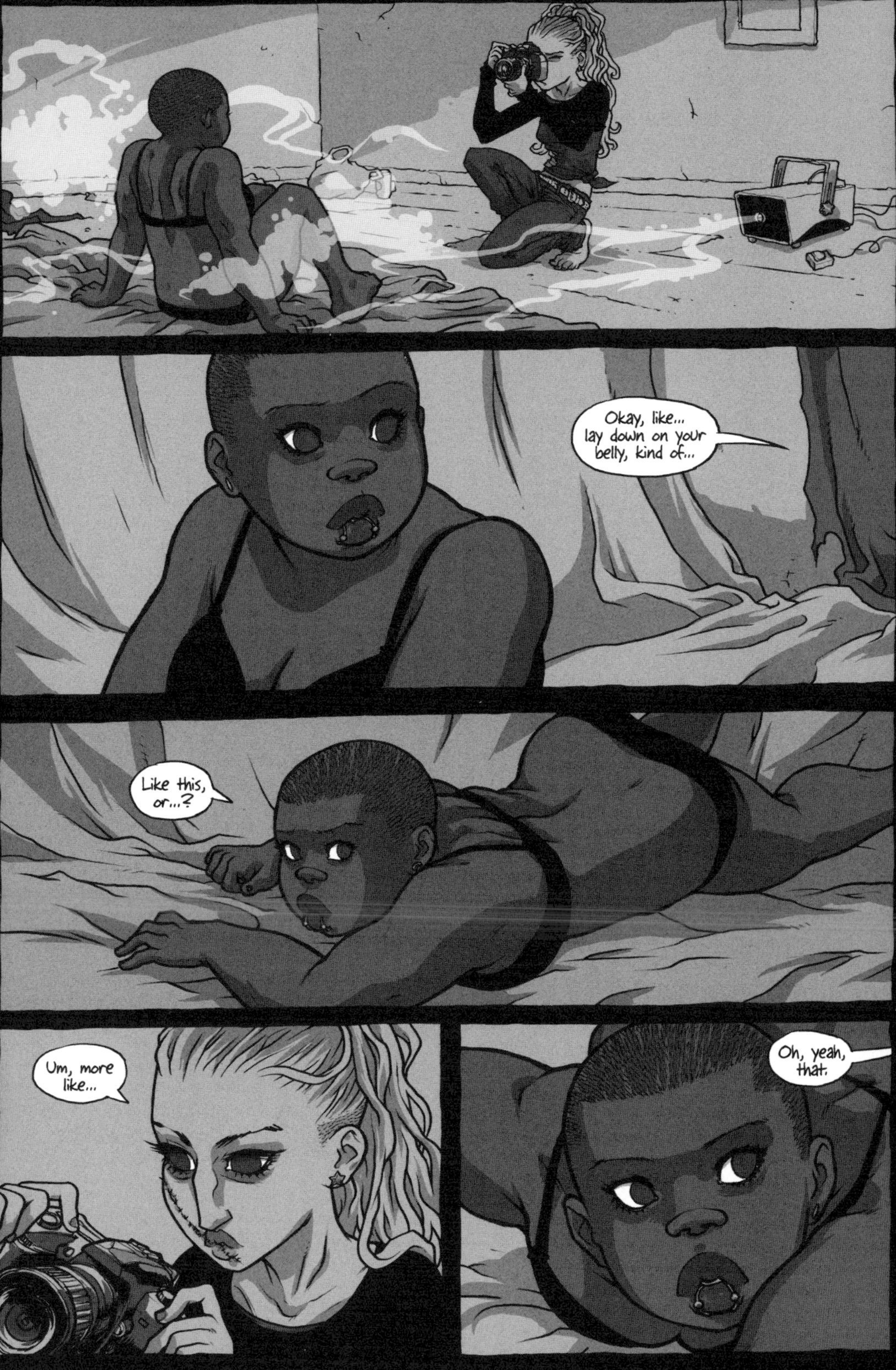
Okay, like... lay down on your belly, kind of...
Like this, or...?
Um, more like...
Oh, yeah, that.

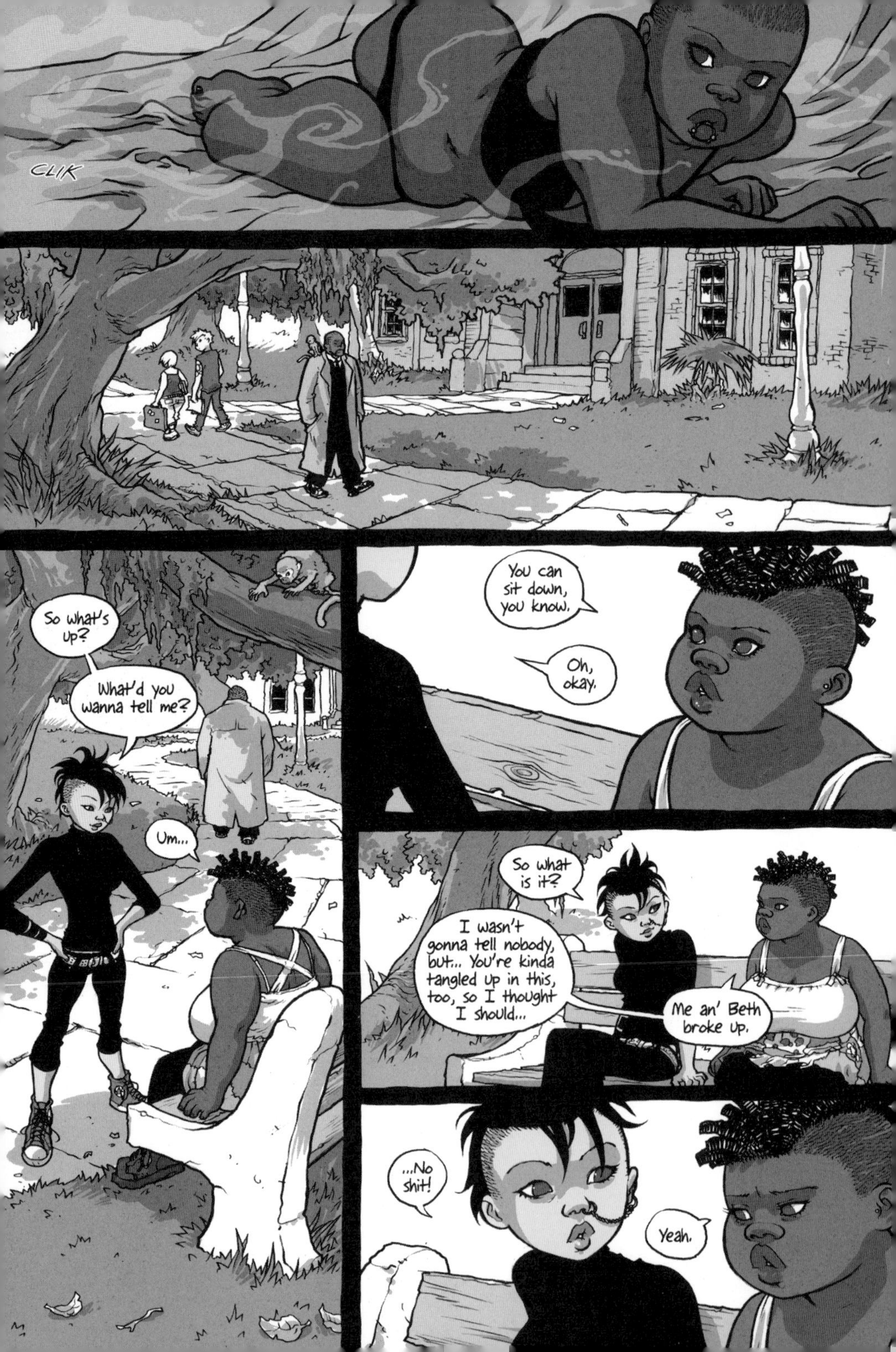

CLIK
So what's up?
What'd you wanna tell me?
Um...
You can sit down, you know.
Oh, okay.
So what is it?
I wasn't gonna tell nobody, but... You're kinda tangled up in this, too, so I thought I should...
Me an' Beth broke up.
...No shit!
Yeah.

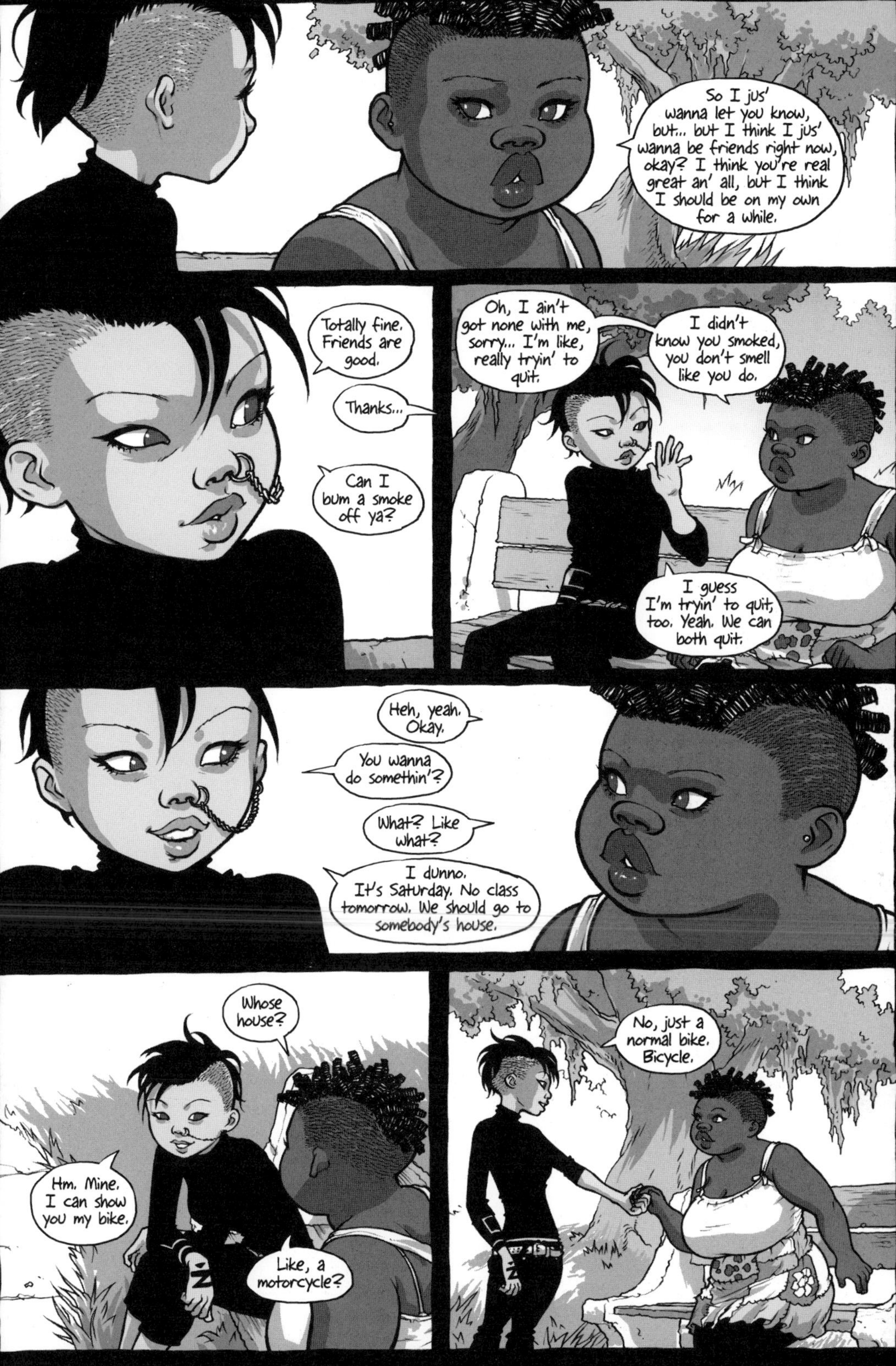
So I jus' wanna let you know, but... but I think I jus' wanna be friends right now, okay? I think you're real great an' all, but I think I should be on my own for a while.
Totally fine. Friends are good.
Thanks...
Can I bum a smoke off ya?
Oh, I ain't got none with me, sorry... I'm like, really tryin' to quit.
I didn't know you smoked, you don't smell like you do.
I guess I'm tryin' to quit, too. Yeah. We can both quit.
Heh, yeah. Okay.
You wanna do somethin'?
What? Like what?
I dunno. It's Saturday. No class tomorrow. We should go to somebody's house.
Whose house?
Hm. Mine. I can show you my bike.
Like, a motorcycle?
No, just a normal bike. Bicycle.

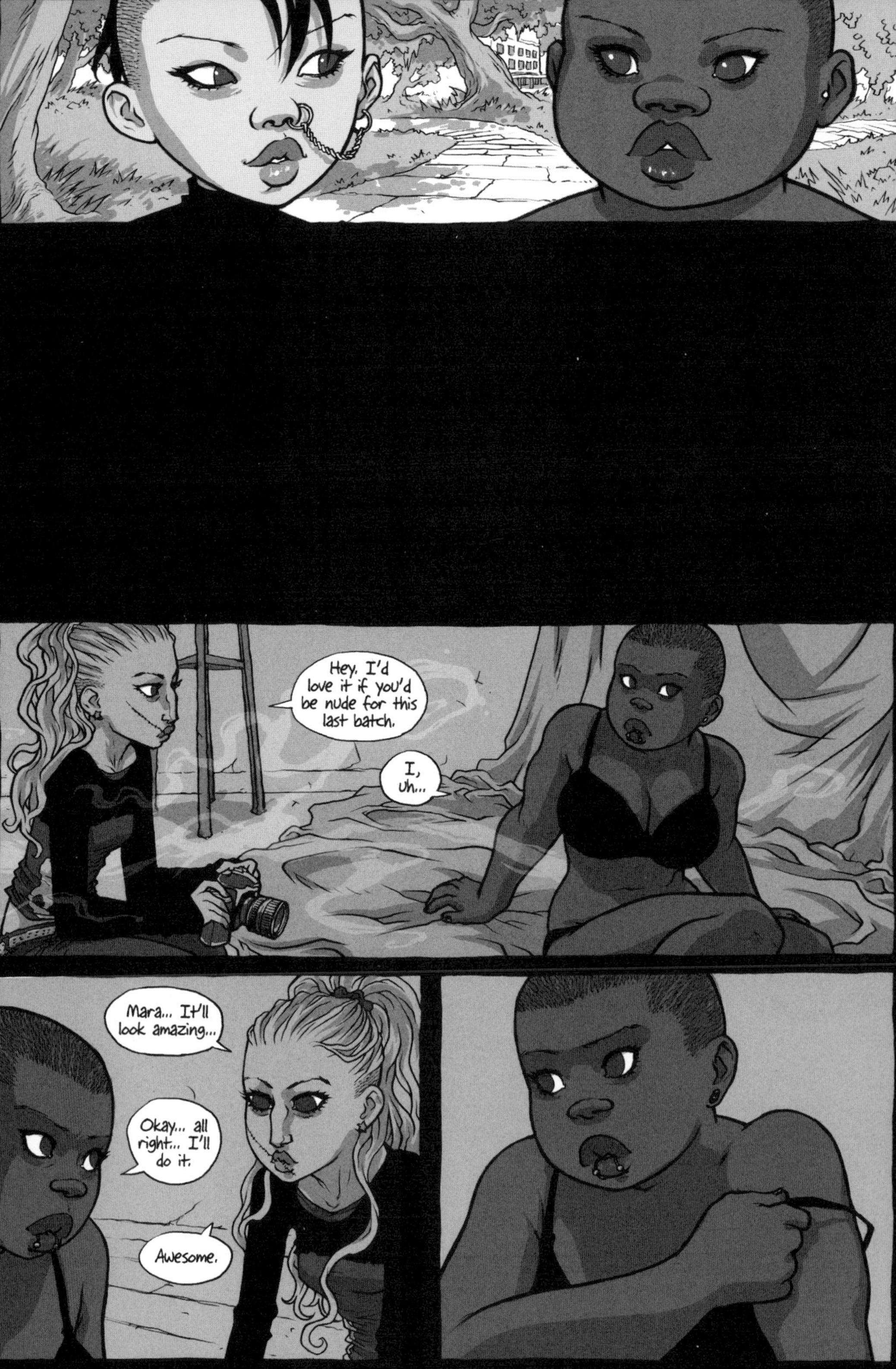
Hey. I'd love it if you'd be nude for this last batch.
I, uh...
Mara... It'll look amazing...
Okay... all right... I'll do it.
Awesome.

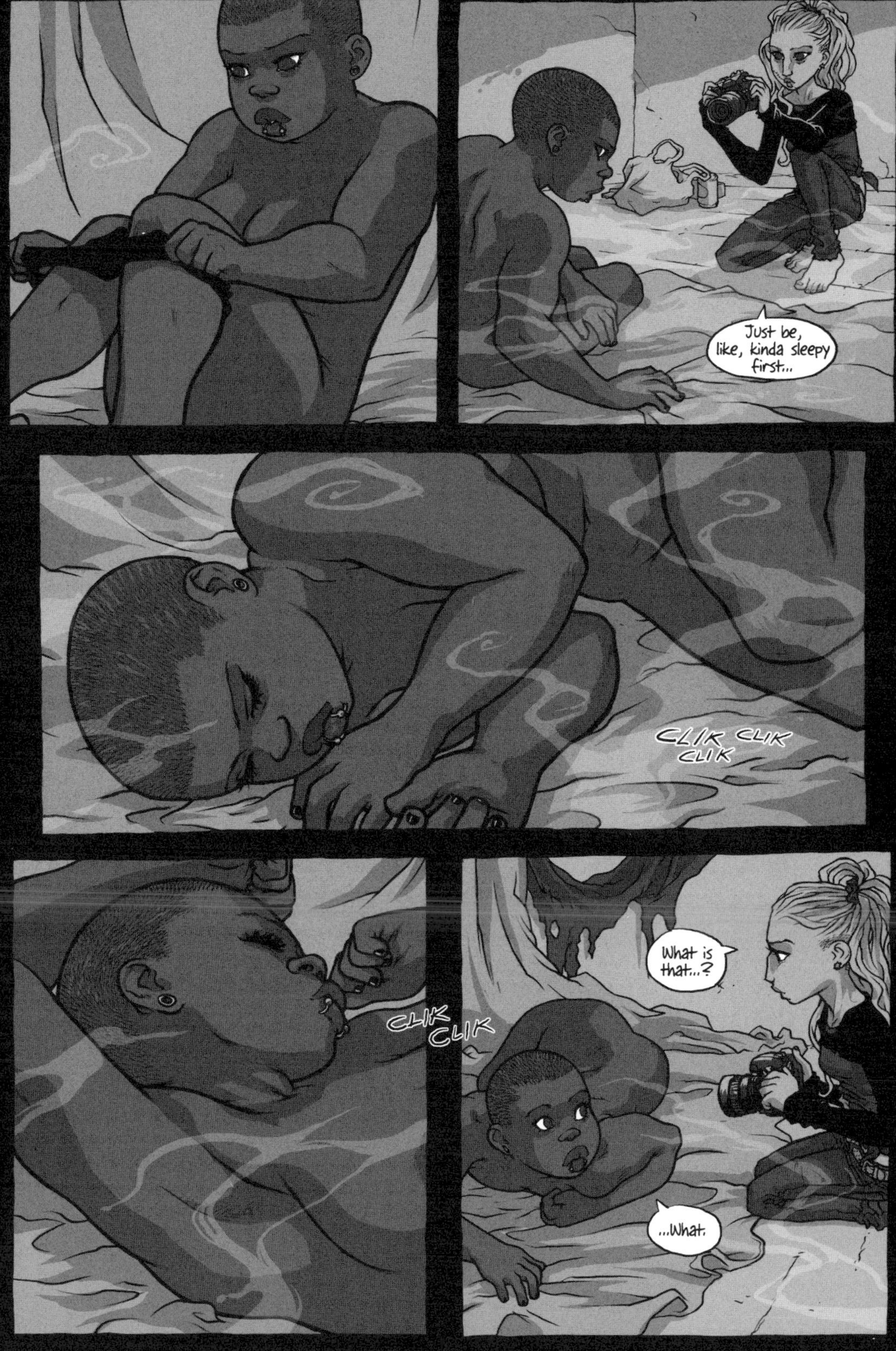
Just be, like, kinda sleepy first...
CLIK CLIK
CLIK
CLIK
CLIK
What is that...?
...What.

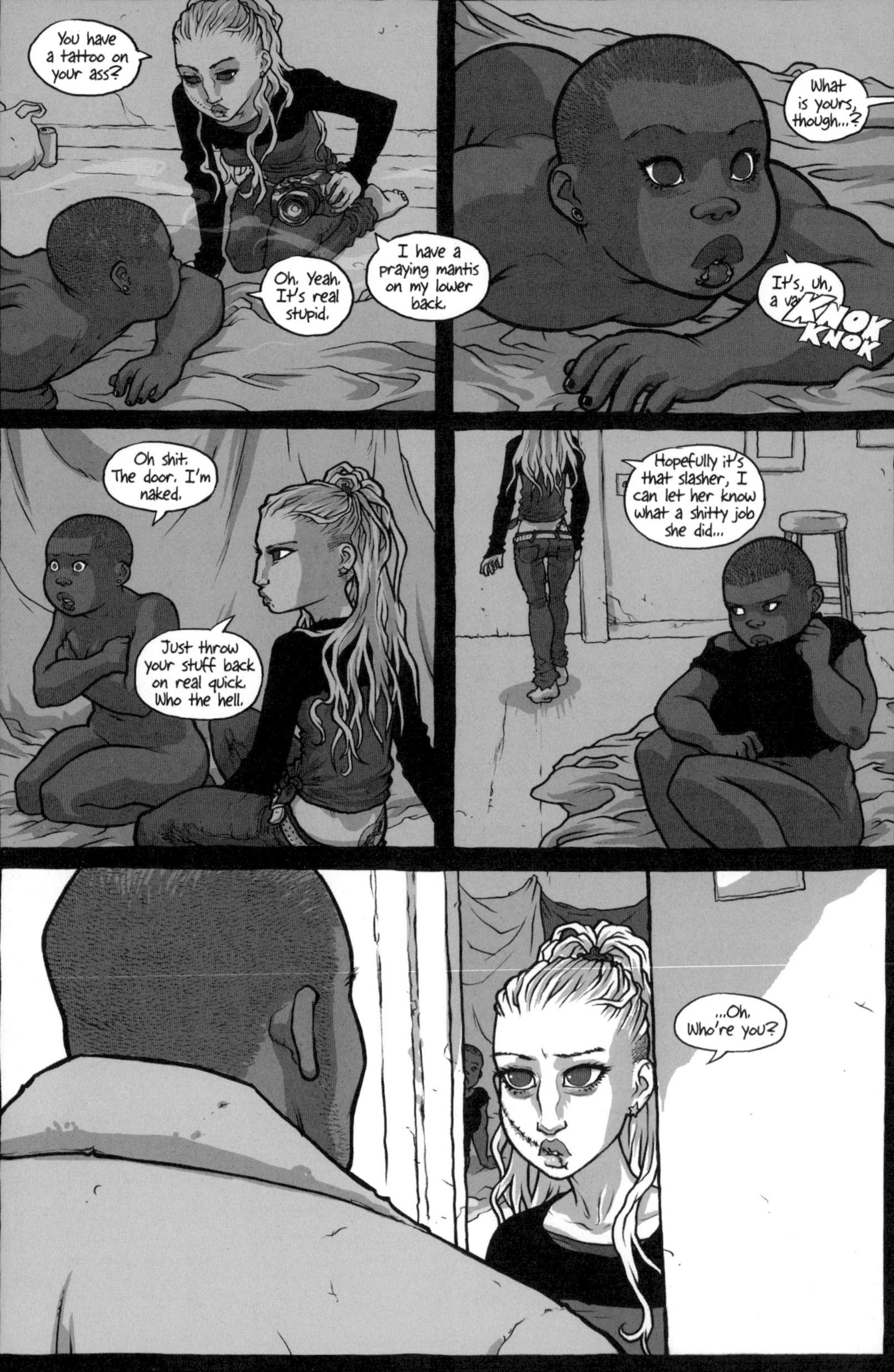
You have a tattoo on your ass?
Oh. Yeah. It's real stupid.
I have a praying mantis on my lower back.
What is yours, though...?
It's, uh, a va
KNOK KNOK
Oh shit. The door. I'm naked.
Just throw your stuff back on real quick. Who the hell.
Hopefully it's that slasher, I can let her know what a shitty job she did...
...Oh. Who're you?

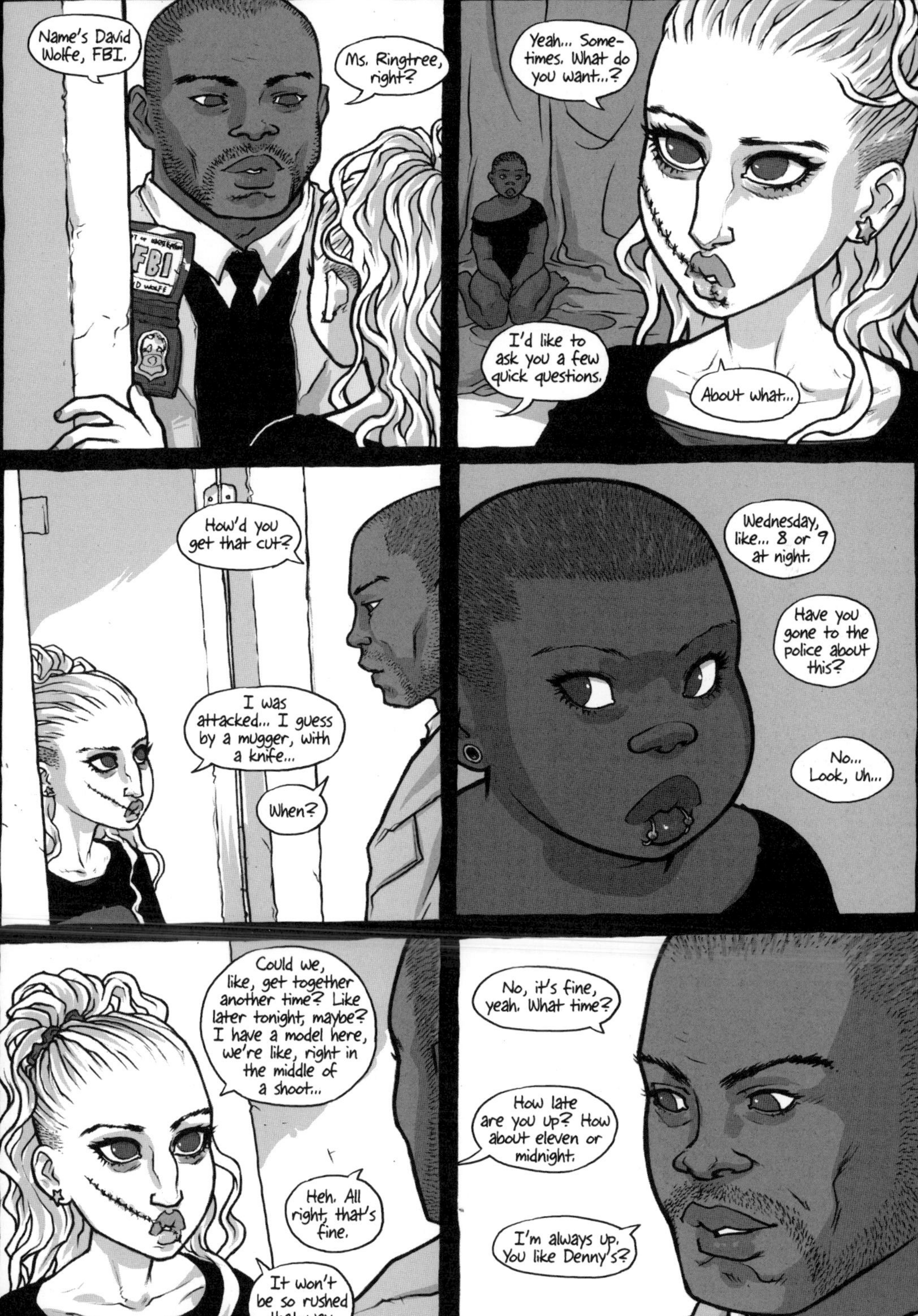
Name's David Wolfe, FBI.
Ms. Ringtree, right?
Yeah... Some-times. What do you want...?
I'd like to ask you a few quick questions.
About what...
How'd you get that cut?
I was attacked... I guess by a mugger, with a knife...
When?
Wednesday, like... 8 or 9 at night.
Have you gone to the police about this?
No... Look, uh...
Could we, like, get together another time? Like later tonight, maybe? I have a model here, we're like, right in the middle of a shoot...
Heh. All right, that's fine.
It won't be so rushed that way, either.
No, it's fine, yeah. What time?
How late are you up? How about eleven or midnight.
I'm always up. You like Denny's?

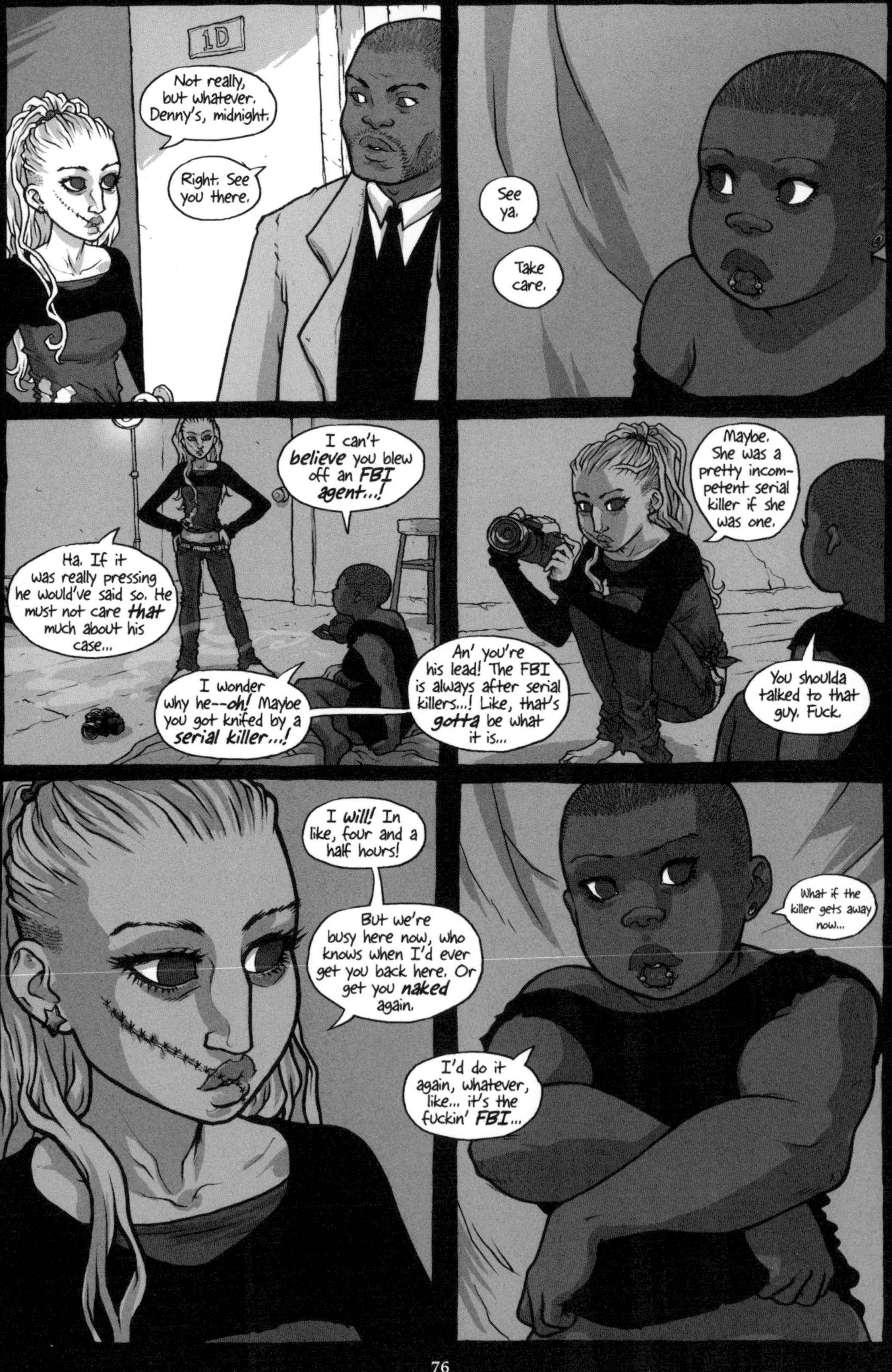
1D
Not really, but whatever. Denny's, midnight.
Right. See you there.
See ya.
Take care.
I can't *believe* you blew off an *FBI agent*...!
Ha. If it was really pressing he would've said so. He must not care *that* much about his case...
I wonder why he--*oh!* Maybe you got knifed by a *serial killer*...!
An' you're his lead! The FBI is always after serial killers...! Like, that's *gotta* be what it is...
Maybe. She was a pretty incompetent serial killer if she was one.
You shoulda talked to that guy. Fuck.
I *will!* In like, four and a half hours!
But we're busy here now, who knows when I'd ever get you back here. Or get you *naked* again.
What if the killer gets away now...
I'd do it again, whatever, like... it's the fuckin' *FBI*...

24

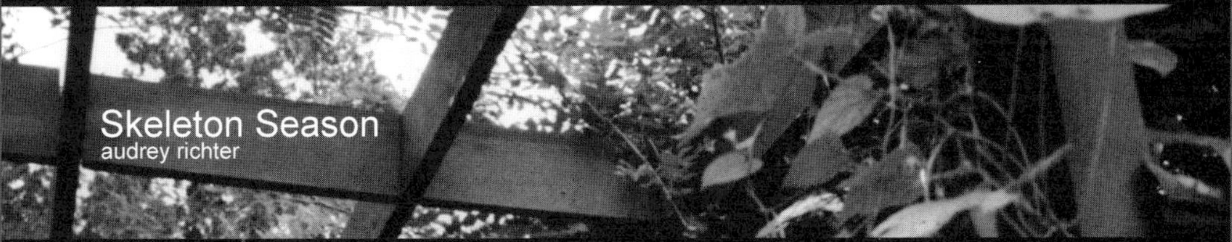
Skeleton Season
audrey richter

Profile

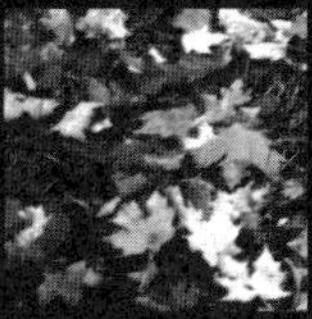

kittyhawk1

Latest Month

November

S	M	T	W	T	F	S
1	2	3	4	5	6	7
8	9	10	11	12	13	14
15	16	17	18	19	20	21
22	23	24	25	26	27	28
29	30	31				

View All Archives

Links

trilbyhatescomics

friendtoroaches

drop-dead

Backyard Birds

Vegans of Color

iamtheshadows.com

kenosha's tomb

230,000 Years Hence

Sisters of Battle

secretcrystal

Evil Galaxy

wetflame

hollow oasis

Twinfold Halfnot

Previous 20

sigh.

November 10th, 3:50pm

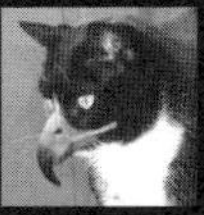

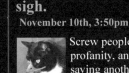

Screw people. No, I don't mean that, but I sure feel like it right now. I dislike profanity, and I like that my blog is potentially child-friendly, but I feel like saying another word instead of "screw"... however, we'll leave it at that. My, admittedly short-term, girlfriend and I broke up. Kind of violently, at least for me, I'm not used to be knocked down to the floor by an angry partner. So that was that, I won't tolerate stuff like that. Nobody ever thinks about domestic violence between two teenage girls, or even between two romantically involved adult WOMEN (which I legally am, but I'm still a teenager and think of myself like one), but it happens whether people decide to see it or not. And I'm so mad already about the whole thing, that my ex-gf would ever do something like that, that I know it's also happening to other girls (and anyone else) out there, but I'm even madder because I know as soon as I open dialogue with my friends or whoever about it, I'll be dismissed. Because I got knocked over by a seventeen year old girl so it's not "serious" and they'll probably laugh, at least at first. I can't brush it aside, though. I shouldn't have to feel awkward about it. I've also had it with the biphobia that seems to be creeping in all over the place in the dyke scene around here. The "B" is in LGBT for a reason!!! >:(That's a WHOLE other thing, I'll work on something about that for a future post. I'M SO MAD, you guys.

And another thing I can't brush aside (maybe a private post would be better for this because it involves private stuff and people I know, but I think it's important to have stuff like this out in the open where we can talk about it) is that my roommate had sex at least once with a 15 year old girl, one I was supposed to be babysitting at the time when it first happened. Apparently they'd met before, but my RM told me that the sex was the first time. I haven't had a chance to really talk to him yet, he's extraordinarily slippery. It's also slipperier because me and him used to date years ago, when I was about 15 and he was 21, so it's like... do I even have a leg to stand on? I don't know. I did the same thing as this other girl, with the same guy who did the same things with me, too. I don't regret it, and it's weird because at the time and I guess even now, I still remember it all clearly, I don't remember feeling like I was being taken advantage of or seduced or manipulated, even though the guy in question is a big slimy jerk. So what if this other girl feels the same way? What do I do? Even if she genuinely likes this guy (ugh), the guy should still know better, but how do I deal with it without making the girl feel stupid or feel like I'm talking down to her because she "doesn't know better"? And how do I wrangle the guy? But then regardless of all that, it's still rape in our society, there's no way around that, no matter the situation you can't look at sex between a 15 year old and a 26 year old in any other way (and yes regardless of gender). And my roommate has uh... quite a history of lawbreaking, and even though he's a boorish smelly stupid dummy, I still care about him and I don't want him to go to prison for the rest of his life, but... I don't know what else to do except talk to them both, if that's even my place (I feel it is because I do care, they're my friends, and because my RM is sort of my ward (long story) and I was also the girl's ward at the time when they had sex). I wonder what I would do if it came to that, the guy going to prison. I don't know. I'm sorry for the disorganized post, I'm really scatterbrained right now and this entry is all over the place. There's just too much to cover in these topics.

Mood: frustrated

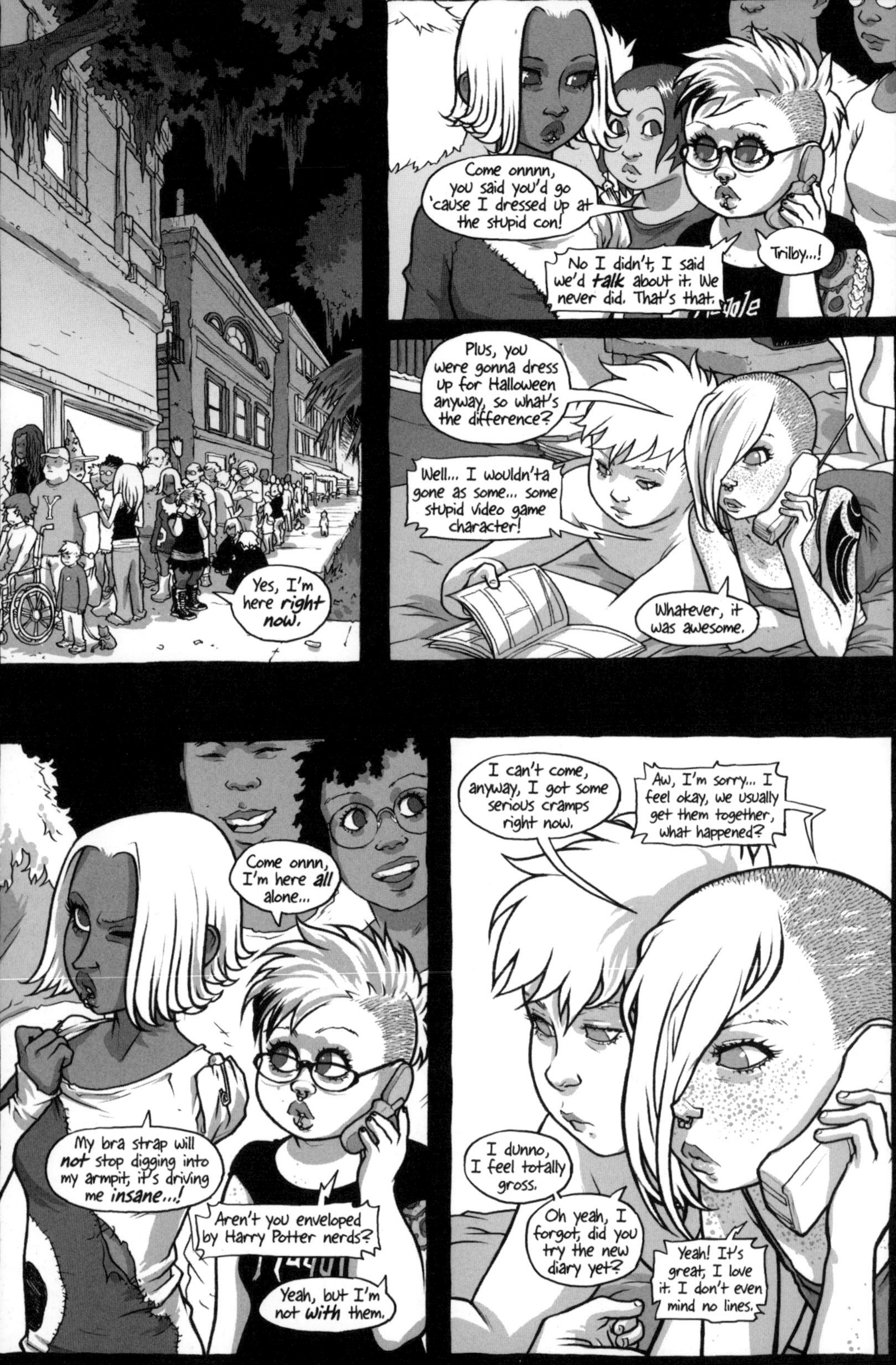
Yes, I'm here **right now.**
Come onnnn, you said you'd go 'cause I dressed up at the stupid con!
No I didn't, I said we'd **talk** about it. We never did. That's that.
Trilby...!
Plus, you were gonna dress up for Halloween anyway, so what's the difference?
Well... I wouldn'ta gone as some... some stupid video game character!
Whatever, it was awesome.
Come onnn, I'm here **all** alone...
My bra strap will **not** stop digging into my armpit, it's driving me **insane**...!
Aren't you enveloped by Harry Potter nerds?
Yeah, but I'm not **with** them.
I can't come, anyway, I got some serious cramps right now.
Aw, I'm sorry... I feel okay, we usually get them together, what happened?
I dunno, I feel totally gross.
Oh yeah, I forgot, did you try the new diary yet?
Yeah! It's great, I love it. I don't even mind no lines.

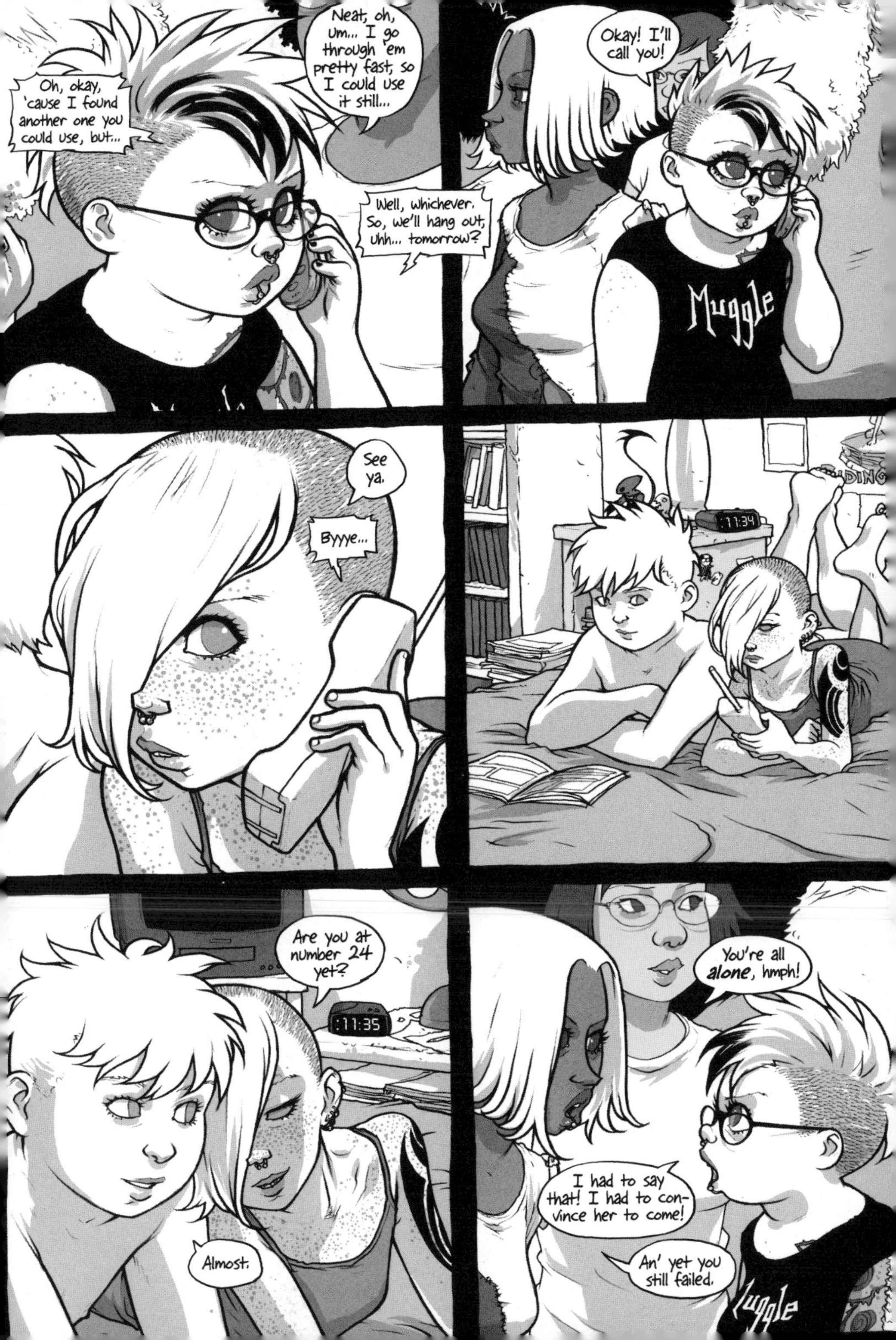

Oh, okay, 'cause I found another one you could use, but...
Neat, oh, um... I go through 'em pretty fast, so I could use it still...
Well, whichever. So, we'll hang out, uhh... tomorrow?
Okay! I'll call you!
Muggle
See ya.
Byyye...
11:34
Are you at number 24 yet?
11:35
Almost.
You're all **alone**, hmph!
I had to say that! I had to convince her to come!
An' yet you still failed.

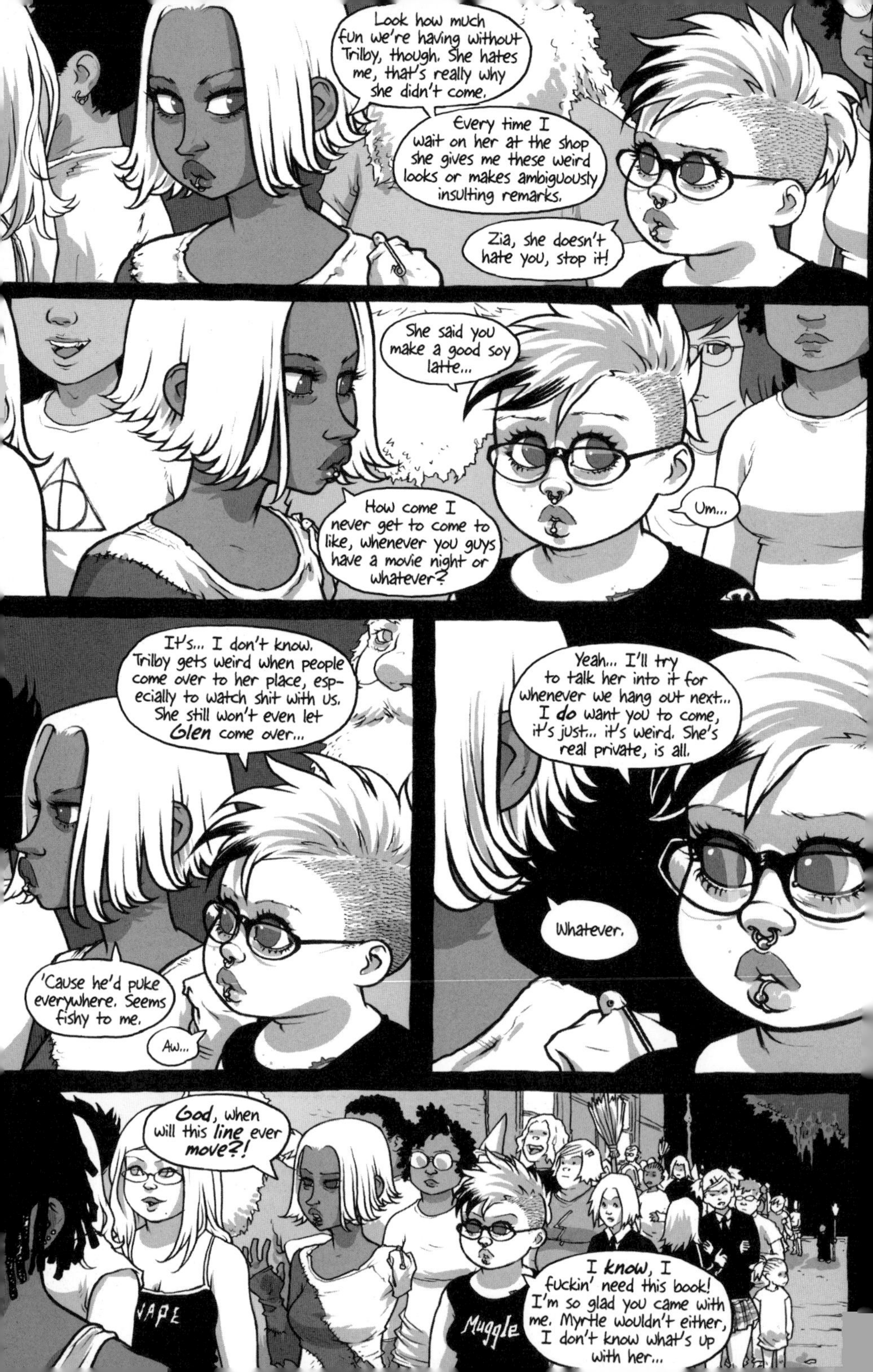
Look how much fun we're having without Trilby, though. She hates me, that's really why she didn't come.
Every time I wait on her at the shop she gives me these weird looks or makes ambiguously insulting remarks.
Zia, she doesn't hate you, stop it!
She said you make a good soy latte...
How come I never get to come to like, whenever you guys have a movie night or whatever?
Um...
It's... I don't know. Trilby gets weird when people come over to her place, especially to watch shit with us. She still won't even let Glen come over...
'Cause he'd puke everywhere. Seems fishy to me.
Aw...
Yeah... I'll try to talk her into it for whenever we hang out next... I do want you to come, it's just... it's weird. She's real private, is all.
Whatever.
God, when will this line ever move?!
I know, I fuckin' need this book! I'm so glad you came with me. Myrtle wouldn't either, I don't know what's up with her...
SNAPE
Muggle

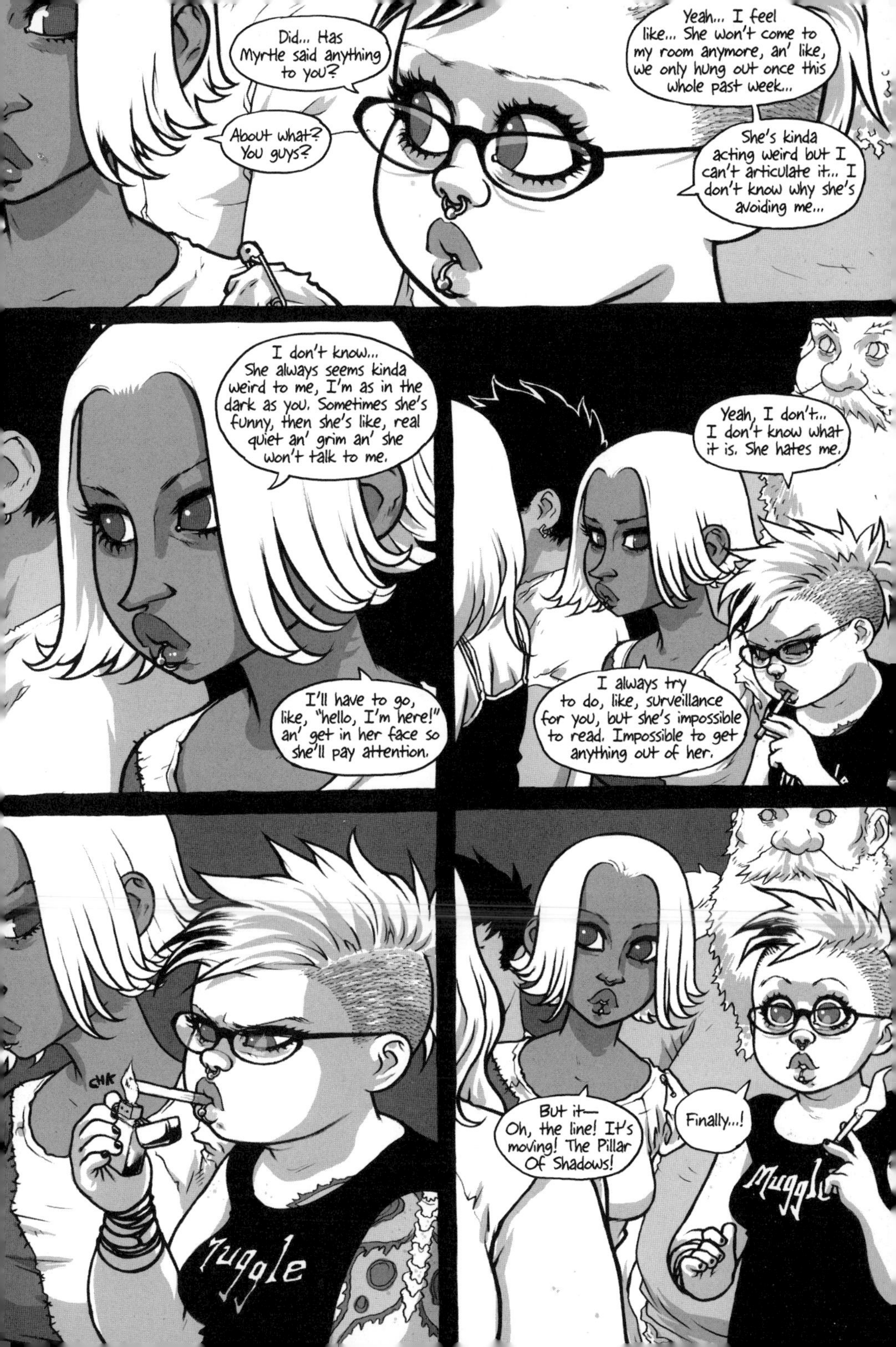
Did... Has Myrtle said anything to you?
About what? You guys?
Yeah... I feel like... She won't come to my room anymore, an' like, we only hung out once this whole past week...
She's kinda acting weird but I can't articulate it... I don't know why she's avoiding me...
I don't know... She always seems kinda weird to me, I'm as in the dark as you. Sometimes she's funny, then she's like, real quiet an' grim an' she won't talk to me.
I'll have to go, like, "hello, I'm here!" an' get in her face so she'll pay attention.
Yeah, I don't... I don't know what it is. She hates me.
I always try to do, like, surveillance for you, but she's impossible to read. Impossible to get anything out of her.
CHK
Muggle
But it— Oh, the line! It's moving! The Pillar Of Shadows!
Finally...!

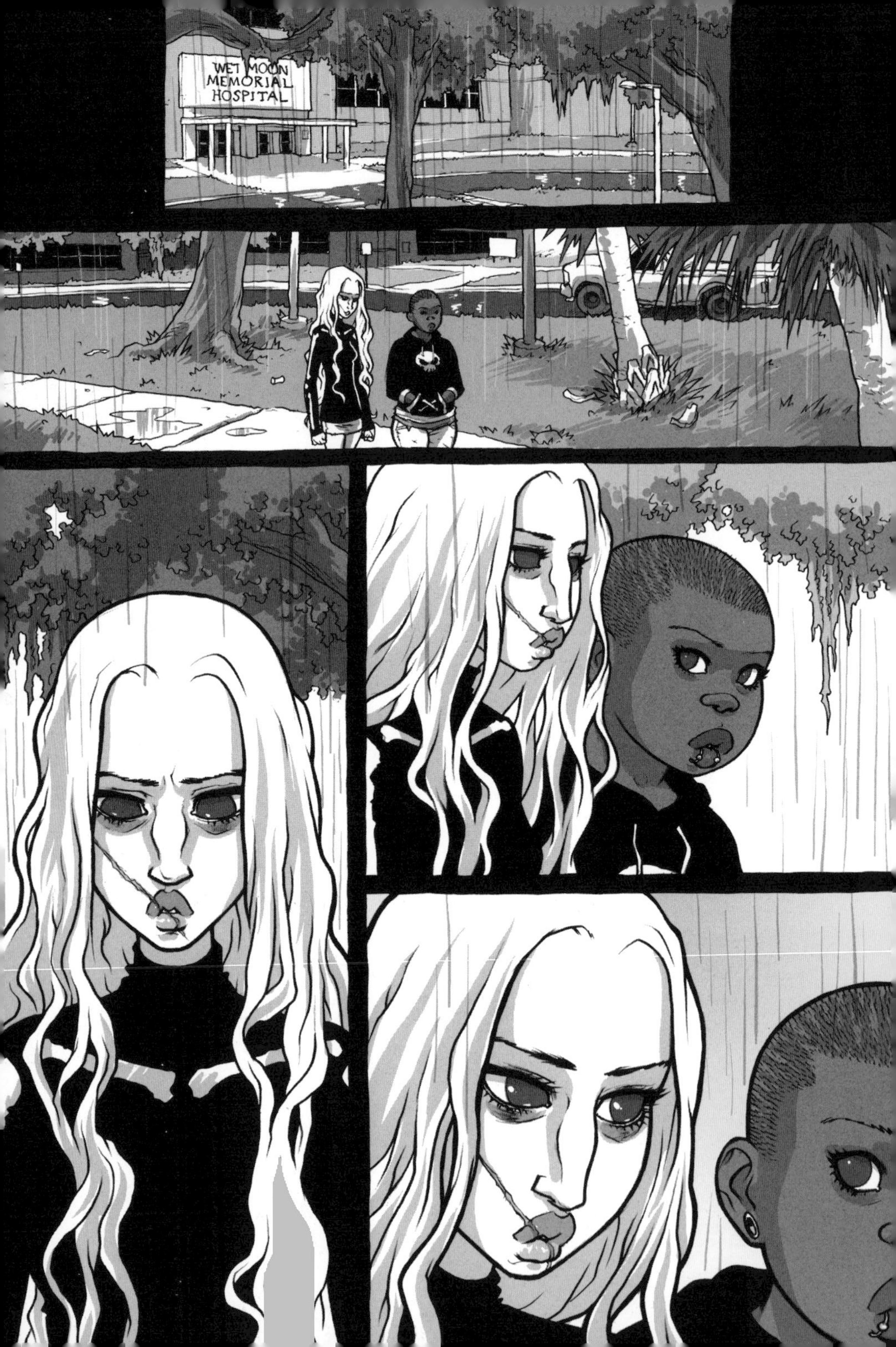
WET MOON
MEMORIAL
HOSPITAL

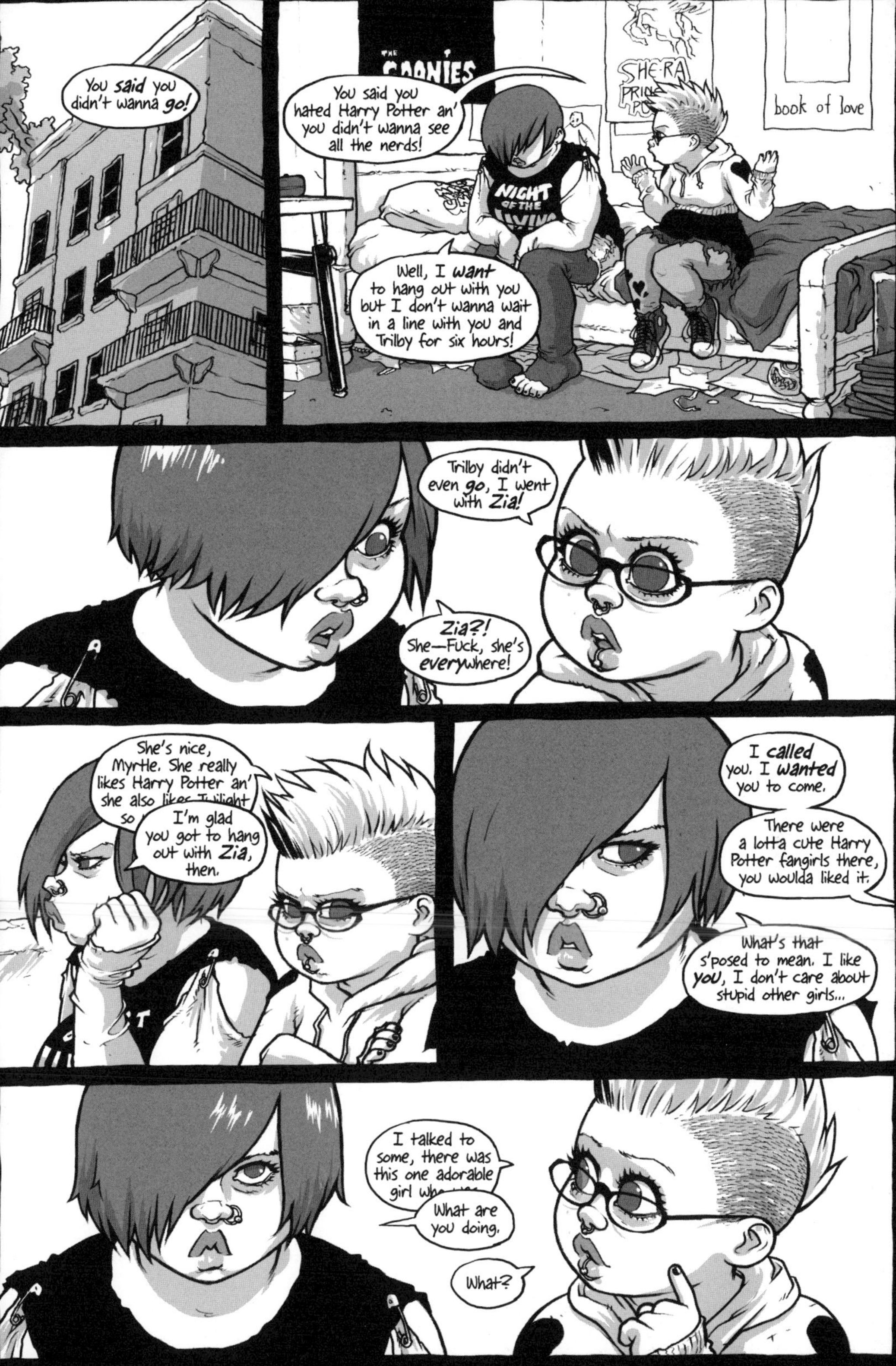
You said you didn't wanna go!
You said you hated Harry Potter an' you didn't wanna see all the nerds!
SHE-RA
book of love
Well, I want to hang out with you but I don't wanna wait in a line with you and Trilby for six hours!
Trilby didn't even go, I went with Zia!
Zia?! She—Fuck, she's everywhere!
She's nice, Myrtle. She really likes Harry Potter an' she also
I'm glad you got to hang out with Zia, then.
I called you. I wanted you to come.
There were a lotta cute Harry Potter fangirls there, you woulda liked it.
What's that s'posed to mean. I like you, I don't care about stupid other girls...
I talked to some, there was this one adorable girl
What are you doing.
What?

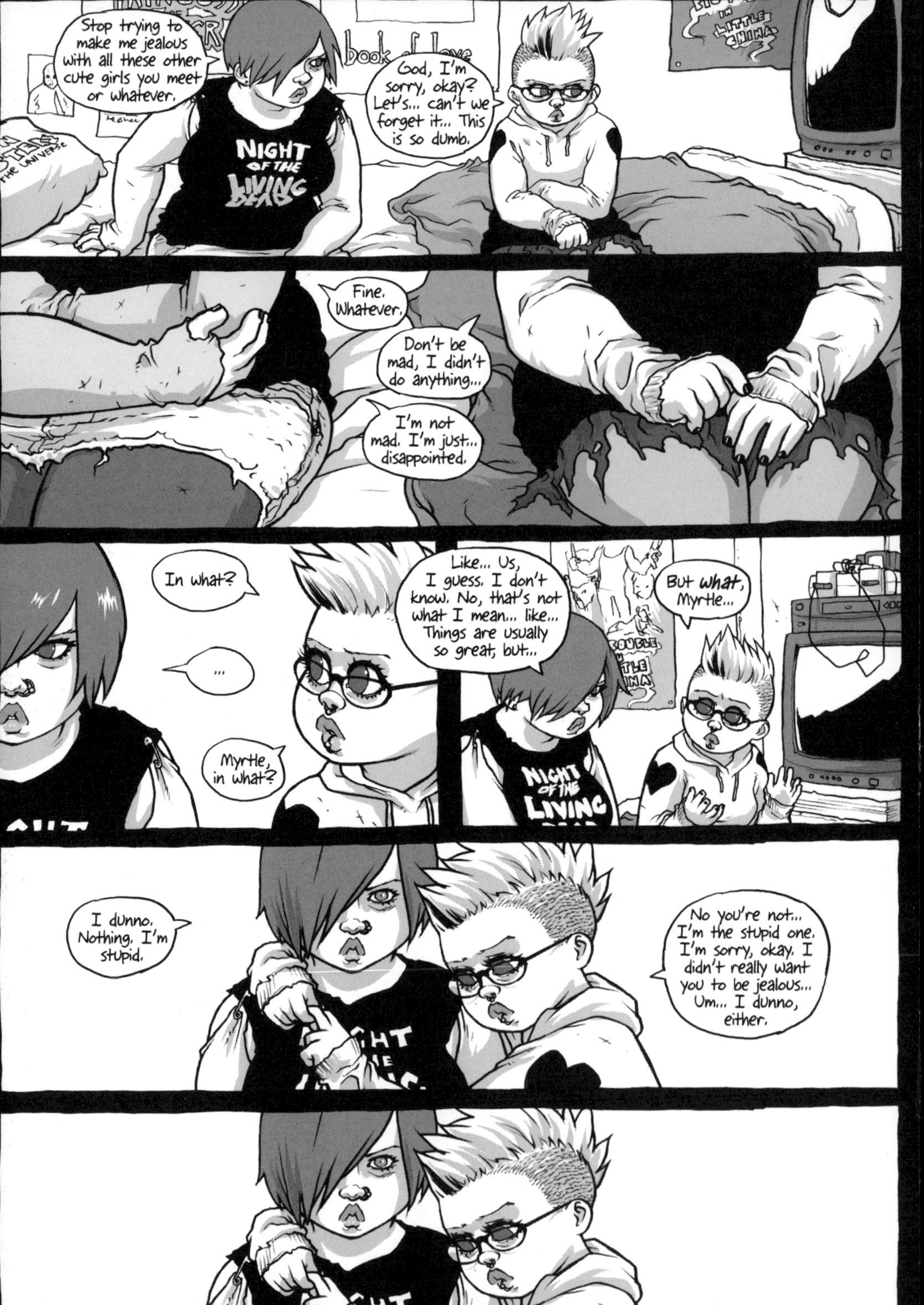

Stop trying to make me jealous with all these other cute girls you meet or whatever.
God, I'm sorry, okay? Let's... can't we forget it... This is so dumb.
NIGHT OF THE LIVING DEAD
Fine. Whatever.
Don't be mad, I didn't do anything...
I'm not mad. I'm just... disappointed.
In what?
...
Myrtle, in what?
Like... Us, I guess. I don't know. No, that's not what I mean... like... Things are usually so great, but...
But what, Myrtle...
I dunno. Nothing. I'm stupid.
No you're not... I'm the stupid one. I'm sorry, okay. I didn't really want you to be jealous... Um... I dunno, either.

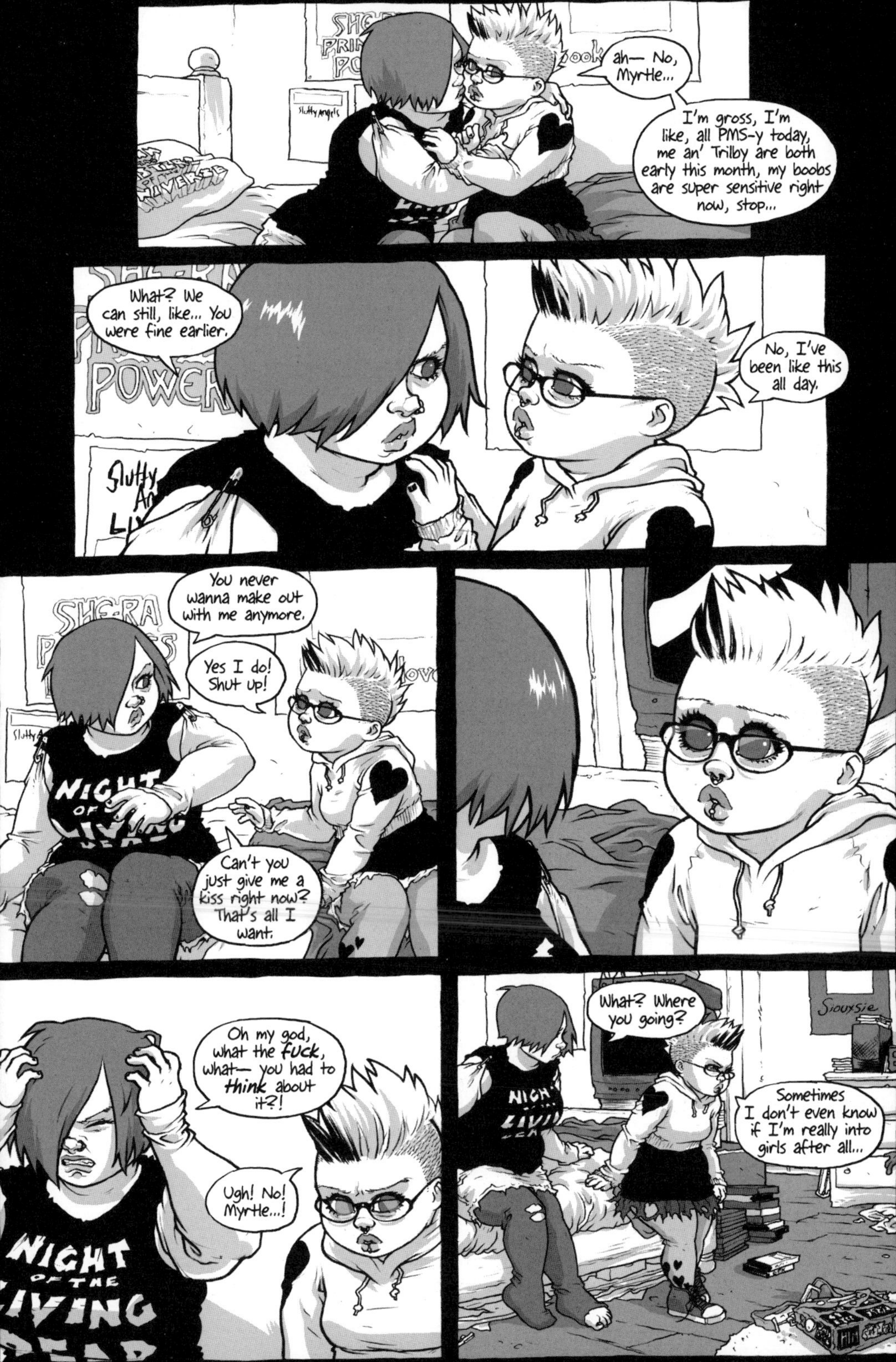
ah— No, Myrtle...
I'm gross, I'm like, all PMS-y today, me an' Trilby are both early this month, my boobs are super sensitive right now, stop...
What? We can still, like... You were fine earlier.
No, I've been like this all day.
You never wanna make out with me anymore.
Yes I do! Shut up!
Can't you just give me a kiss right now? That's all I want.
Oh my god, what the fuck, what— you had to think about it?!
Ugh! No! Myrtle...!
What? Where you going?
Sometimes I don't even know if I'm really into girls after all...

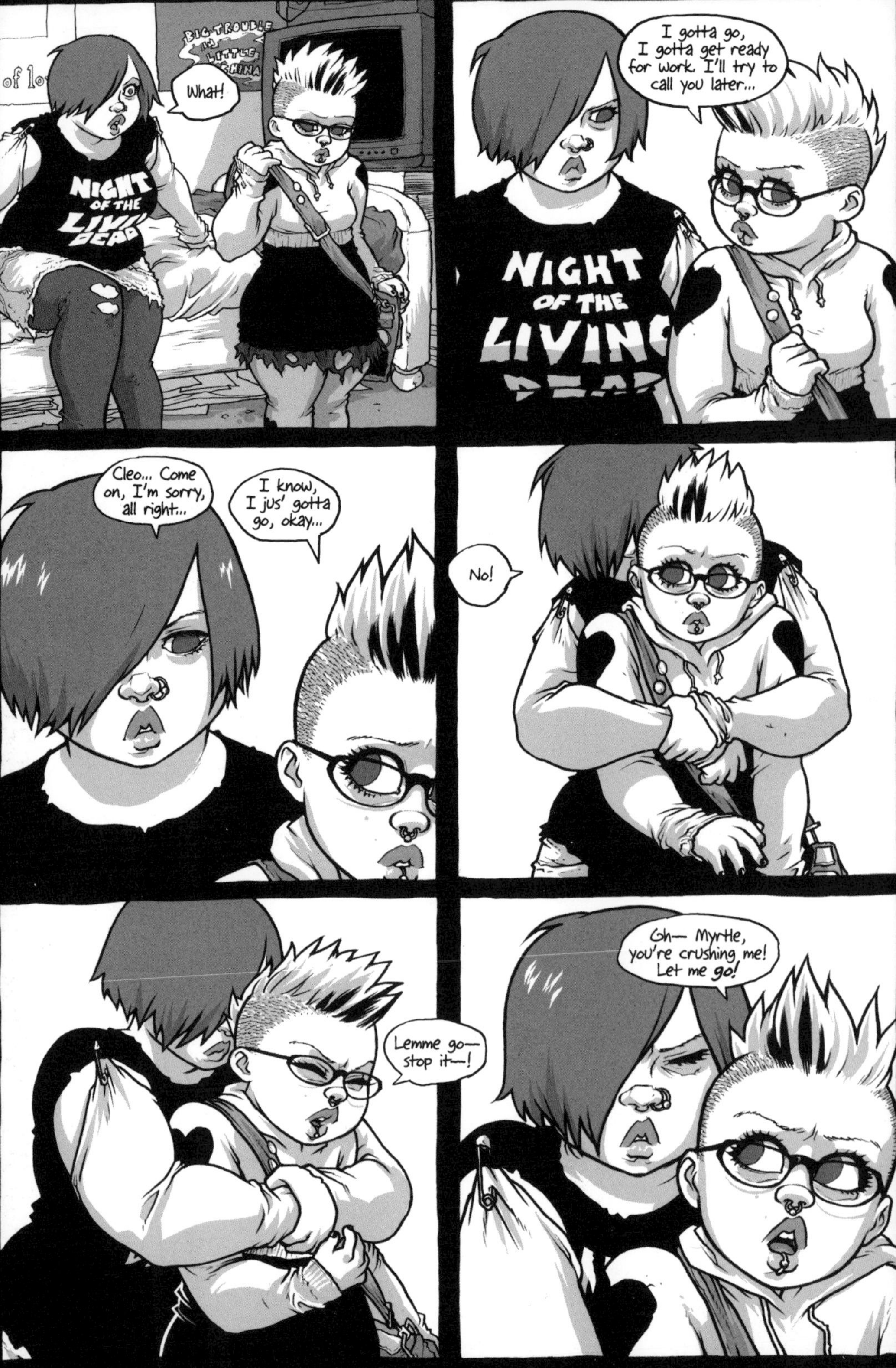
BIG TROUBLE IN LITTLE CHINA
What!
NIGHT OF THE LIVING DEAD
I gotta go, I gotta get ready for work. I'll try to call you later...
NIGHT OF THE LIVING
Cleo... Come on, I'm sorry, all right...
I know, I jus' gotta go, okay...
No!
Lemme go— stop it—!
Gh— Myrtle, you're crushing me! Let me go!

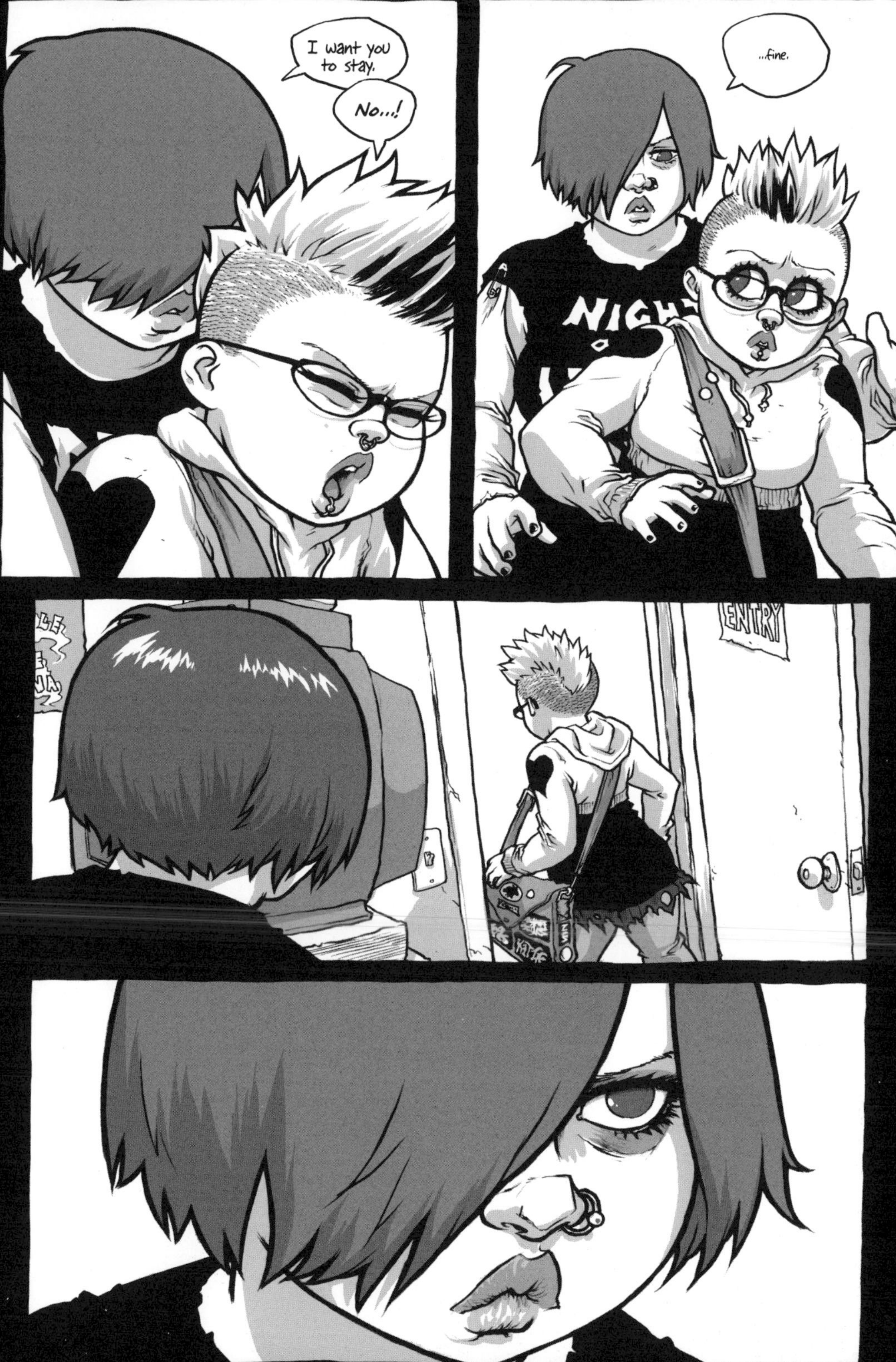

I want you to stay.
No...!
...fine.
ENTRY

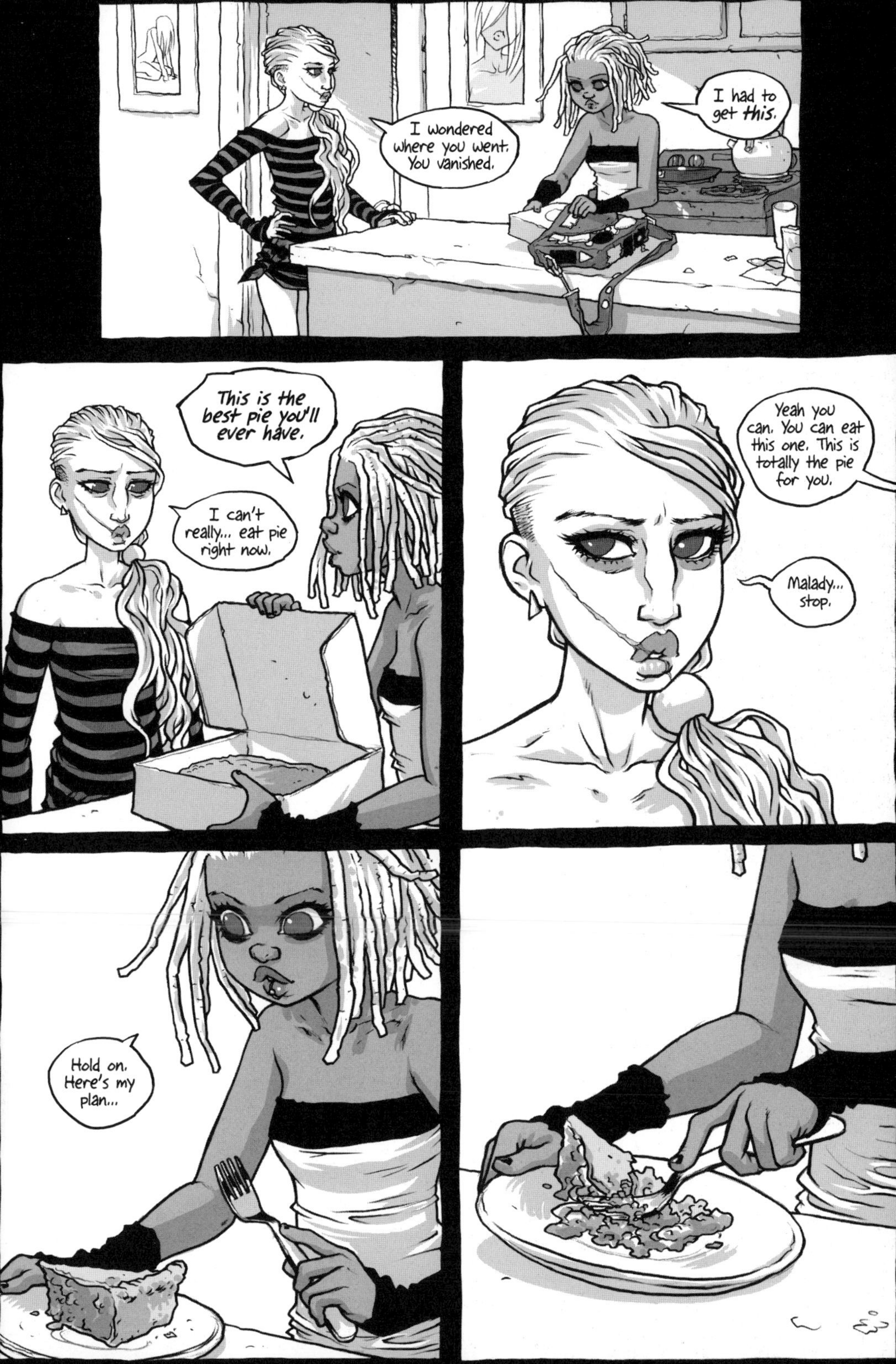
I wondered where you went. You vanished.
I had to get *this*.
This is the best pie you'll ever have.
I can't really... eat pie right now.
Yeah you can. You can eat this one. This is totally the pie for you.
Malady... stop.
Hold on. Here's my plan...

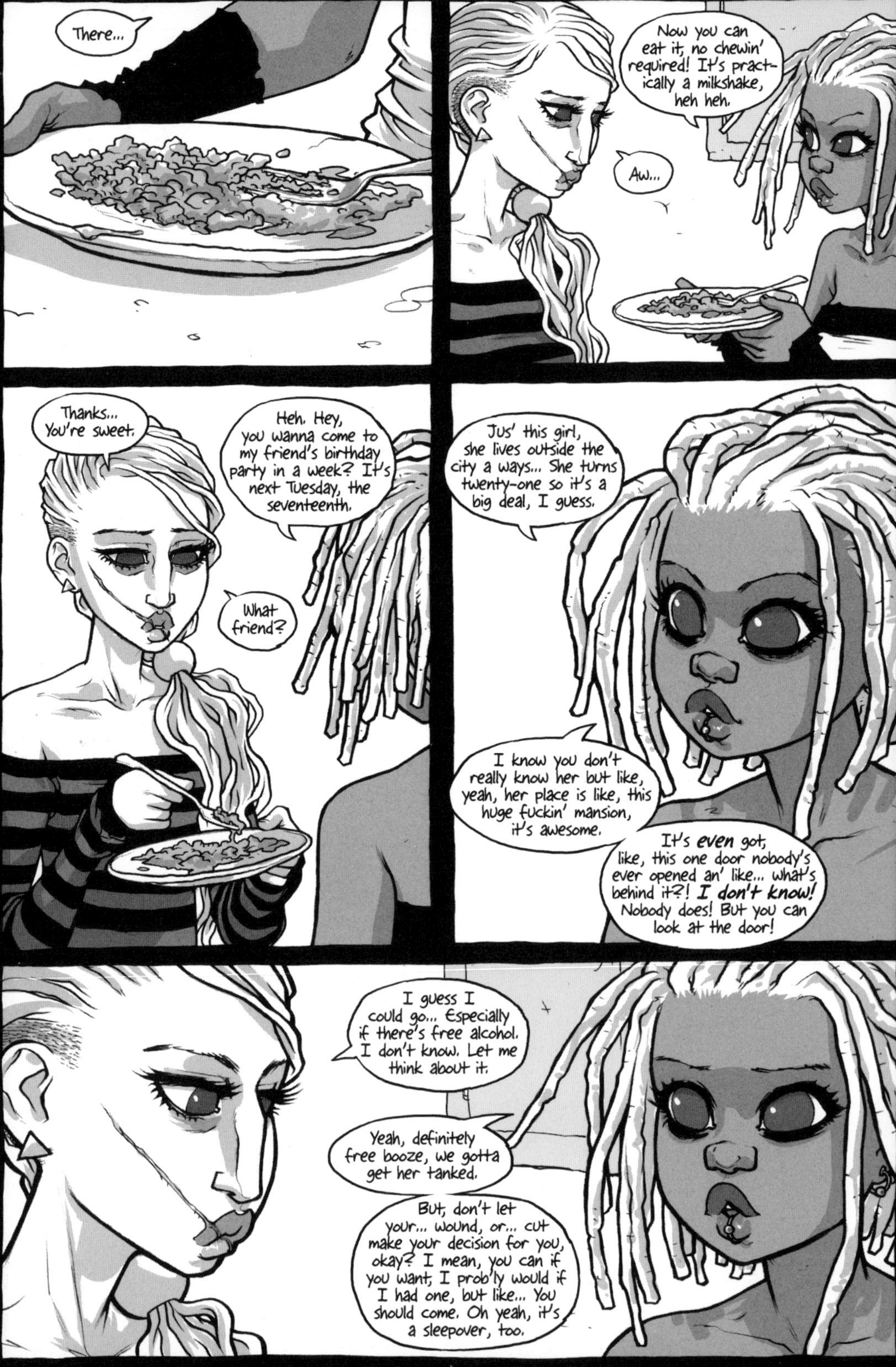
There...
Now you can eat it, no chewin' required! It's practically a milkshake, heh heh.
Aw...
Thanks... You're sweet.
Heh. Hey, you wanna come to my friend's birthday party in a week? It's next Tuesday, the seventeenth.
What friend?
Jus' this girl, she lives outside the city a ways... She turns twenty-one so it's a big deal, I guess.
I know you don't really know her but like, yeah, her place is like, this huge fuckin' mansion, it's awesome.
It's *even* got, like, this one door nobody's ever opened an' like... what's behind it?! ***I don't know!*** Nobody does! But you can look at the door!
I guess I could go... Especially if there's free alcohol. I don't know. Let me think about it.
Yeah, definitely free booze, we gotta get her tanked.
But, don't let your... wound, or... cut make your decision for you, okay? I mean, you can if you want, I prob'ly would if I had one, but like... You should come. Oh yeah, it's a sleepover, too.

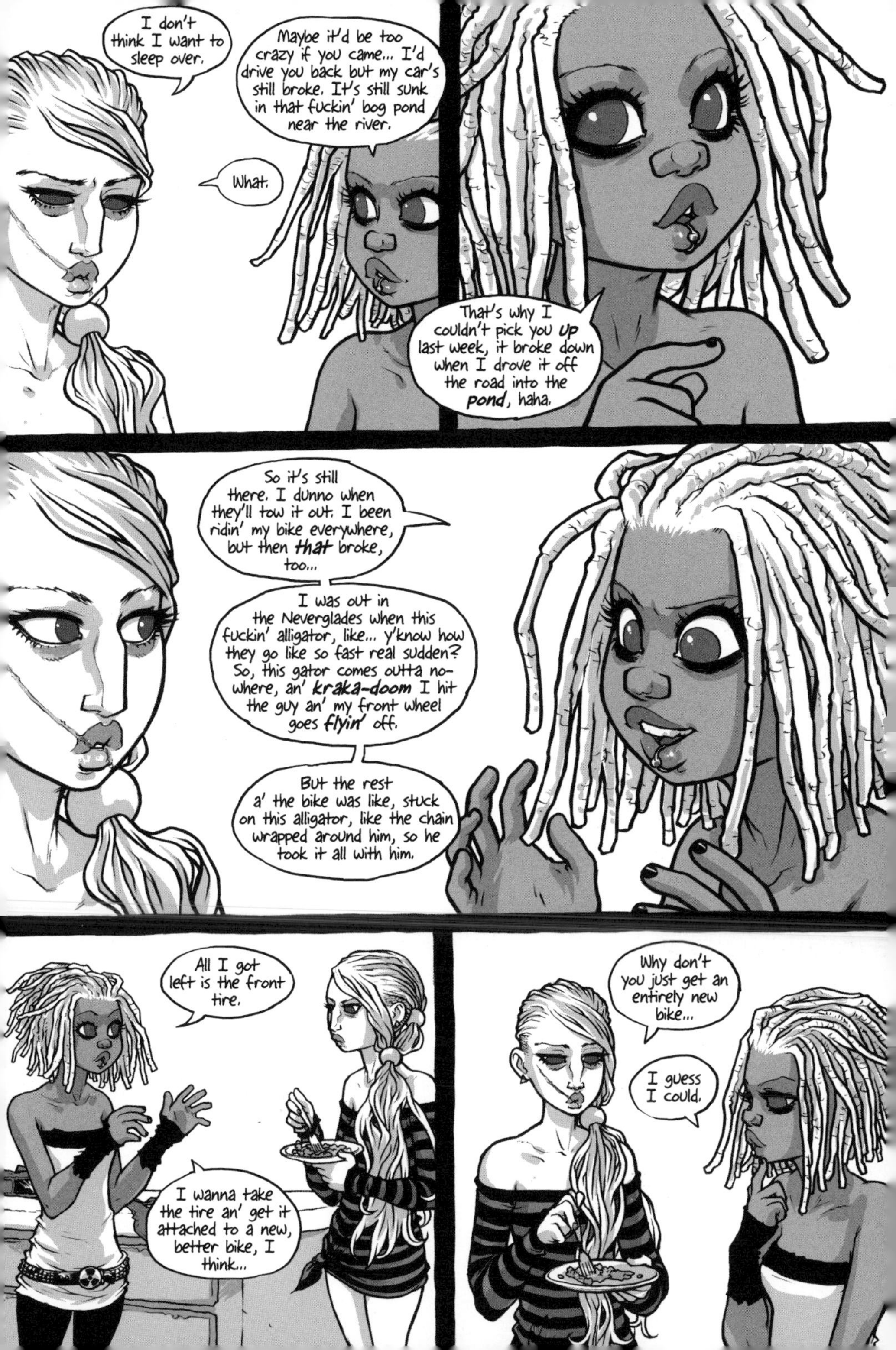

I don't think I want to sleep over.
Maybe it'd be too crazy if you came... I'd drive you back but my car's still broke. It's still sunk in that fuckin' bog pond near the river.
What.
That's why I couldn't pick you UP last week, it broke down when I drove it off the road into the pond, haha.
So it's still there. I dunno when they'll tow it out. I been ridin' my bike everywhere, but then that broke, too...
I was out in the Neverglades when this fuckin' alligator, like... y'know how they go like so fast real sudden? So, this gator comes outta no-where, an' kraka-doom I hit the guy an' my front wheel goes flyin' off.
But the rest a' the bike was like, stuck on this alligator, like the chain wrapped around him, so he took it all with him.
All I got left is the front tire.
I wanna take the tire an' get it attached to a new, better bike, I think...
Why don't you just get an entirely new bike...
I guess I could.

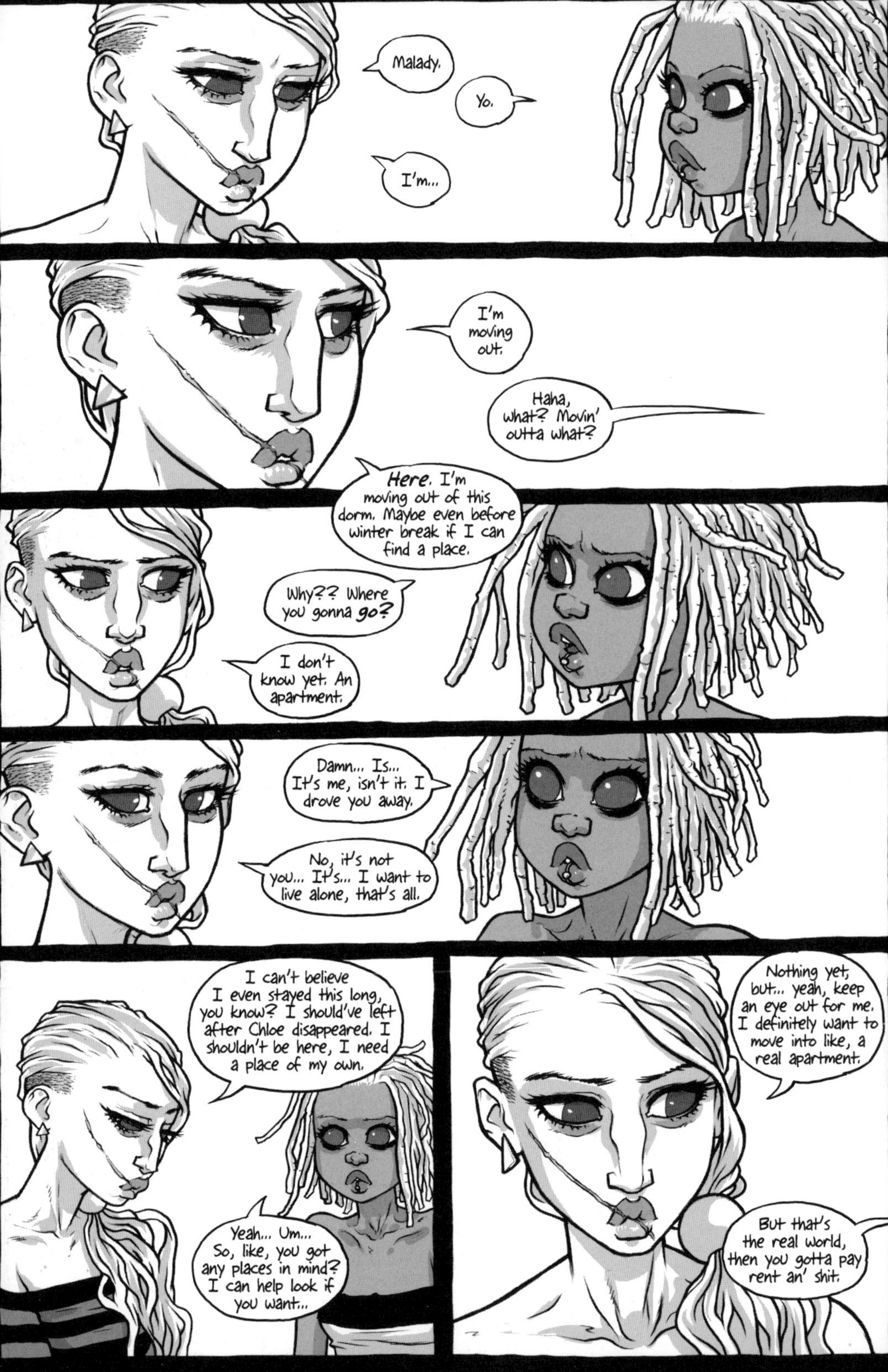
Malady.
Yo.
I'm...
I'm moving out.
Haha, what? Movin' outta what?
Here. I'm moving out of this dorm. Maybe even before winter break if I can find a place.
Why?? Where you gonna go?
I don't know yet. An apartment.
Damn... Is... It's me, isn't it. I drove you away.
No, it's not you... It's... I want to live alone, that's all.
I can't believe I even stayed this long, you know? I should've left after Chloe disappeared. I shouldn't be here, I need a place of my own.
Yeah... Um... So, like, you got any places in mind? I can help look if you want...
Nothing yet, but... yeah, keep an eye out for me. I definitely want to move into like, a real apartment.
But that's the real world, then you gotta pay rent an' shit.

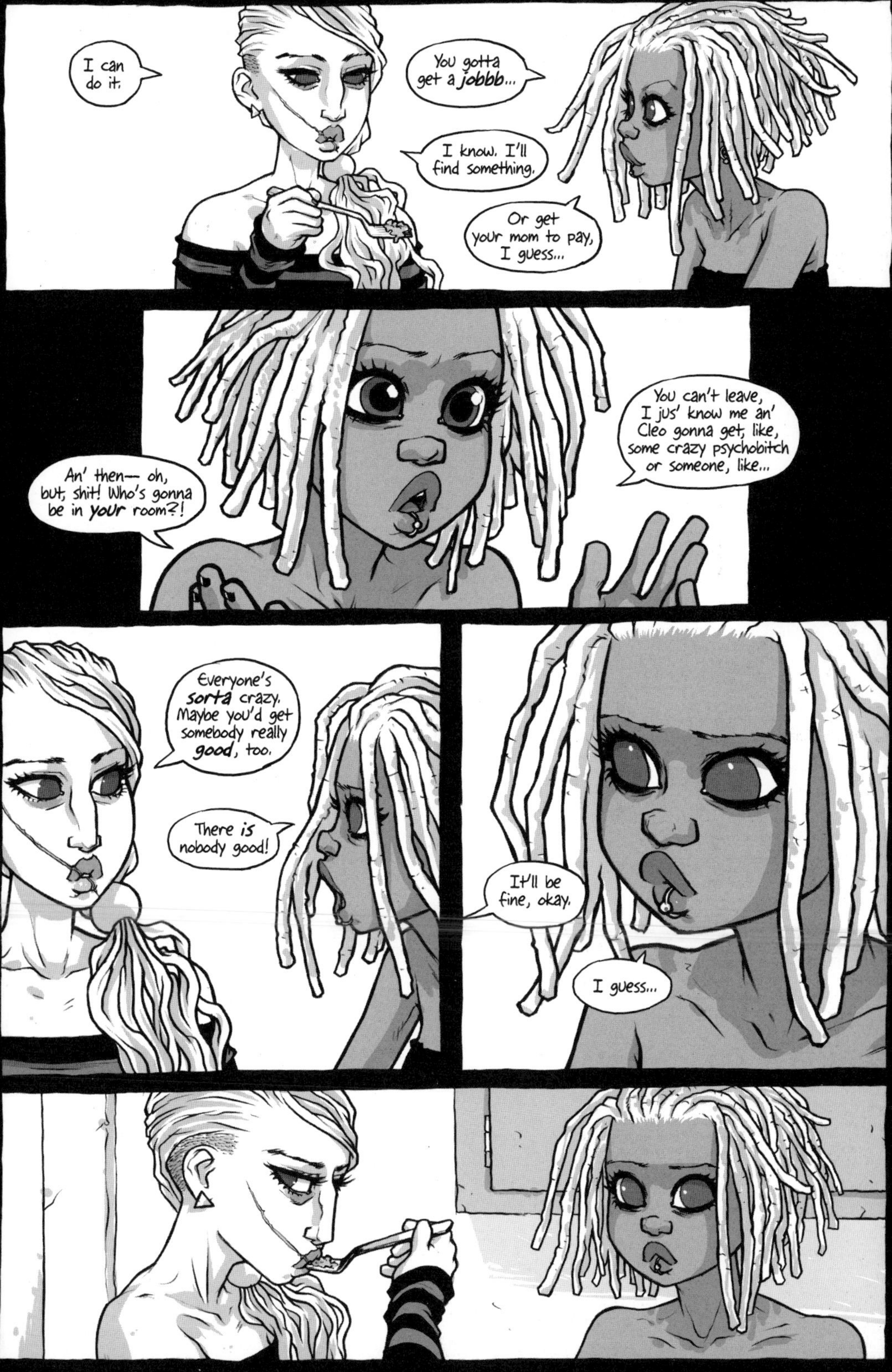
I can do it.
You gotta get a *jobbb*...
I know. I'll find something.
Or get your mom to pay, I guess...
An' then— oh, but, shit! Who's gonna be in *your* room?!
You can't leave, I jus' know me an' Cleo gonna get, like, some crazy psychobitch or someone, like...
Everyone's *sorta* crazy. Maybe you'd get somebody really *good*, too.
There *is* nobody good!
It'll be fine, okay.
I guess...

Nov 12, thursday

myrtle finally fucking showed up but she was so mean, I don't know what her problem is. what am I doing. we had this big dumb fight, and myrtle really gets scary when she's mad. she's also really perceptive, though, and I'm the worst liar, so she was like "stop trying to make me jealous!" when I would talk about other girls, and like ... okay, I am. I'm just trying to... I don't know. I know everybody does that, everybody tries to make their lover jealous, right?? I do it too, so what. I haven't heard from myrtle since the fight, I don't know what'll happen. I'm half furious and half about to cry, teetering between them, but I don't know where I stand. I fucking hate this! I fucking hate ... romance or whatever. why does it have to be like this? I'm so terrible at it, I've never had anything successful or good come from it, and now I'm fucking around with my best friend and what if it doesn't work, what if I lose her because of it? God what the fuck am I doing?!! the next slutty angels show is the 22nd, and myrtle said they're going to play my song, but what if we aren't together anymore? How do you know if you're still with a person after the last time you see them is a huge fight? should I just assume we're broken up and start sobbing? I can't talk to her, I'll lose it. And she hasn't even tried to talk to me yet, so fuck that. I was going to invite her to thanksgiving at my house but now I guess not. I wish unknown would show up and sweep me off my feet and rescue me. The only good thing I can think of is that the new HARRY POTTER book is awesome. I cried.

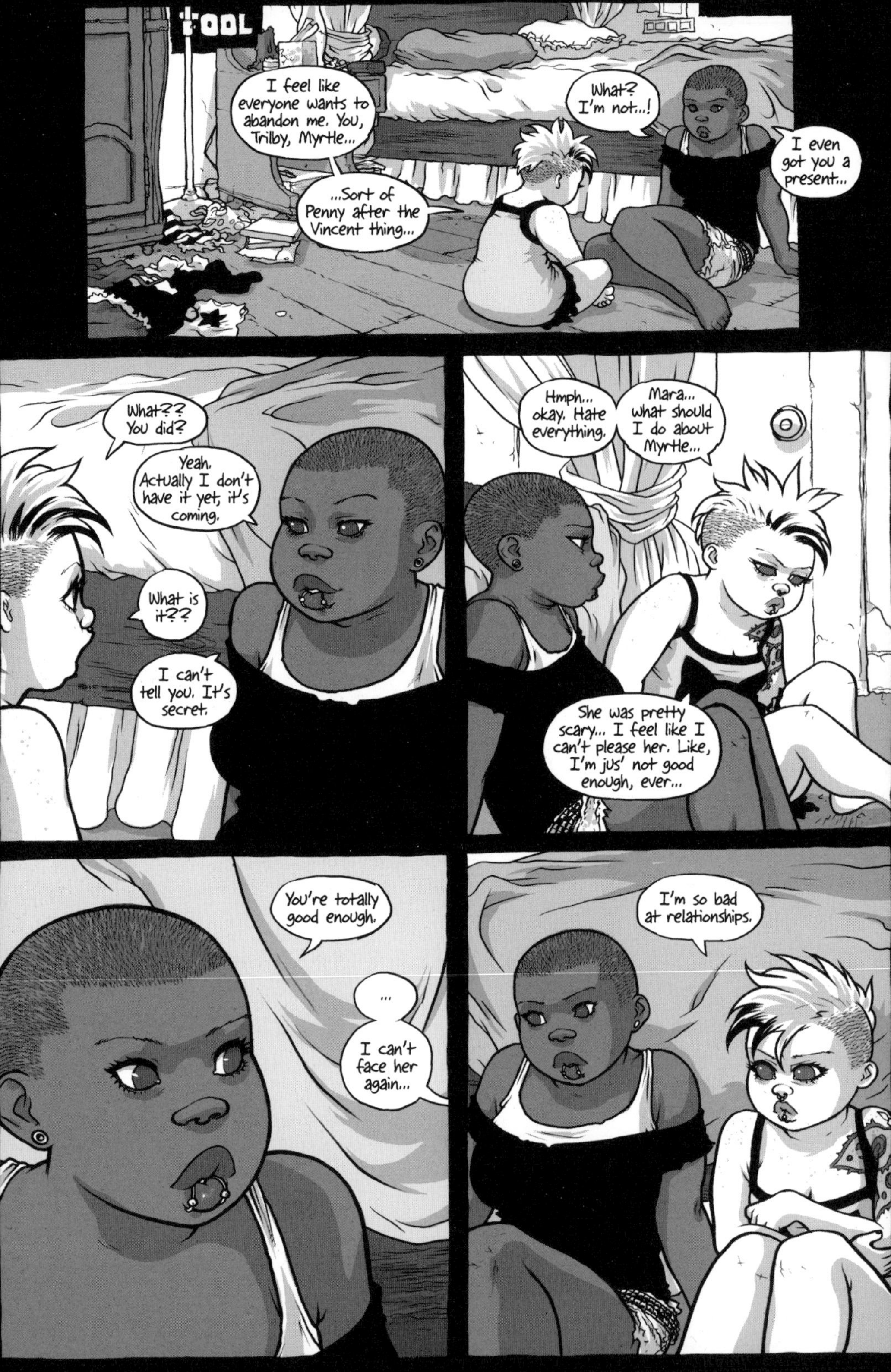
TOOL
I feel like everyone wants to abandon me. You, Trilby, Myrtle...
...Sort of Penny after the Vincent thing...
What? I'm not...!
I even got you a present...
What?? You did?
Yeah. Actually I don't have it yet; it's coming.
What is it??
I can't tell you. It's secret.
Hmph... okay. Hate everything.
Mara... what should I do about Myrtle...
She was pretty scary... I feel like I can't please her. Like, I'm jus' not good enough, ever...
You're totally good enough.
...
I can't face her again...
I'm so bad at relationships.

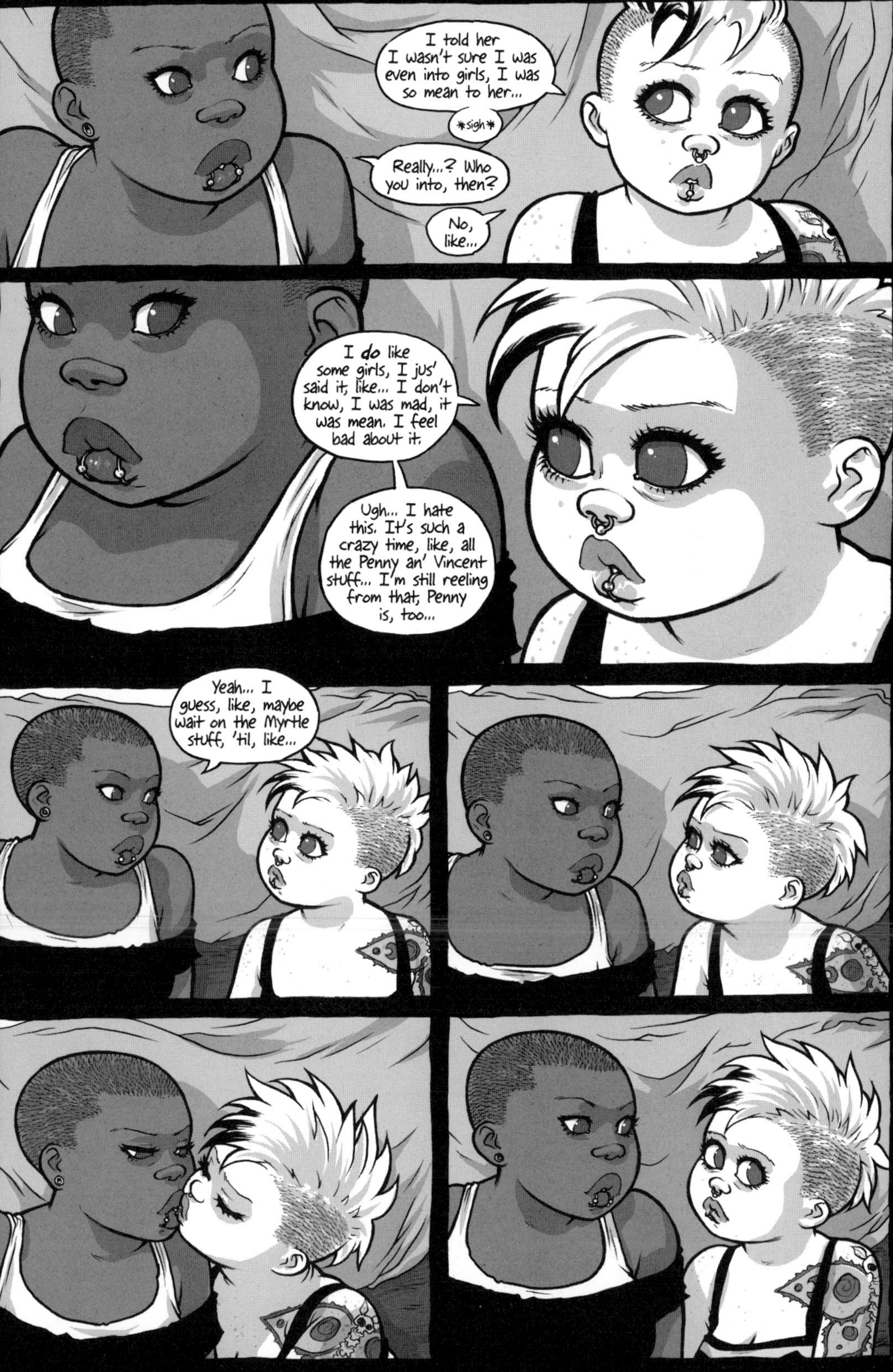

I told her I wasn't sure I was even into girls, I was so mean to her...
sigh
Really...? Who you into, then?
No, like...
I do like some girls, I jus' said it, like... I don't know, I was mad, it was mean. I feel bad about it.
Ugh... I hate this. It's such a crazy time, like, all the Penny an' Vincent stuff... I'm still reeling from that, Penny is, too...
Yeah... I guess, like, maybe wait on the Myrtle stuff, 'til, like...

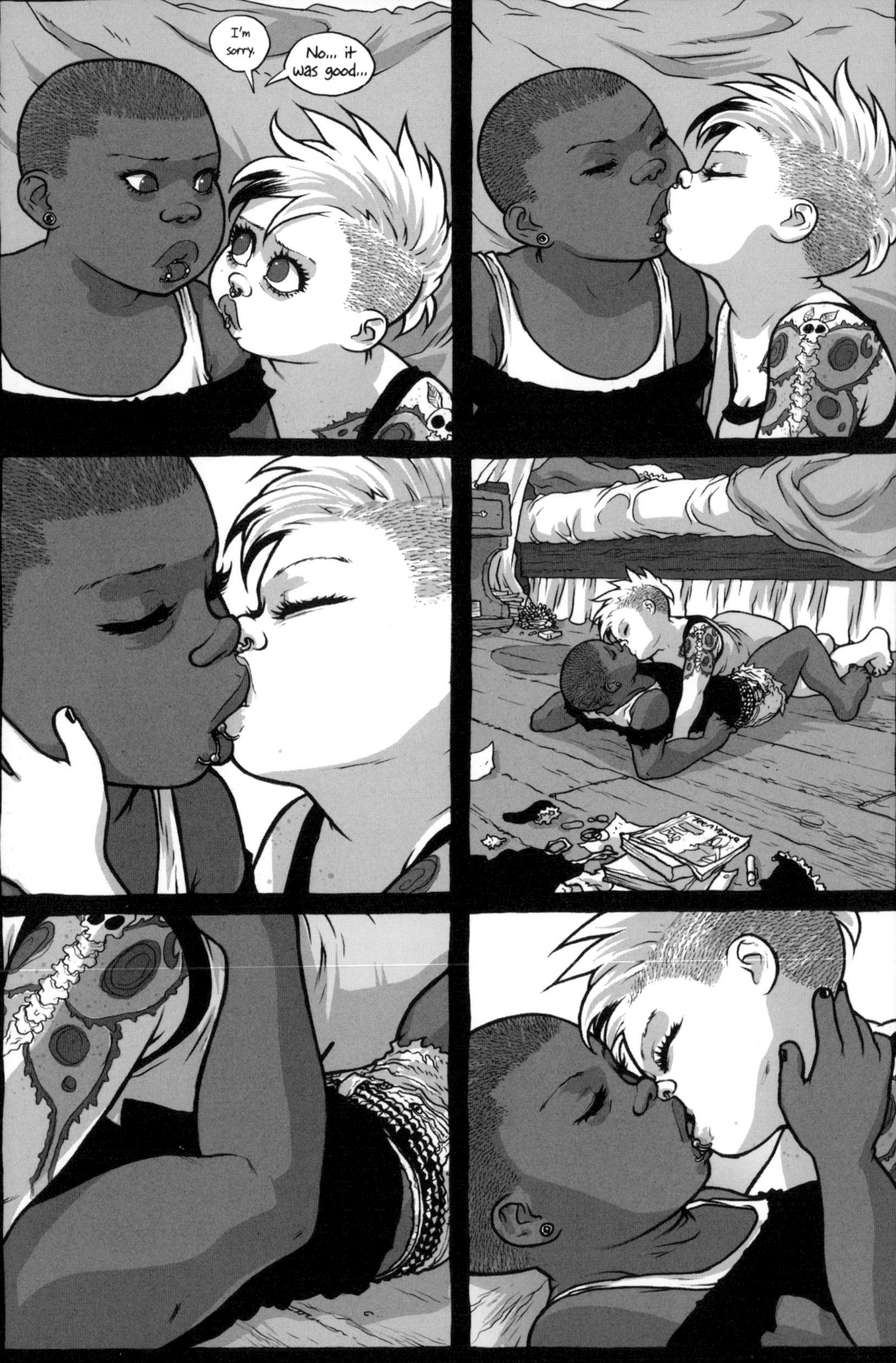
I'm sorry.
No... it was good...

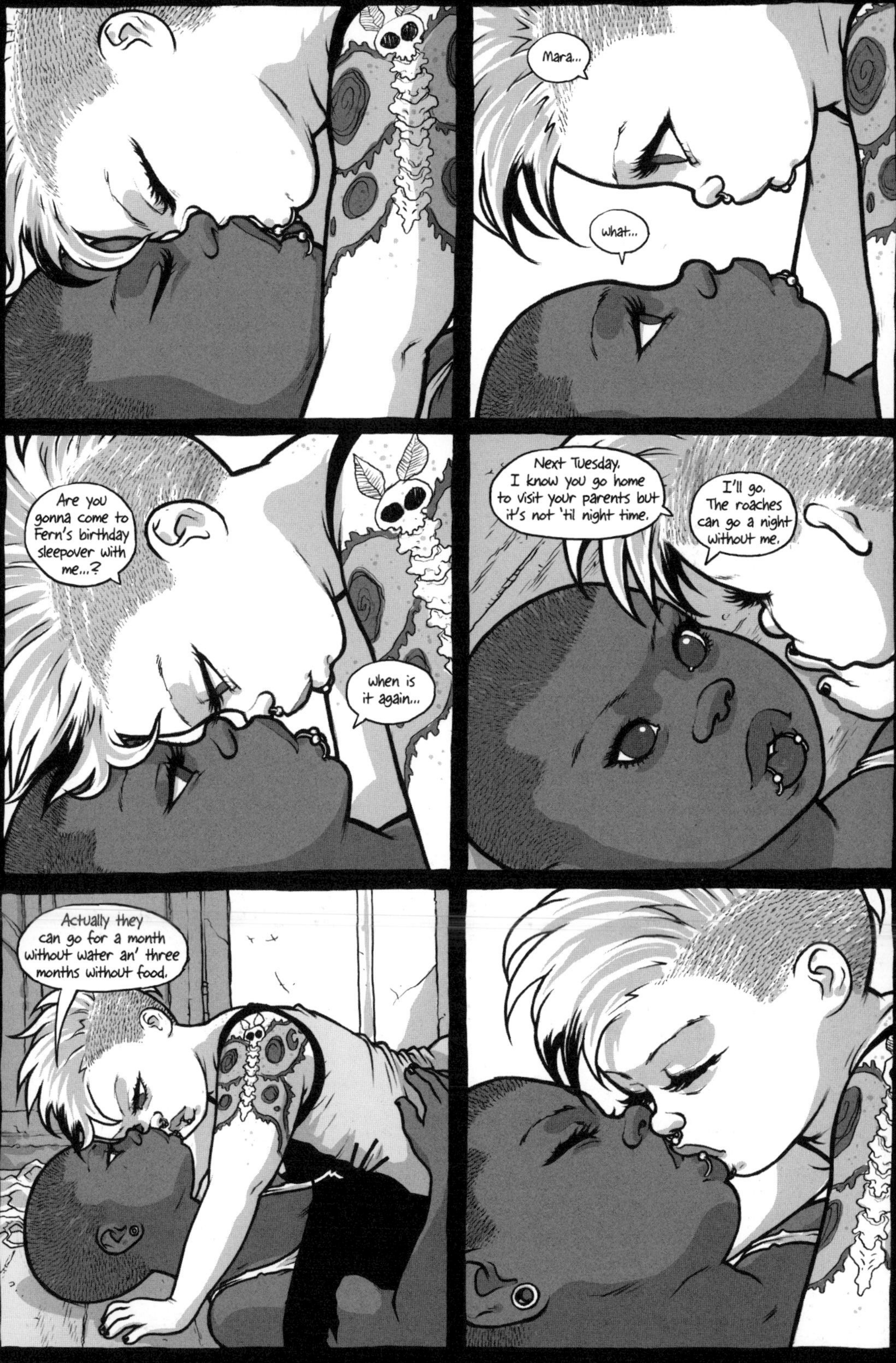
Mara...
what...
Are you gonna come to Fern's birthday sleepover with me...?
when is it again...
Next Tuesday. I know you go home to visit your parents but it's not 'til night time.
I'll go. The roaches can go a night without me.
Actually they can go for a month without water an' three months without food.

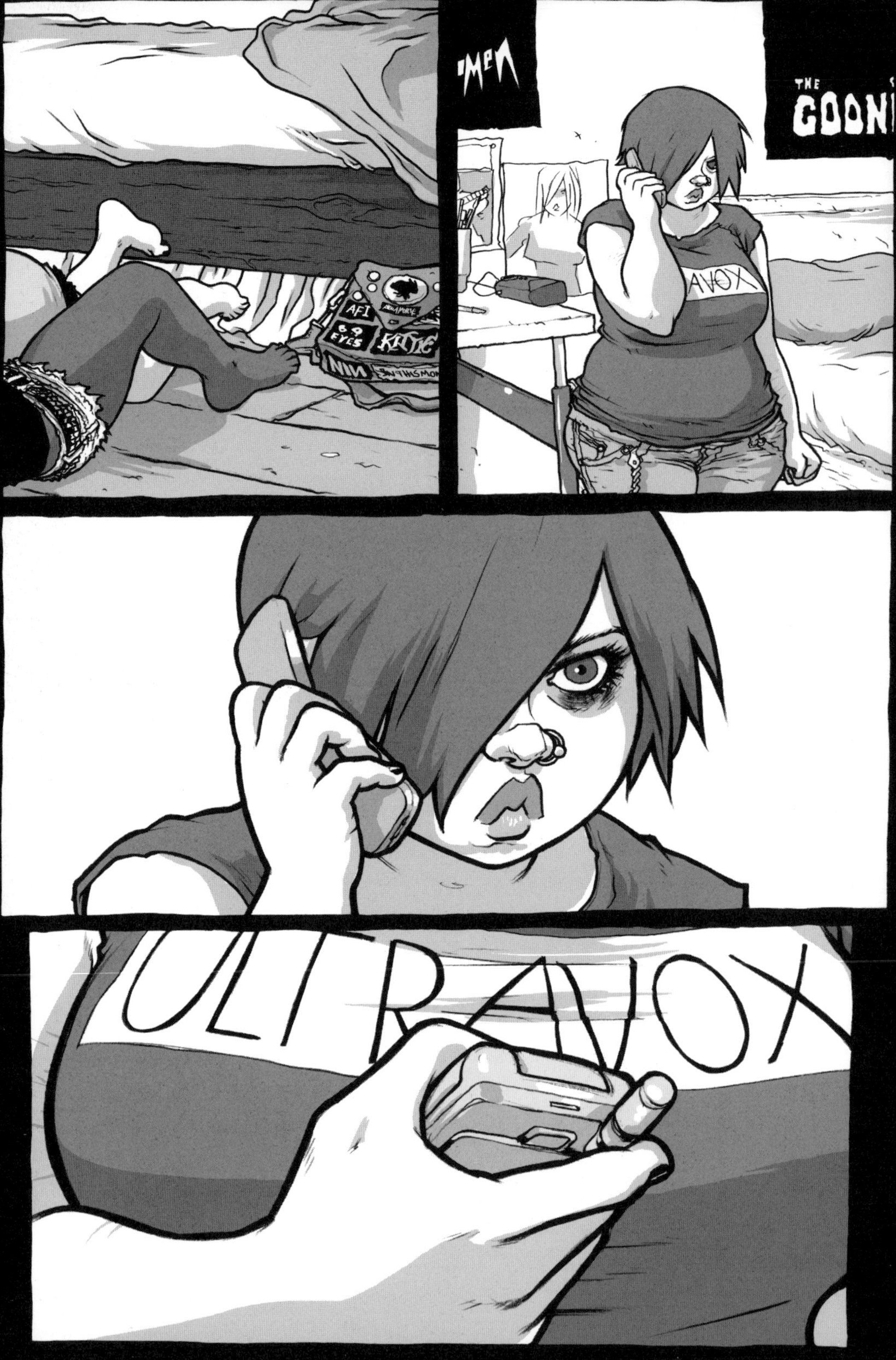
AFI
64 EYES
NIN
AVOX
ULTRAVOX

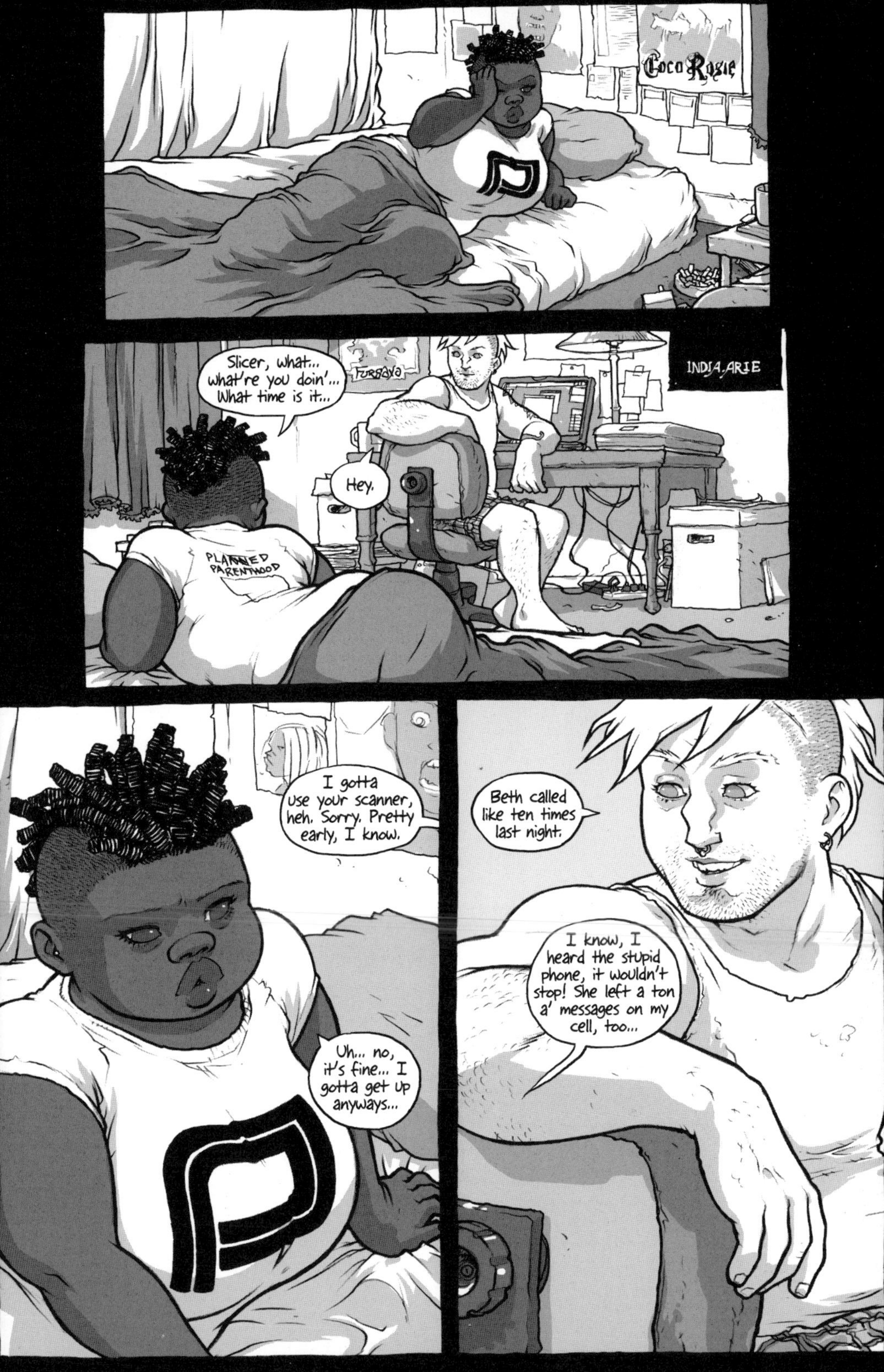
Coco Rosie
INDIA.ARIE
Slicer, what... what're you doin'... What time is it...
Hey.
PLANNED PARENTHOOD
I gotta use your scanner, heh. Sorry. Pretty early, I know.
Uh... no, it's fine... I gotta get up anyways...
Beth called like ten times last night.
I know, I heard the stupid phone, it wouldn't stop! She left a ton a' messages on my cell, too...

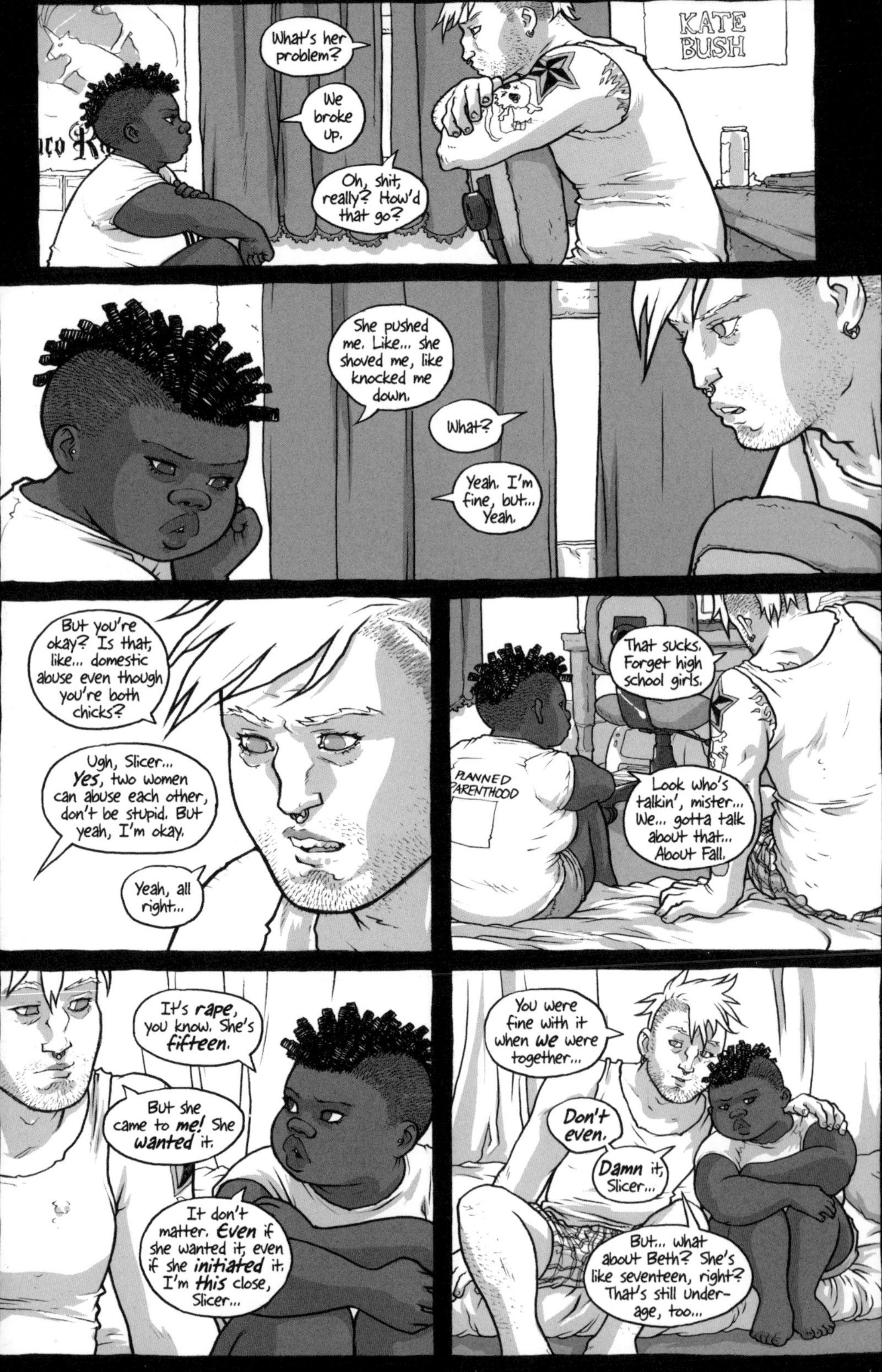
KATE BUSH
What's her problem?
We broke up.
Oh, shit, really? How'd that go?
She pushed me. Like... she shoved me, like knocked me down.
What?
Yeah. I'm fine, but... Yeah.
But you're okay? Is that, like... domestic abuse even though you're both chicks?
Ugh, Slicer... *Yes*, two women can abuse each other, don't be stupid. But yeah, I'm okay.
Yeah, all right...
That sucks. Forget high school girls.
PLANNED PARENTHOOD
Look who's talkin', mister... We... gotta talk about that... About Fall.
It's **rape**, you know. She's **fifteen**.
But she came to **me!** She **wanted** it.
It don't matter. **Even** if she wanted it, even if she **initiated** it. I'm **this** close, Slicer...
You were fine with it when **we** were together...
Don't even.
Damn it, Slicer...
But... what about Beth? She's like seventeen, right? That's still under-age, too...

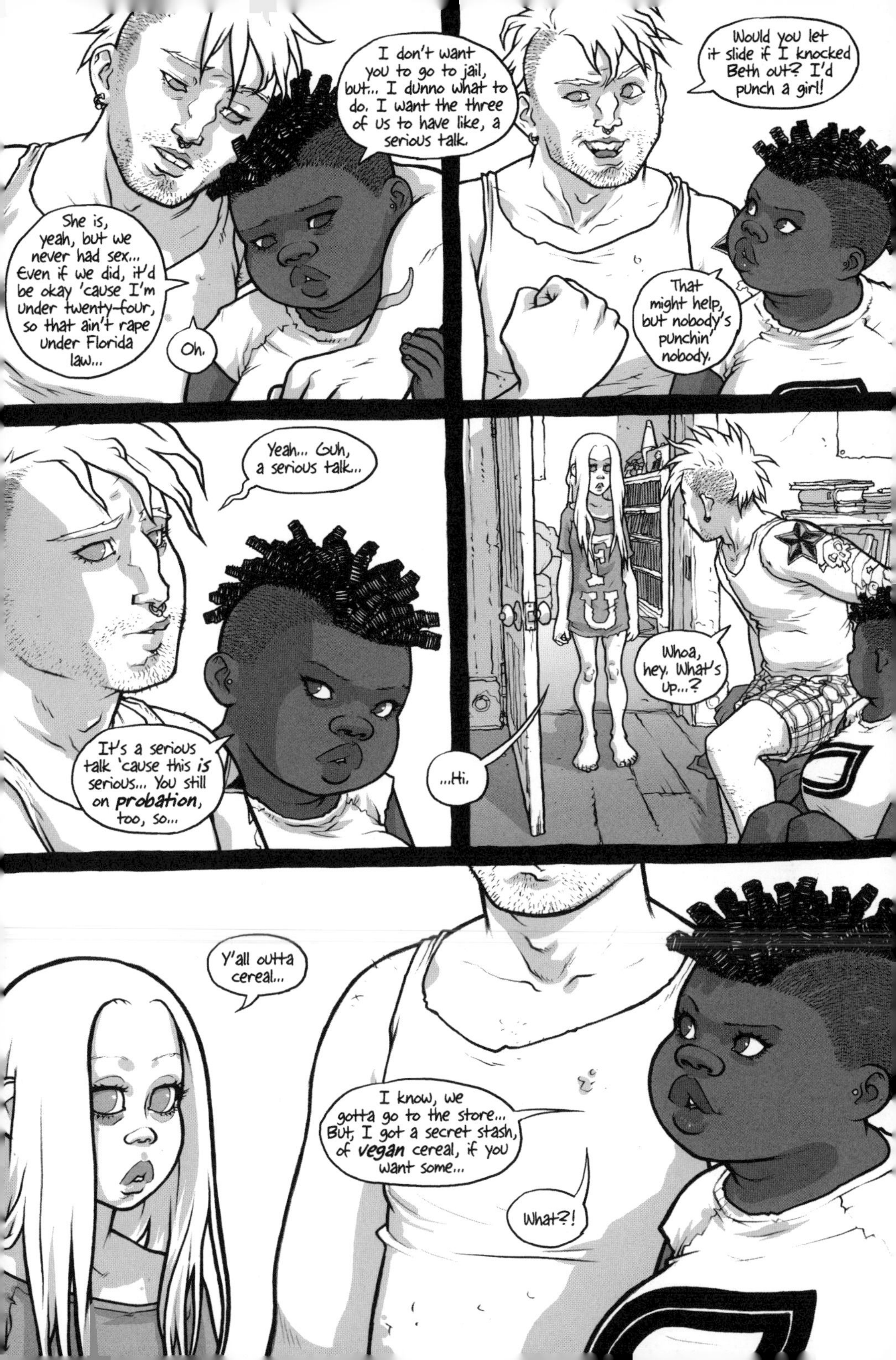
I don't want you to go to jail, but... I dunno what to do. I want the three of us to have like, a serious talk.
She is, yeah, but we never had sex... Even if we did, it'd be okay 'cause I'm under twenty-four, so that ain't rape under Florida law...
Oh.
Would you let it slide if I knocked Beth out? I'd punch a girl!
That might help, but nobody's punchin' nobody.
Yeah... Guh, a serious talk...
It's a serious talk 'cause this *is* serious... You still on **probation**, too, so...
...Hi.
Whoa, hey. What's up...?
Y'all outta cereal...
I know, we gotta go to the store... But, I got a secret stash, of **vegan** cereal, if you want some...
What?!

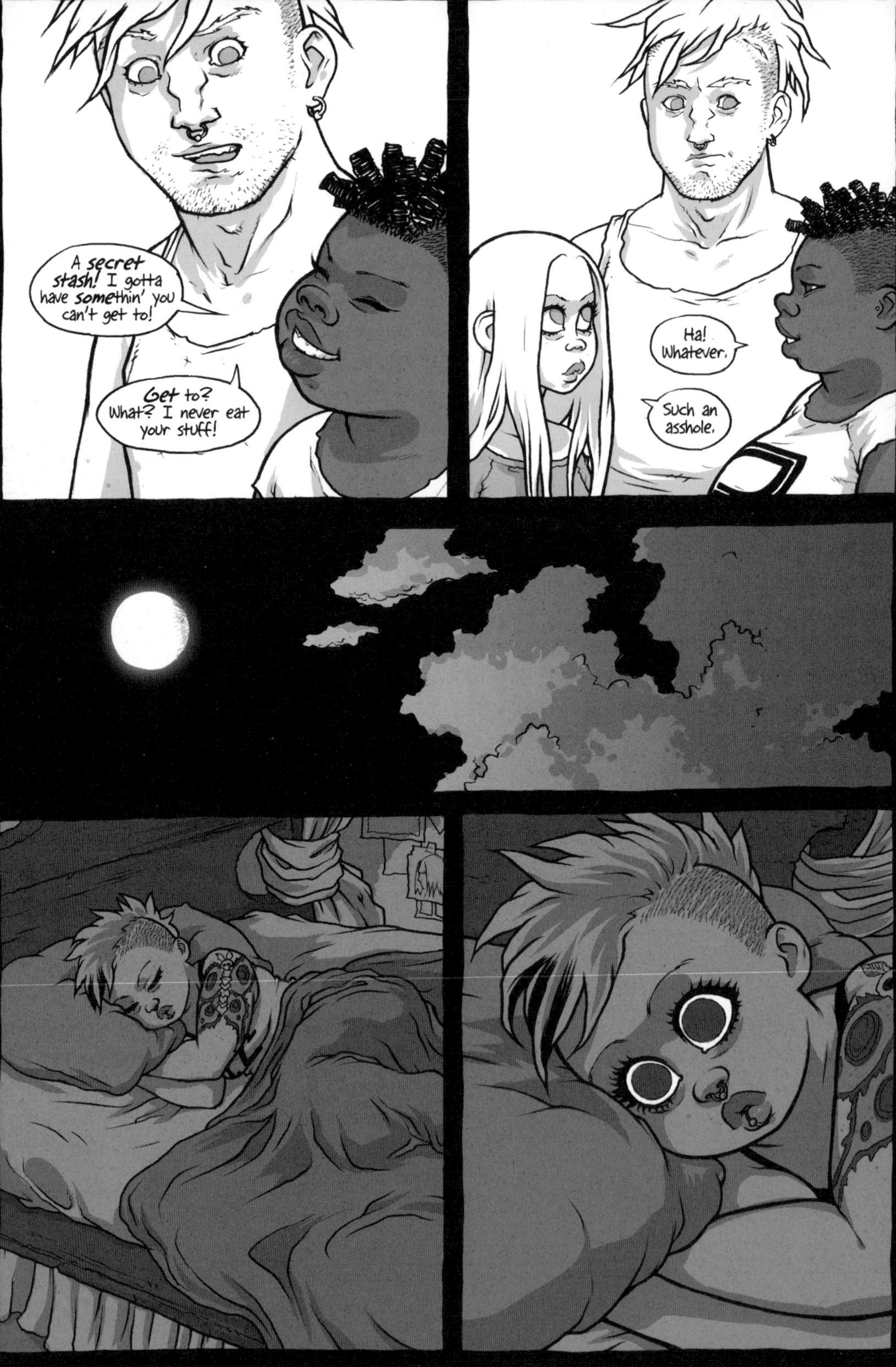
A secret stash! I gotta have somethin' you can't get to!
Get to? What? I never eat your stuff!
Ha! Whatever.
Such an asshole.

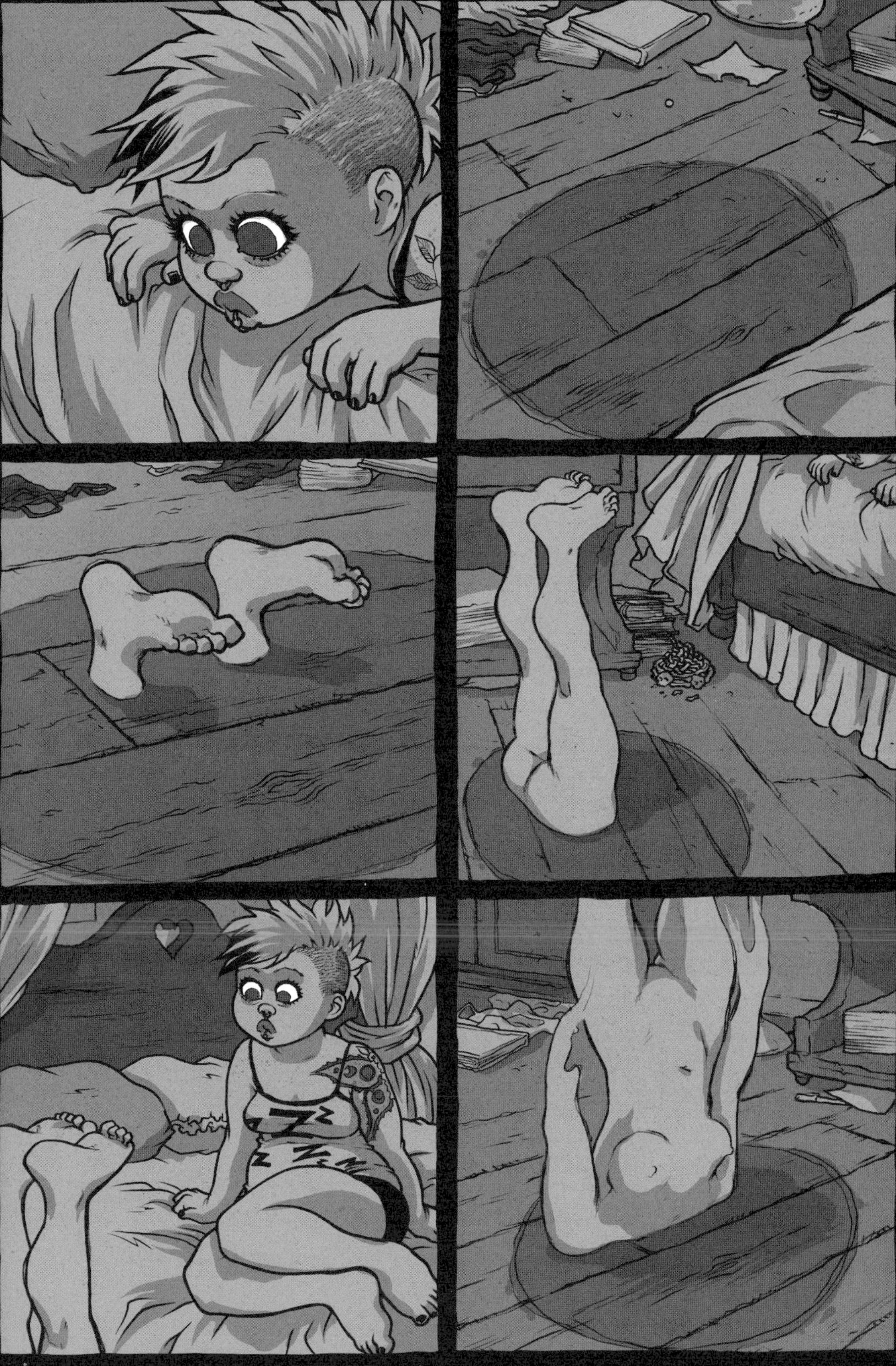

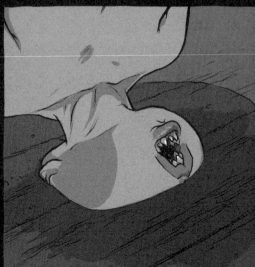
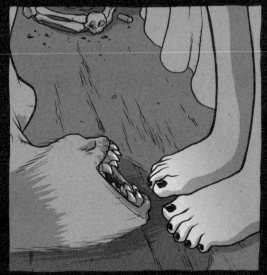

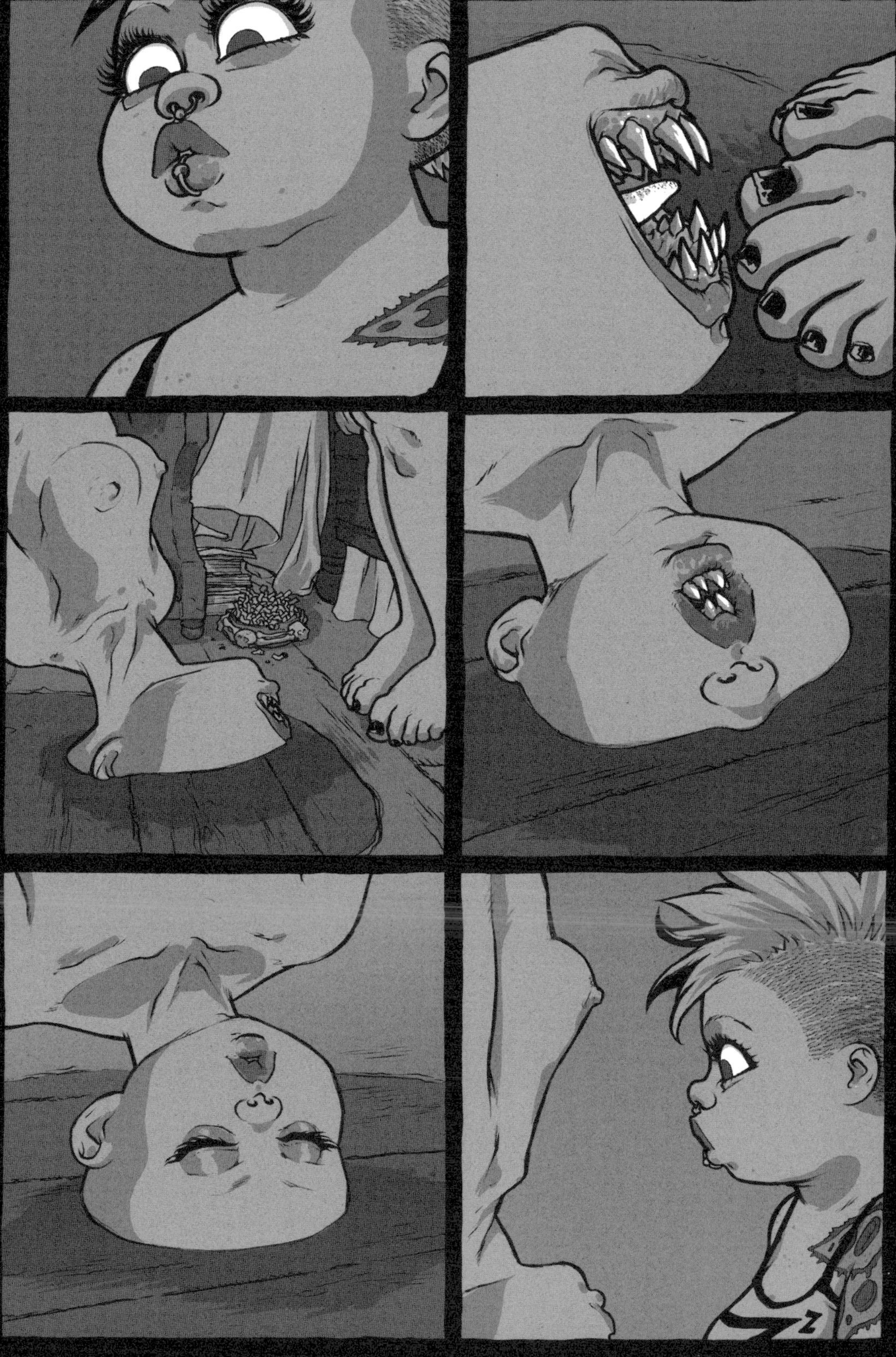

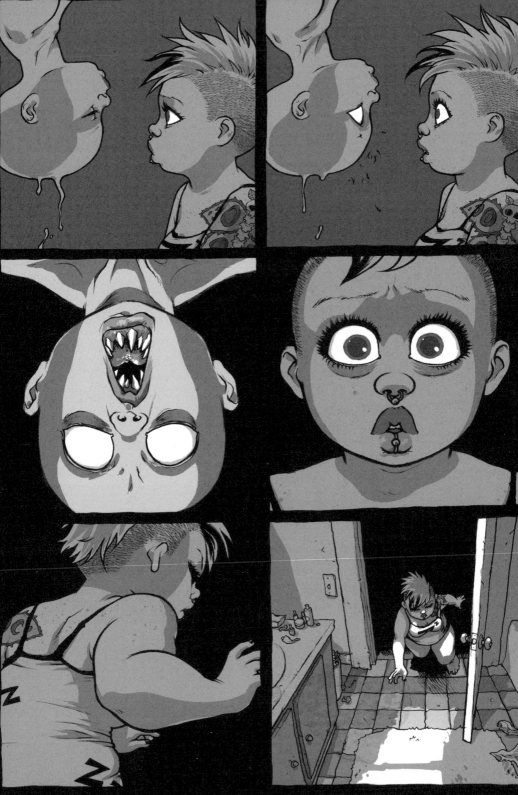

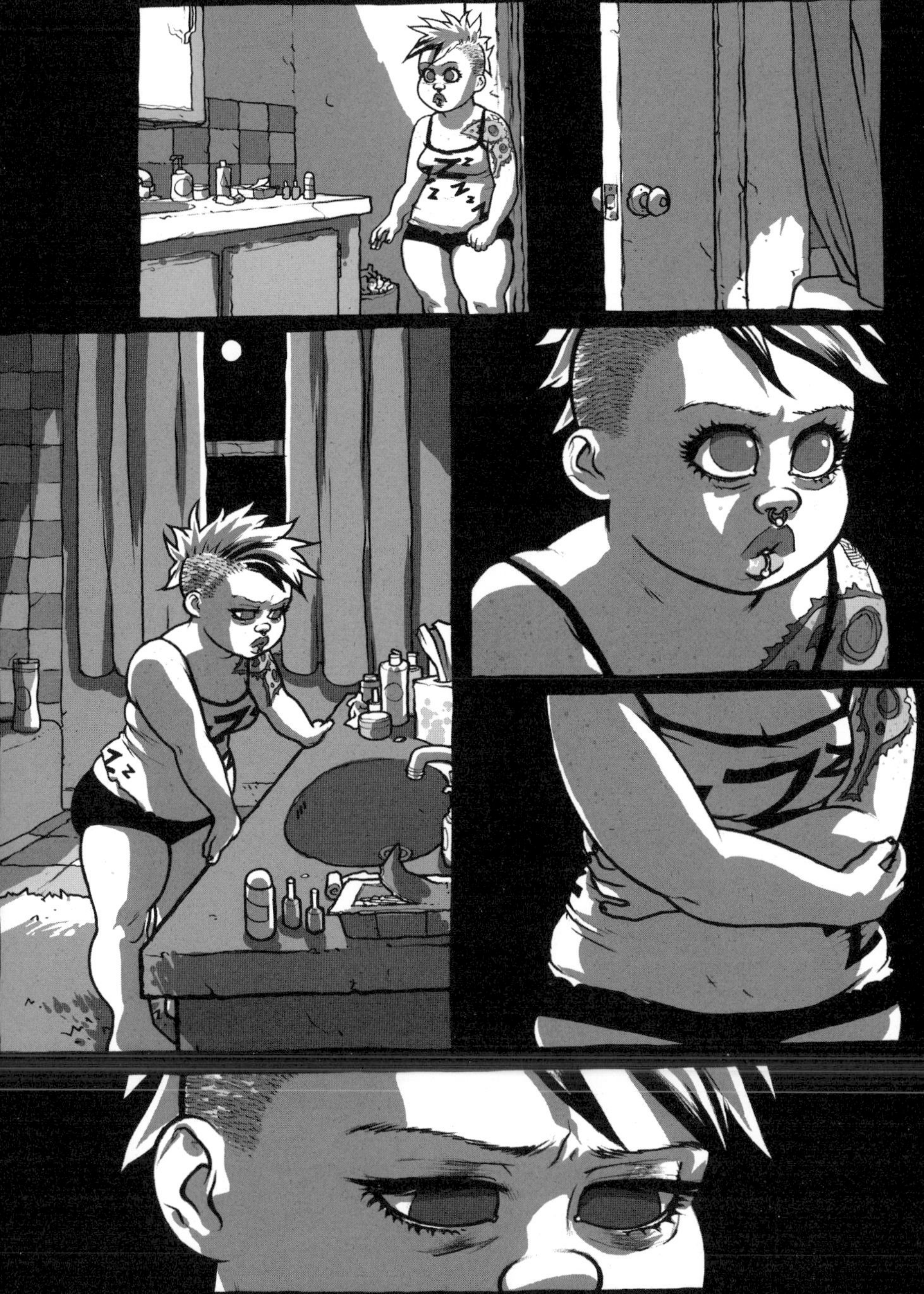

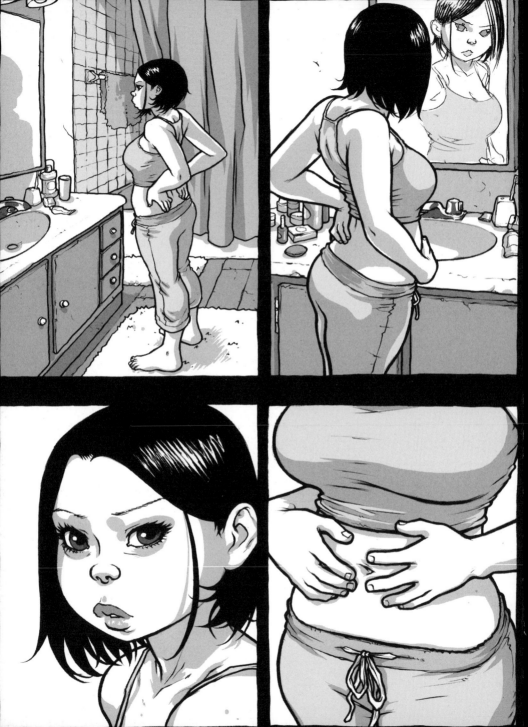

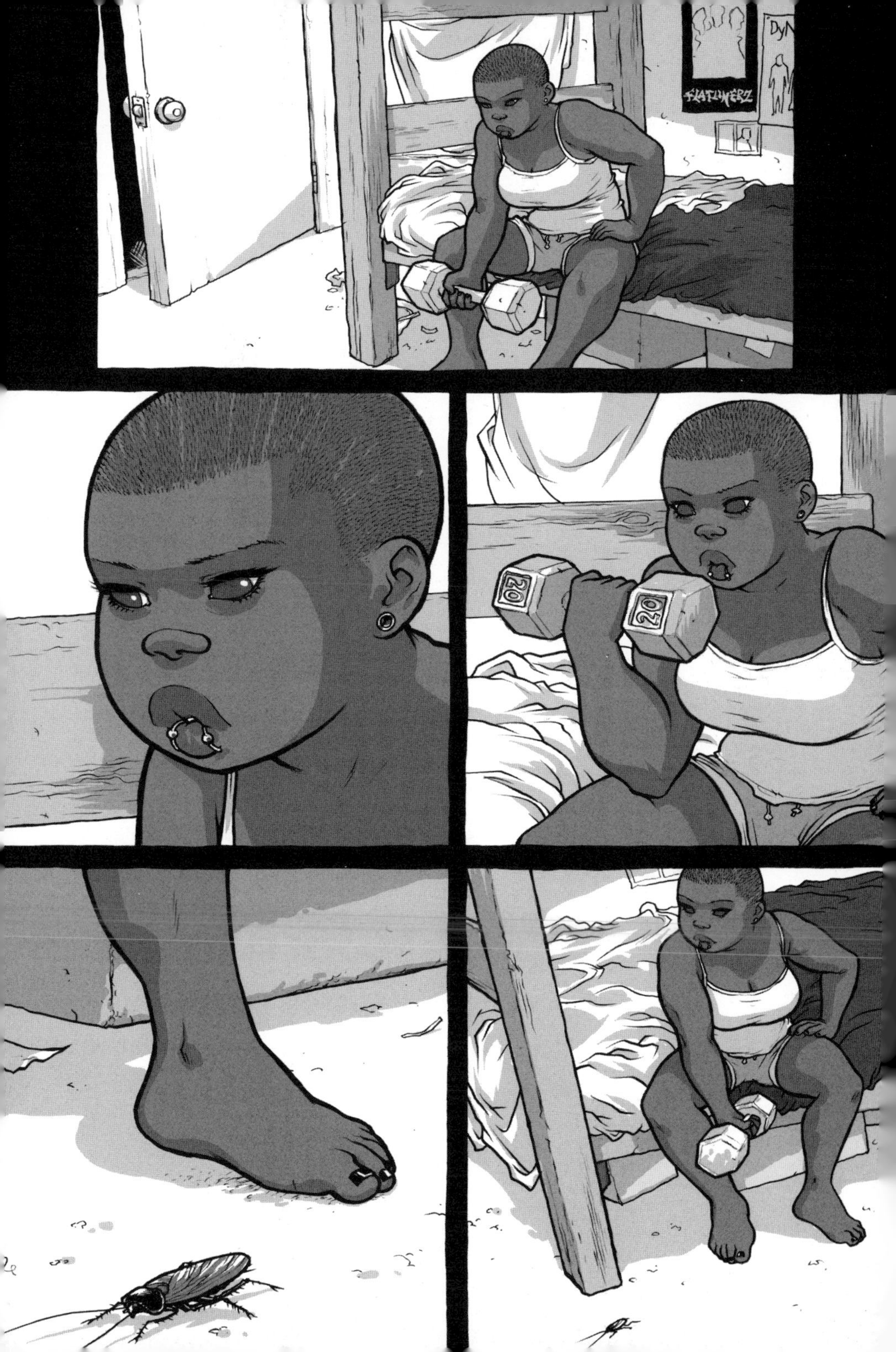
FLATLINERZ
DyN
20
20

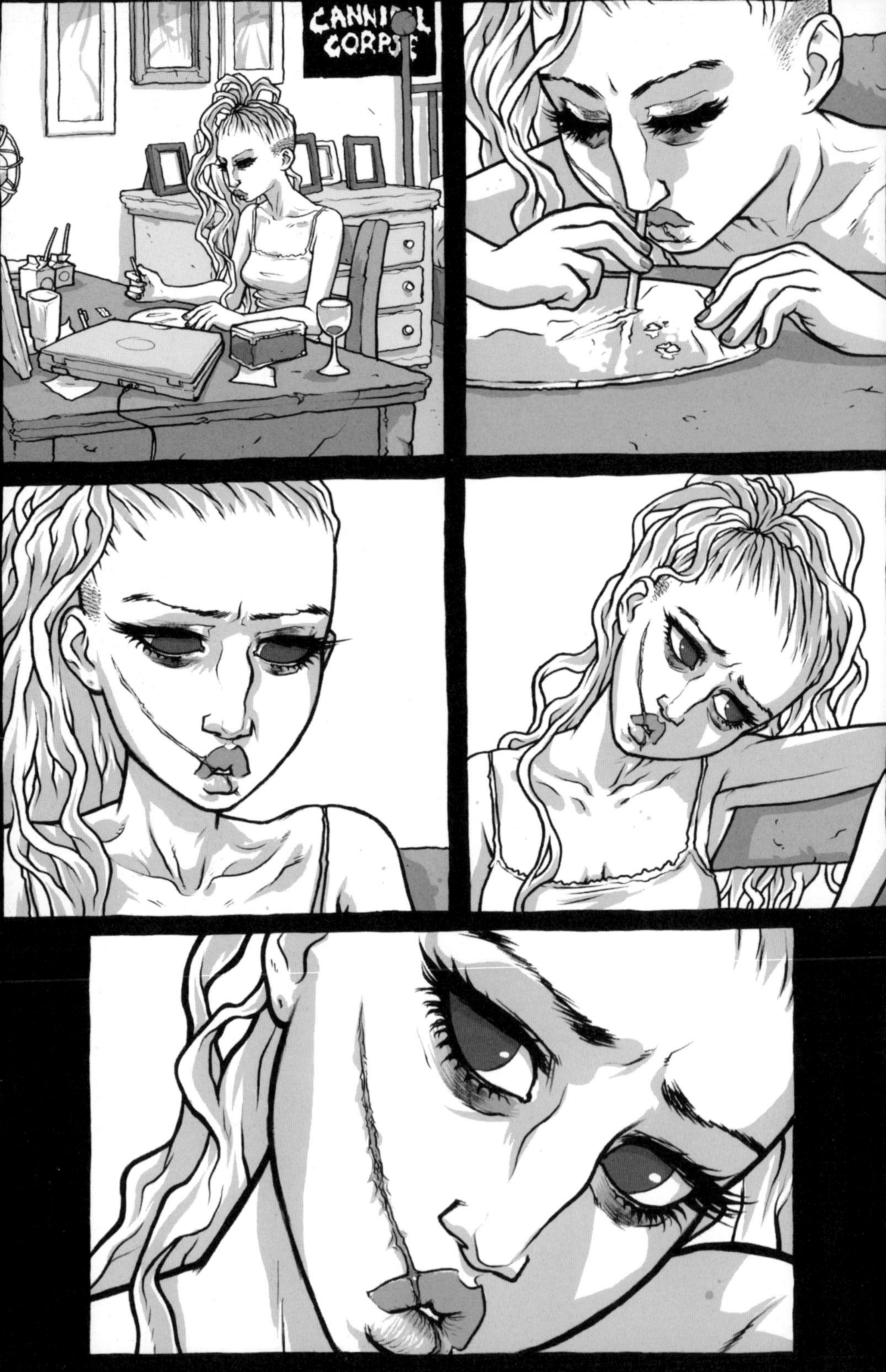

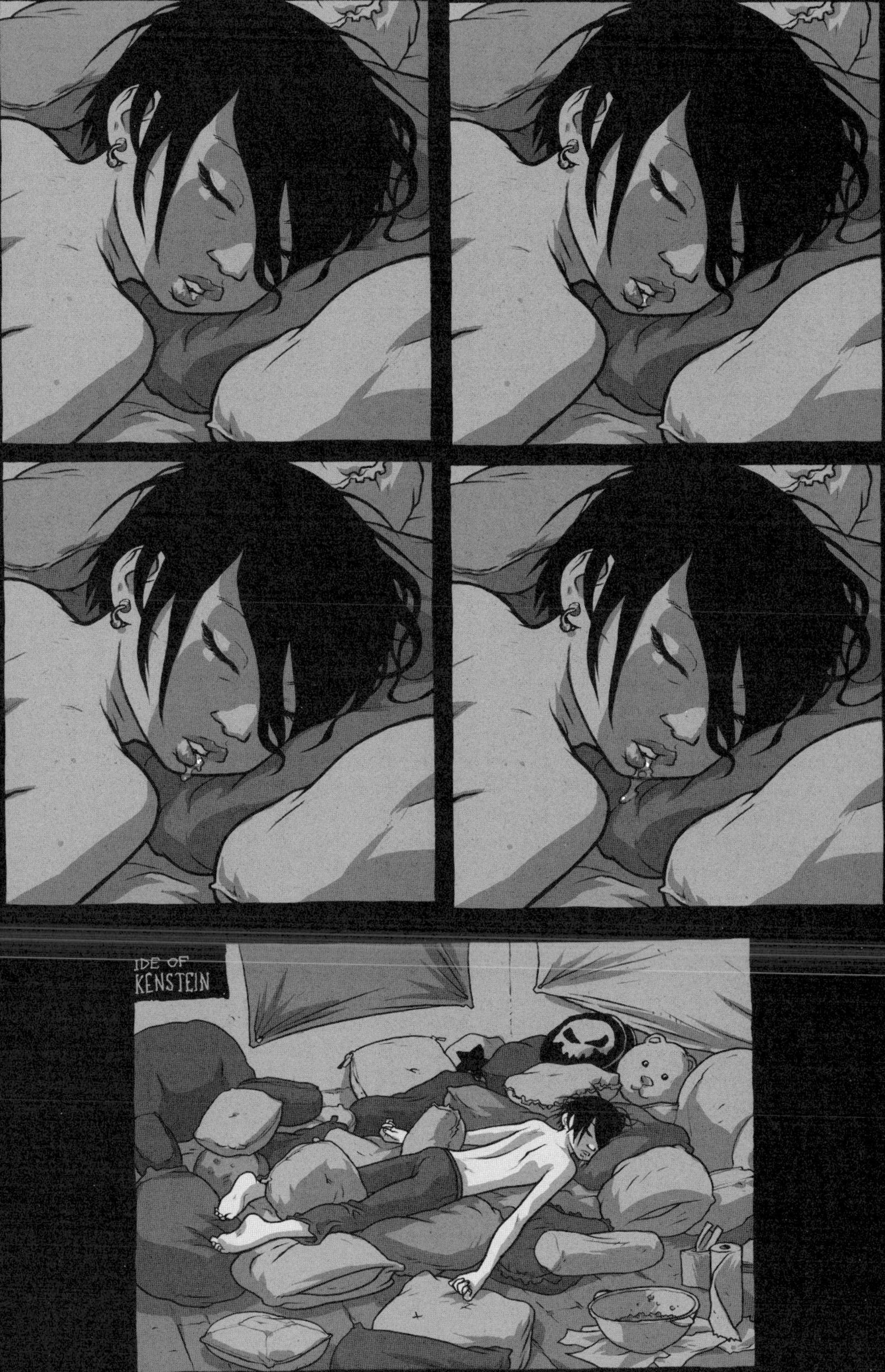
IDE OF
KENSTEIN

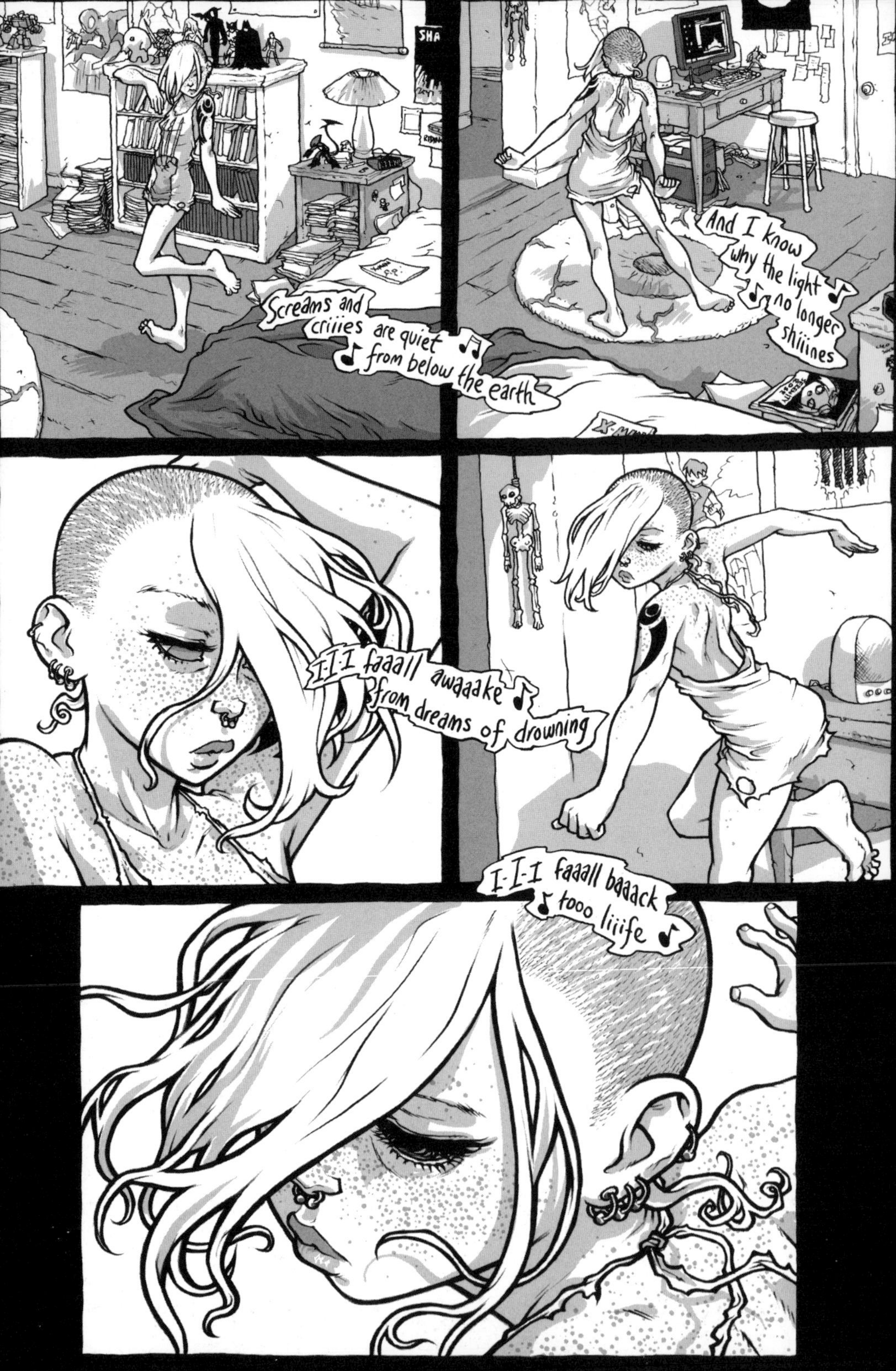

Screams and criiies are quiet ♫ ♪ from below the earth
And I know why the light ♪ ♪ no longer shiiines
I-I-I faaall awaaake ♪ from dreams of drowning
I-I-I faaall baaack ♪ tooo liiife ♪

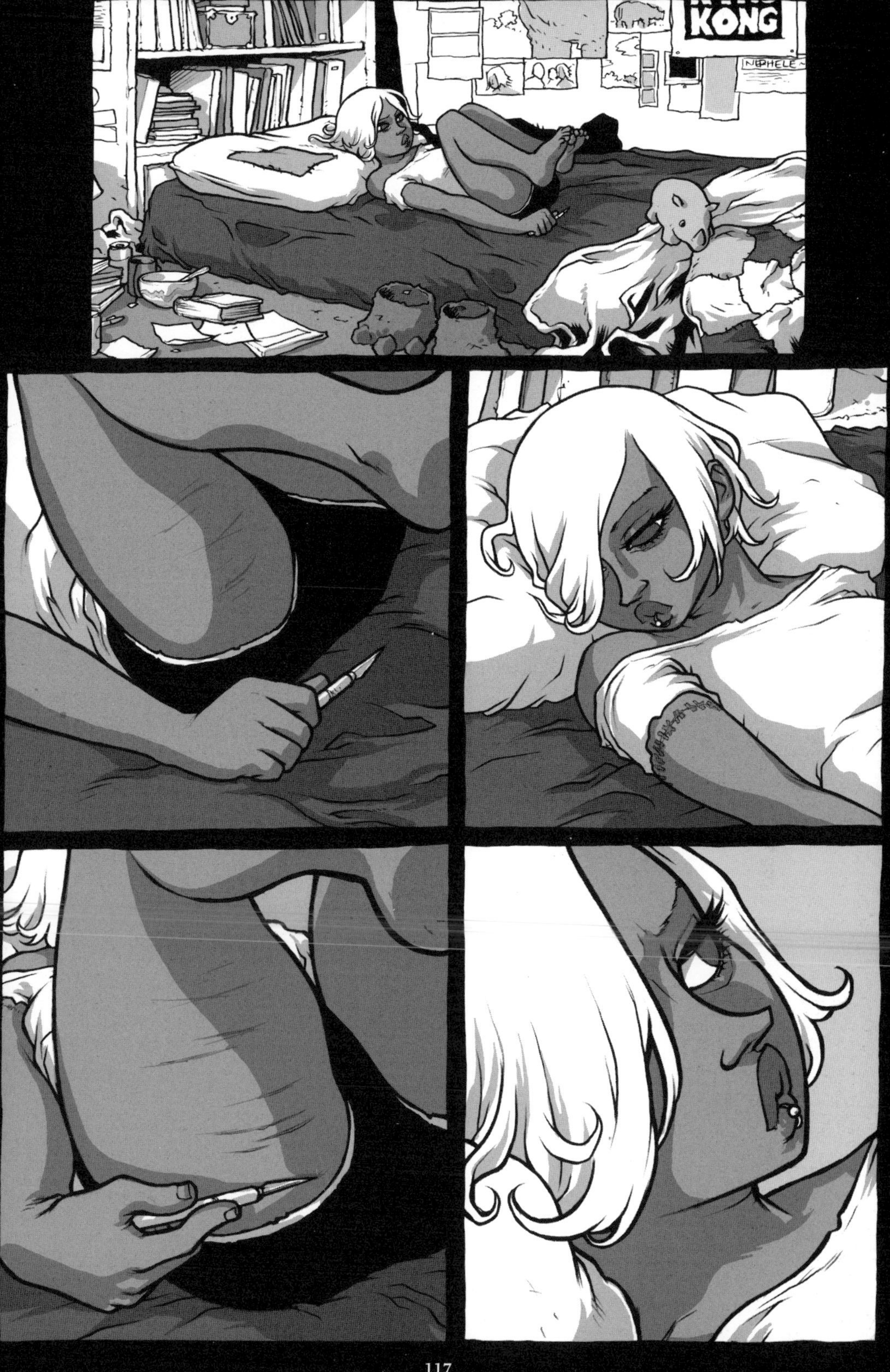
KONG
NEPHELE

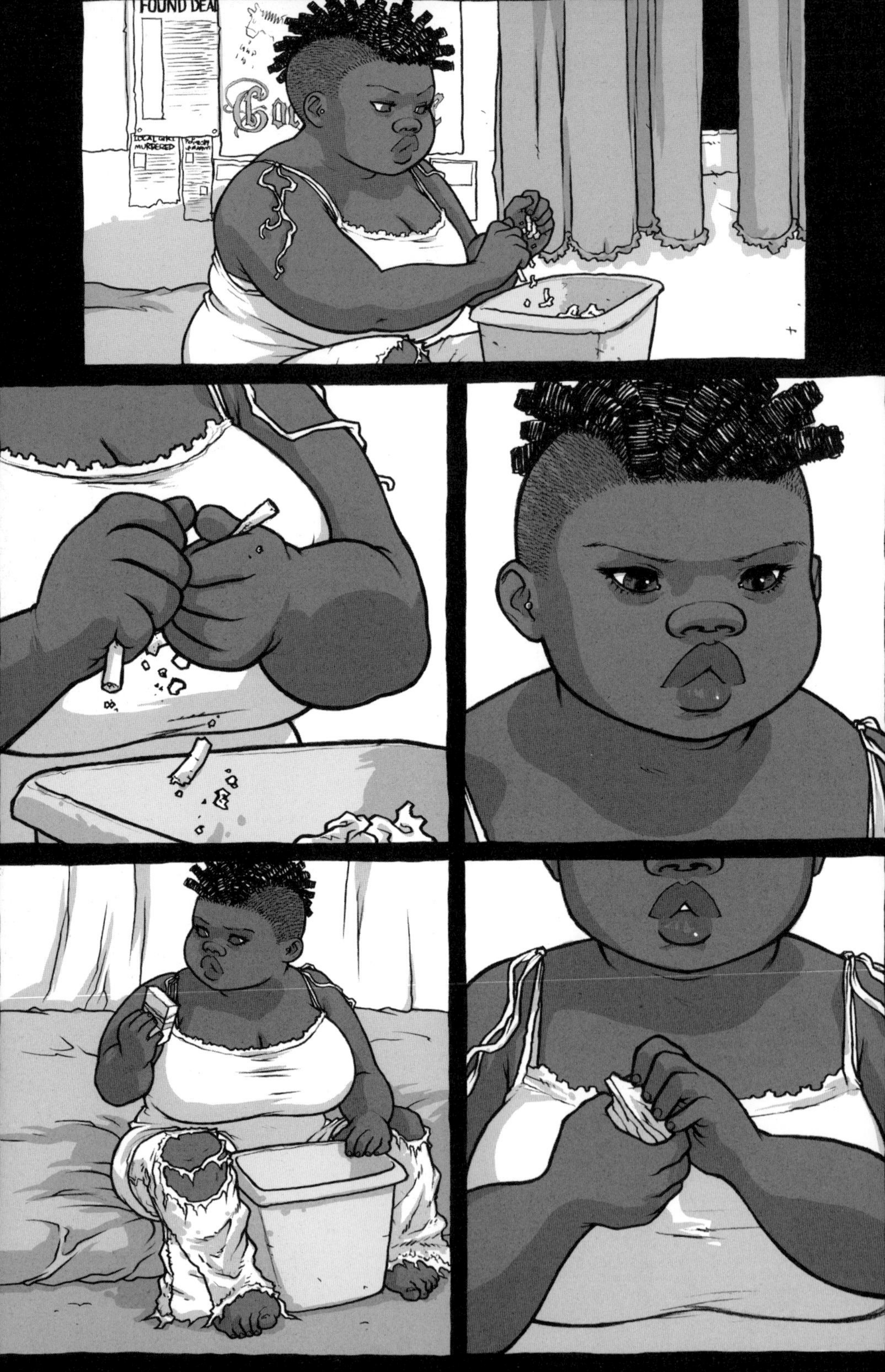
FOUND DEA
LOCAL GIRL
MURDERED

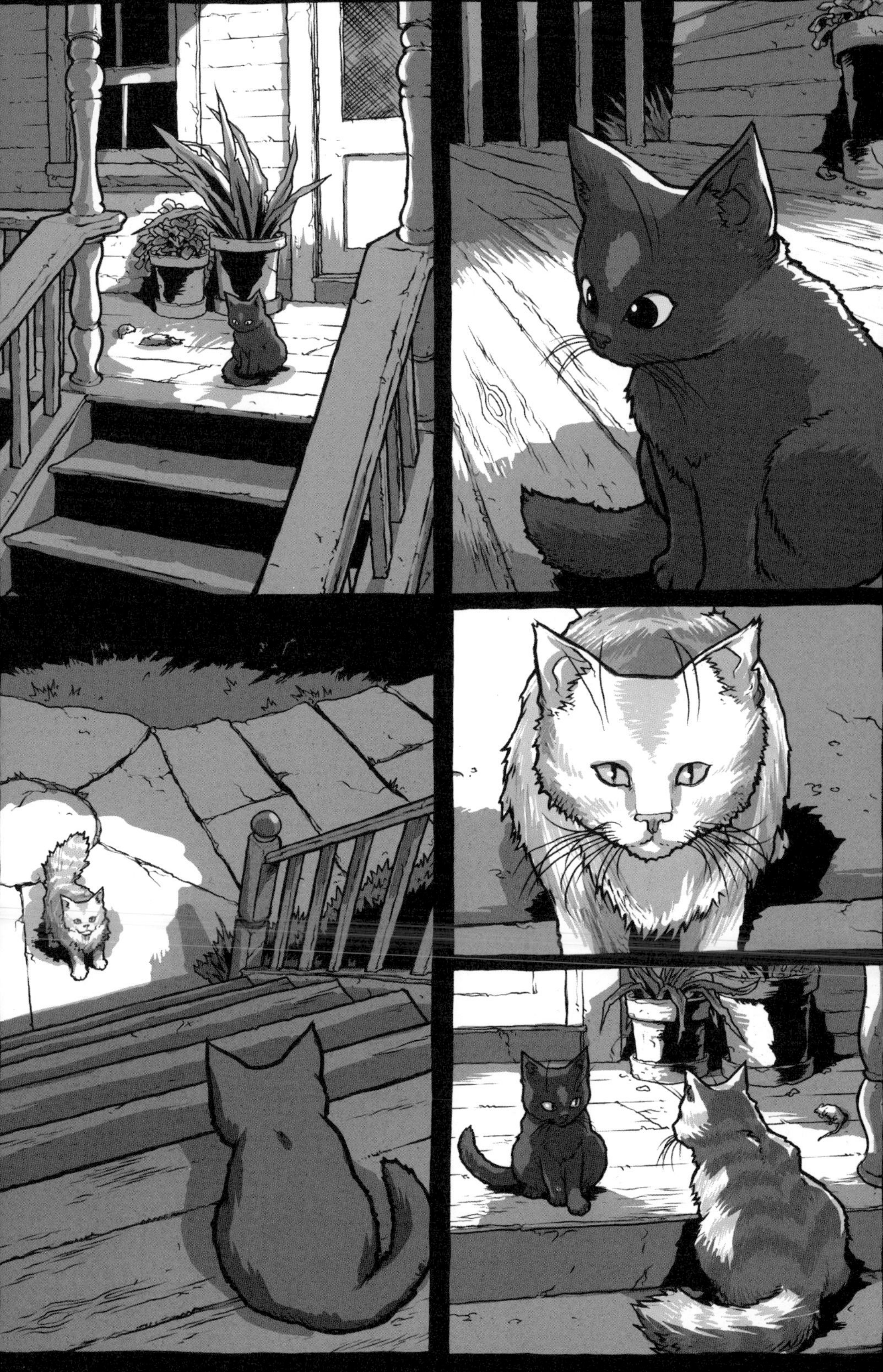

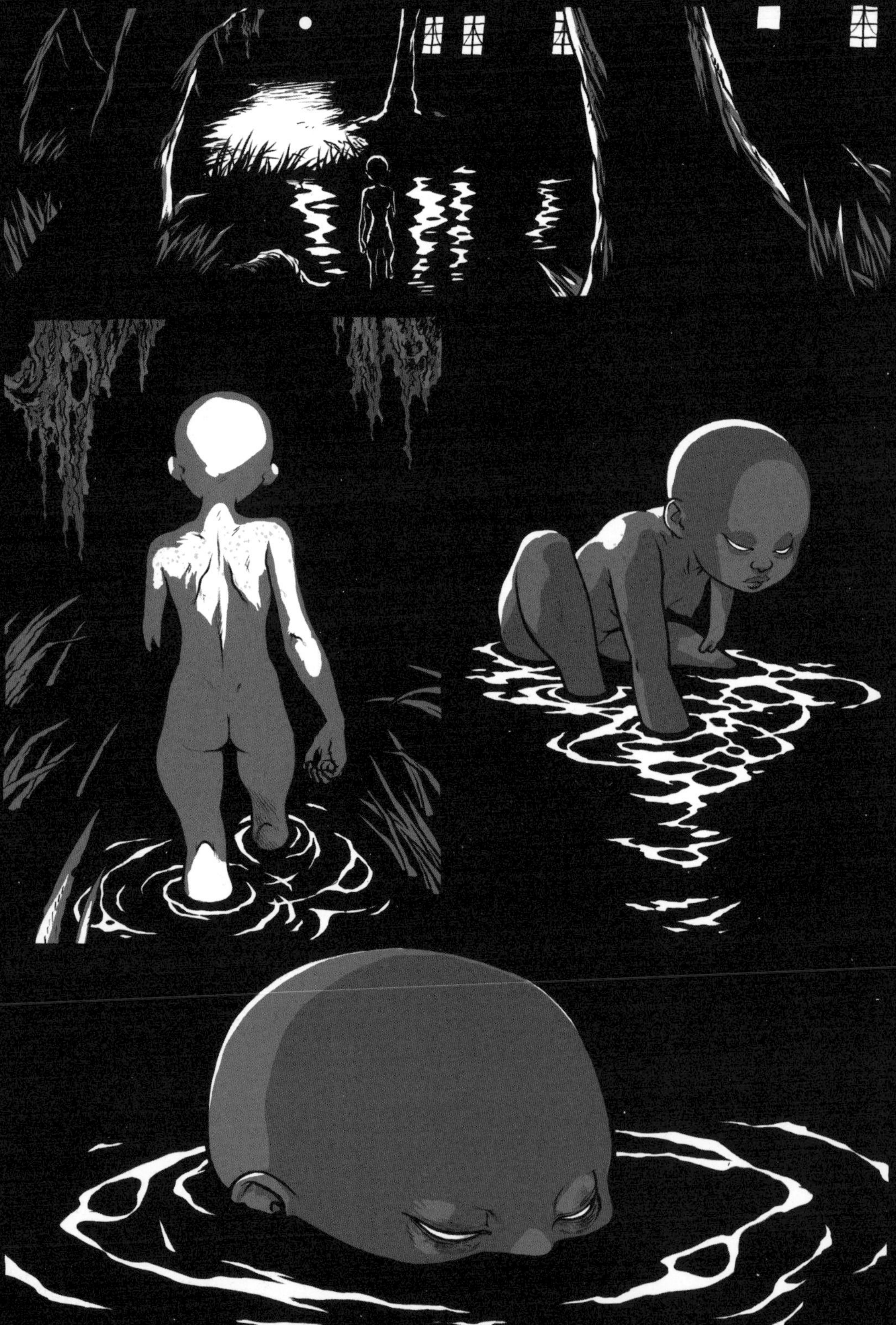

25

The Wonders At Your Feet

[friendtoroaches@gmail.com]

Recent Entries Archive Friends User Info

mara's journal

profile

November 17th, 3:42am

UNDER EVIL.

okay, i'm not growing my hair out. i didn't know you guys cared so much, thanks for the comments. i think from now on i'm going to have code names for everybody i know so things won't turn into big drama. maybe that makes me cowardly but whatever. my new possible girlfriend's name is Lucy. i don't know what's going on. she's with somebody else officially but me and her keep messing around like kissing or making out or whatever, i guess nothin too serious but still. i really have to sit down and be like what's the deal. things seems rocky with her other SO (who is kind of a smug bitch imo), so maybe i won't have to. but even then, we've been friends for a long time and there have been little things over the years that led up to this, i think i always sort of knew how i felt but i was too confused or scared or something and never did anything until recently but now that i did, everything seems like this out of control rollercoaster that could totally like fly off the tracks and everybody gets body parts sliced off by support beams or flung out over the amusement park and they land on a cotton candy stand and everybody's like "AAAAH!!" and screaming and then the people's blood is all spilling and oozing out and goes into the cotton candy spinner machine and the cotton candy starts coming out sickening red instead of happy pink, and then some clueless kid takes one of the red cotton candy and eats it and is like "look, mommy, it's not pink!" and then he's a fucking cannibal. but then the other way is that the rollercoaster finishes and everyone's fine and it was really fun and awesome, then your friend goes "let's go again!!!" then you ride it again but flying off the tracks is still a possible looming thing. that's how it feels i can't really describe it any other way.

i don't know if i'm the "let's go again" friend or the other friend who doesn't say nothin. i really want things to work out. i don't want to be a fling. i don't want to be the one who gets attached but then find out the other person isn't and that i was just a thing or an experiment and then the other friend can move on just fine and go back to normal, but since i'm the one with all the feelings fucking shit up we can't be normal again, can't go back to being just plain old best friends like before, and then those are MY guts making pink candy red. and getting eaten by that bastard kid. i don't know why Lucy is even bothering with me, i feel like i got so many issues and we have such a weird history and she used to be so mean to me when wereyounger. we've both changnd alot obviously but i still think about going back to that time when i was really submissive or subserveint, or what if this is Lucy manipulating me or she could not realize she's manipuatling me. i feel terrible thinking that is even a possiblity or that she's doing that. i'm sorry, Lucy, it's just me fuckin dwelling on all this shit. i know you're not like that. i hate myself for selling her short even for a second. i wish i knew if this was a good idea. but i guess there's no turning back now, we already made out a bunch of times. i even let her touch my ass in a non-joke way. that's pretty much the event horizon, isn't it?

i wish i was completely straight. i always thought i was, i guess, and maybe i'm only not straight for Lucy, but it all smacks you in the face and not only do you get the normal bullshit that comes with love and relationships but then you got this like "oh my god i'm gay or something, it has to be a secret" shit going on. like what the fuck do i say to my parents, you know? i guess if this goes nowhere with Lucy it won't matter, i won't have too. but i'd still need to make up a story why we aren't friends anymore. need another smoke. this quitting thing ain't goin too great.

mood: full of angst
current music: none

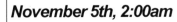

[0 comments | leave a comment]

November 5th, 2:00am

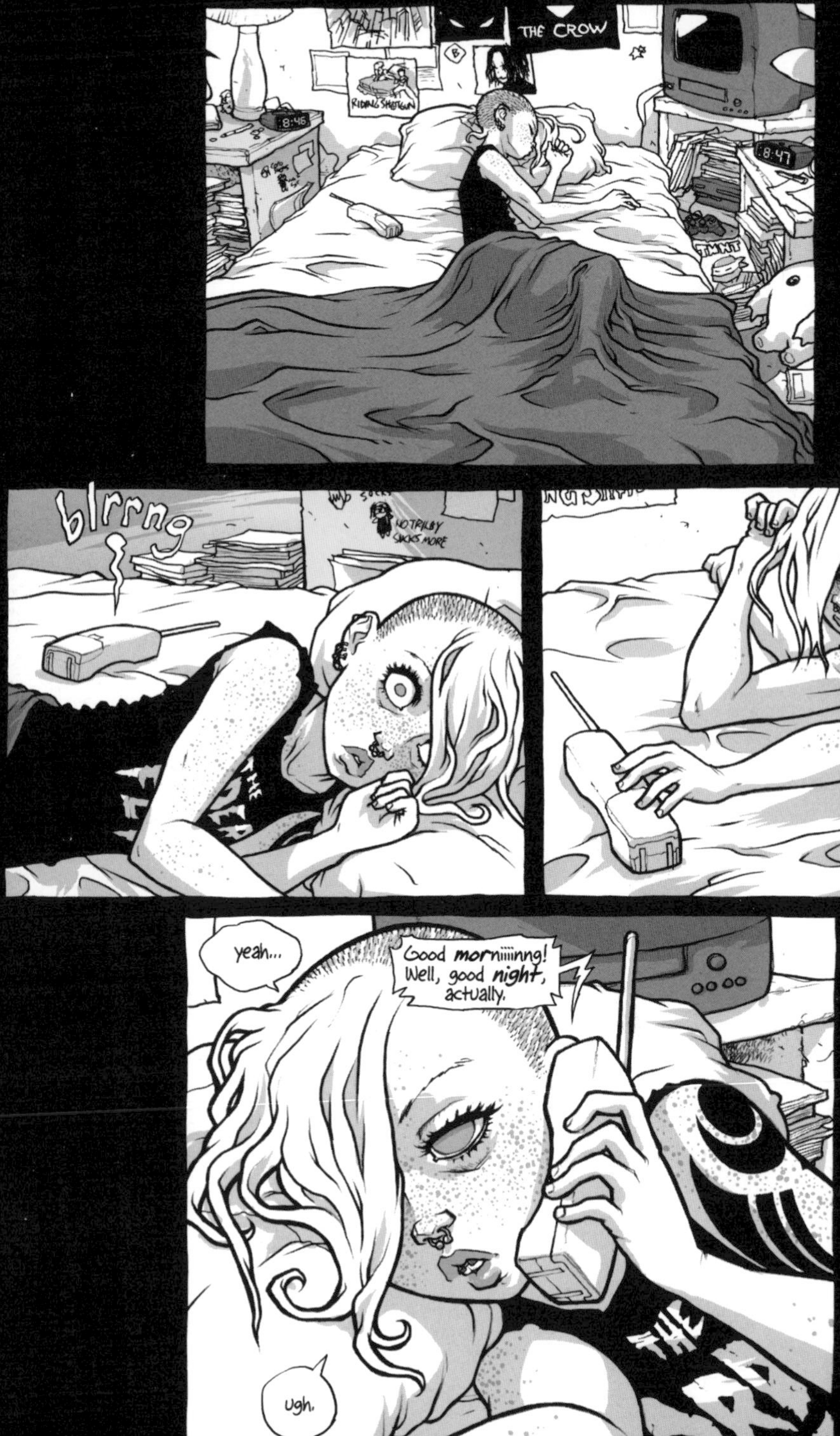
THE CROW
RIDING SHOTGUN
8:46
8:47
TMNT
blrrng
NO TRILBY SUCKS MORE
ORDER OF THE FLY
yeah...
Good **mor**niiiiinng!
Well, good **night**,
actually.
Ugh.

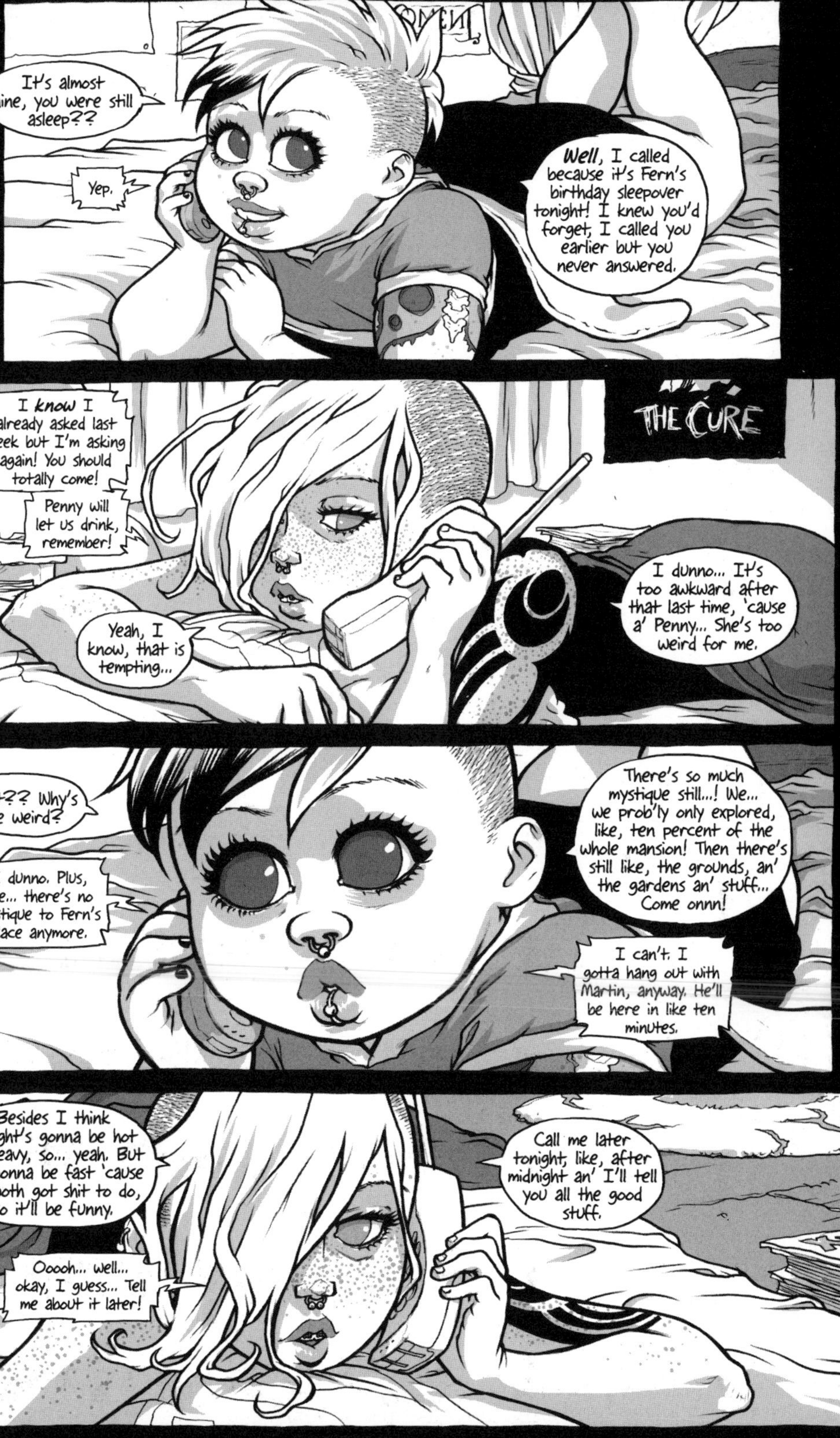
It's almost nine, you were still asleep??
Yep.
Well, I called because it's Fern's birthday sleepover tonight! I knew you'd forget, I called you earlier but you never answered.
I know I already asked last week but I'm asking again! You should totally come!
Penny will let us drink, remember!
Yeah, I know, that is tempting...
I dunno... It's too awkward after that last time, 'cause a' Penny... She's too weird for me.
THE CURE
:49
What?? Why's she weird?
I dunno. Plus, like... there's no mystique to Fern's place anymore.
There's so much mystique still...! We... we prob'ly only explored, like, ten percent of the whole mansion! Then there's still like, the grounds, an' the gardens an' stuff... Come onnn!
I can't. I gotta hang out with Martin, anyway. He'll be here in like ten minutes.
Besides I think tonight's gonna be hot 'n' heavy, so... yeah. But it's gonna be fast 'cause we both got shit to do, so it'll be funny.
Call me later tonight, like, after midnight an' I'll tell you all the good stuff.
Ooooh... well... okay, I guess... Tell me about it later!

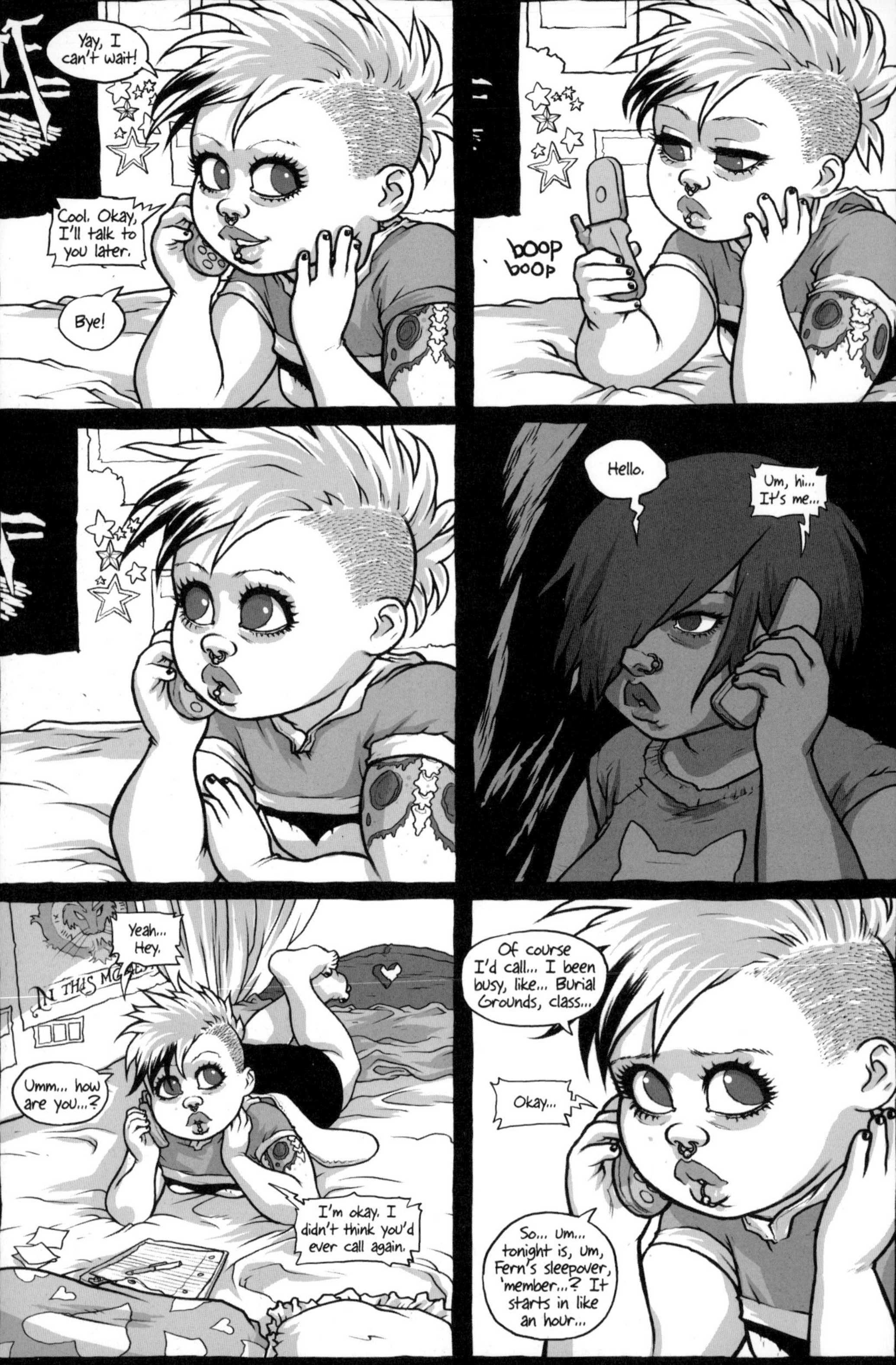

Yay, I can't wait!
Cool. Okay, I'll talk to you later.
Bye!
boop boop
Hello.
Um, hi... It's me...
Yeah... Hey.
Umm... how are you...?
I'm okay. I didn't think you'd ever call again.
Of course I'd call... I been busy, like... Burial Grounds, class...
Okay...
So... um... tonight is, um, Fern's sleepover, 'member...? It starts in like an hour...

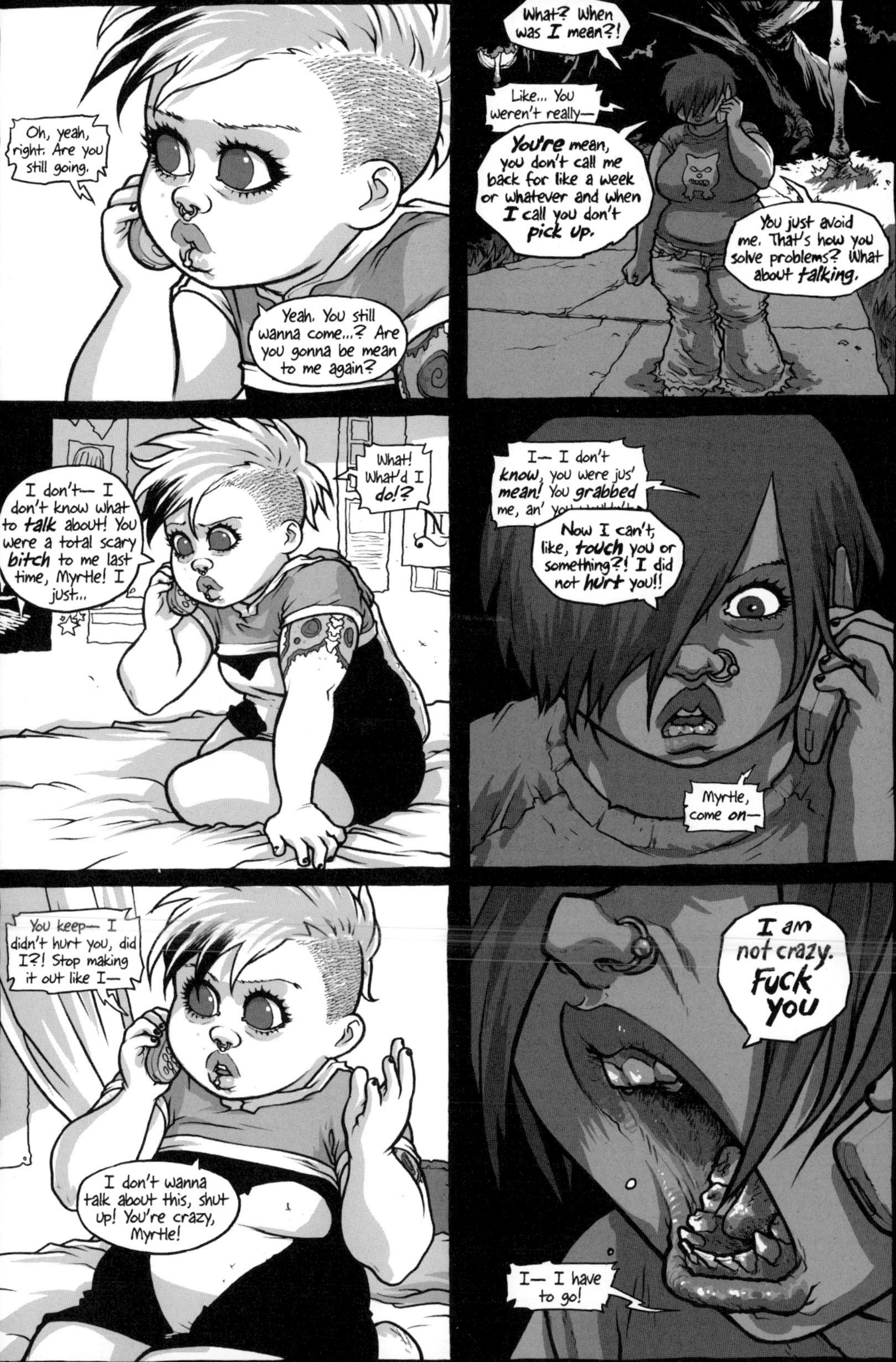
Oh, yeah, right. Are you still going.
Yeah. You still wanna come...? Are you gonna be mean to me again?
What? When was I mean?!
Like... You weren't really—
You're mean, you don't call me back for like a week or whatever and when I call you don't pick up.
You just avoid me. That's how you solve problems? What about talking.
I don't— I don't know what to talk about! You were a total scary bitch to me last time, Myrtle! I just...
What! What'd I do!?
I— I don't know, you were jus' mean! You grabbed me, an'
Now I can't, like, touch you or something?! I did not hurt you!!
Myrtle, come on—
You keep— I didn't hurt you, did I?! Stop making it out like I—
I don't wanna talk about this, shut up! You're crazy, Myrtle!
I am not crazy. Fuck you
I— I have to go!

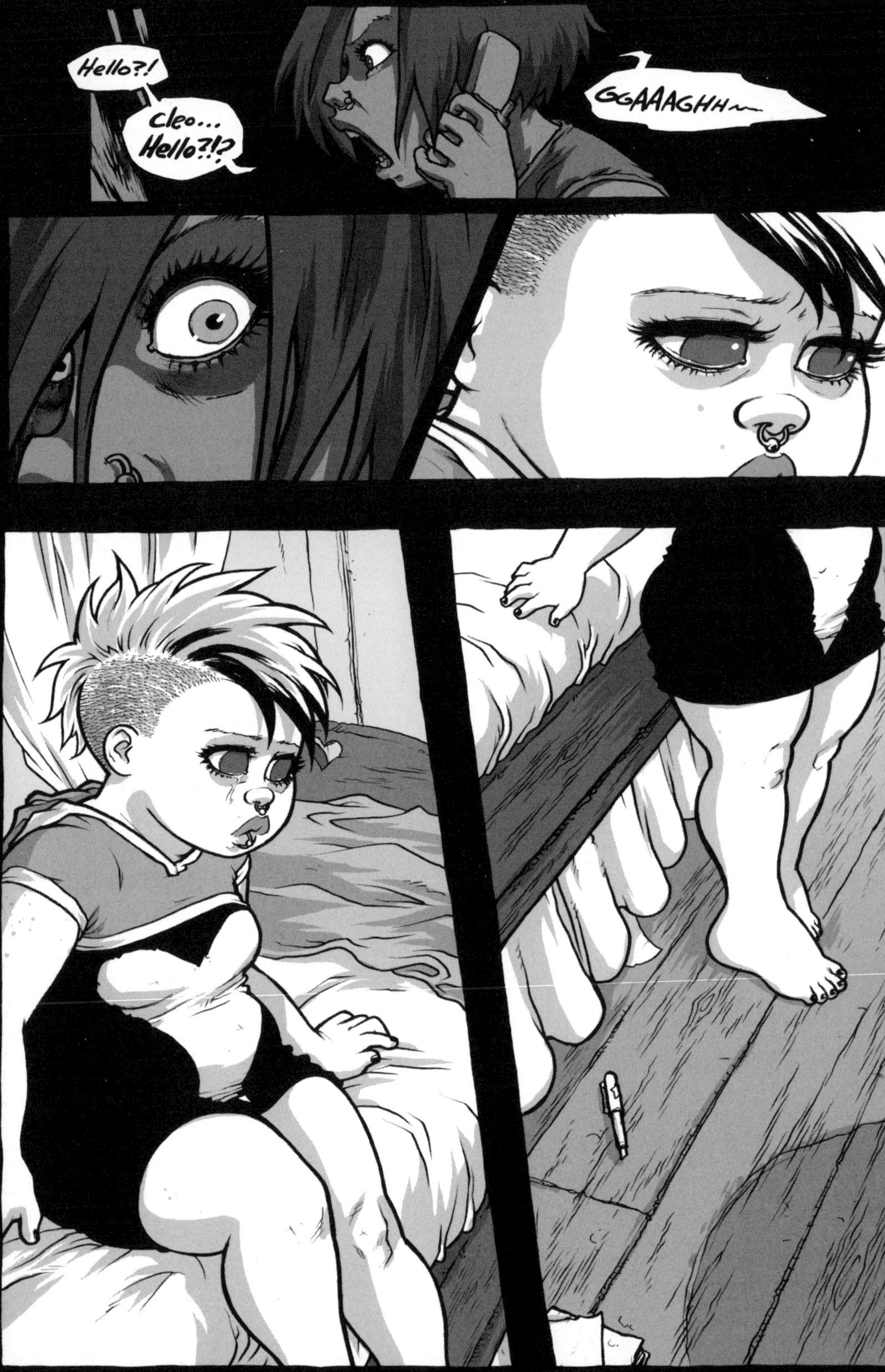
Hello?!
Cleo... Hello?!?
GGAAAAGHH~

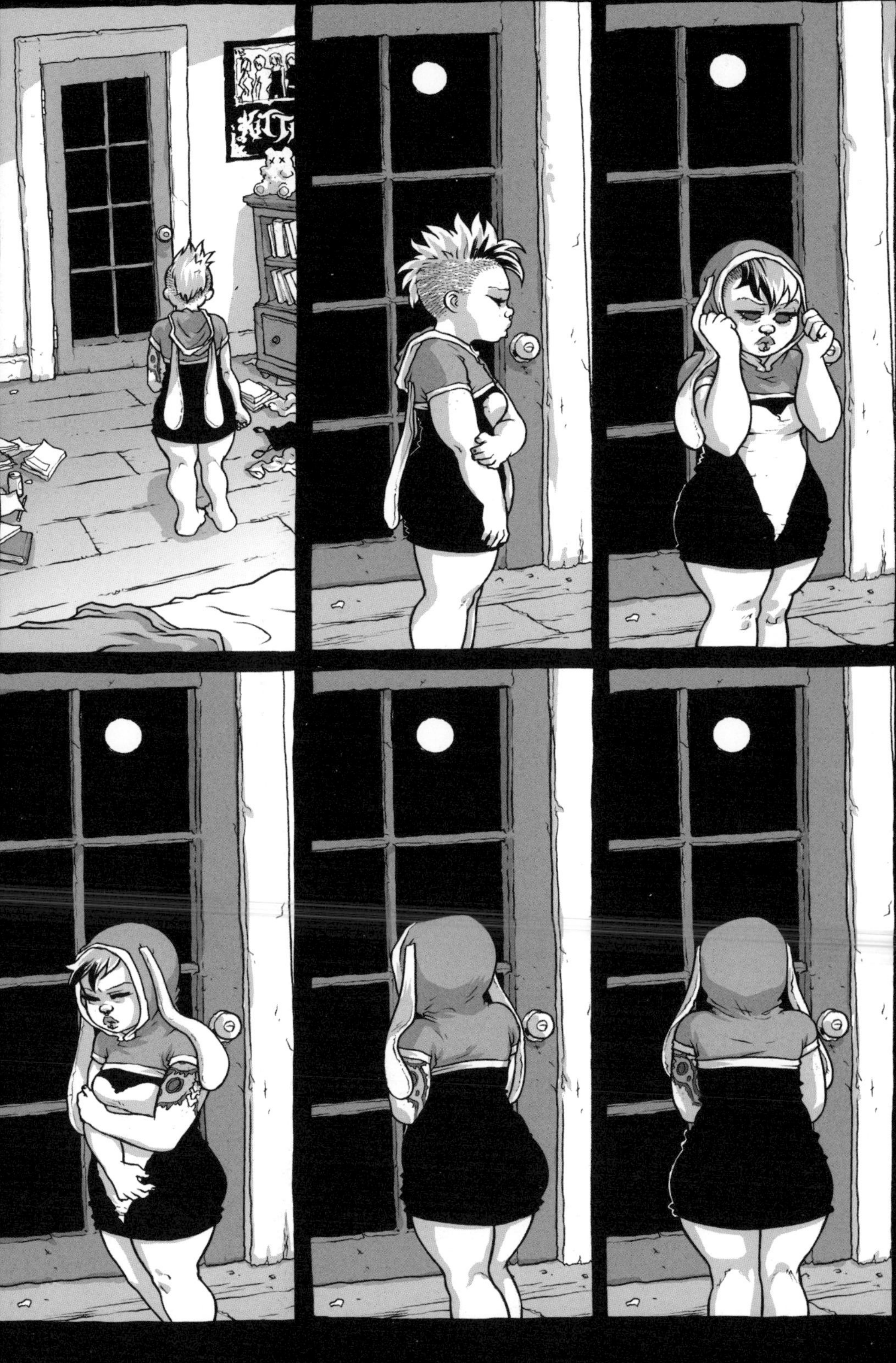

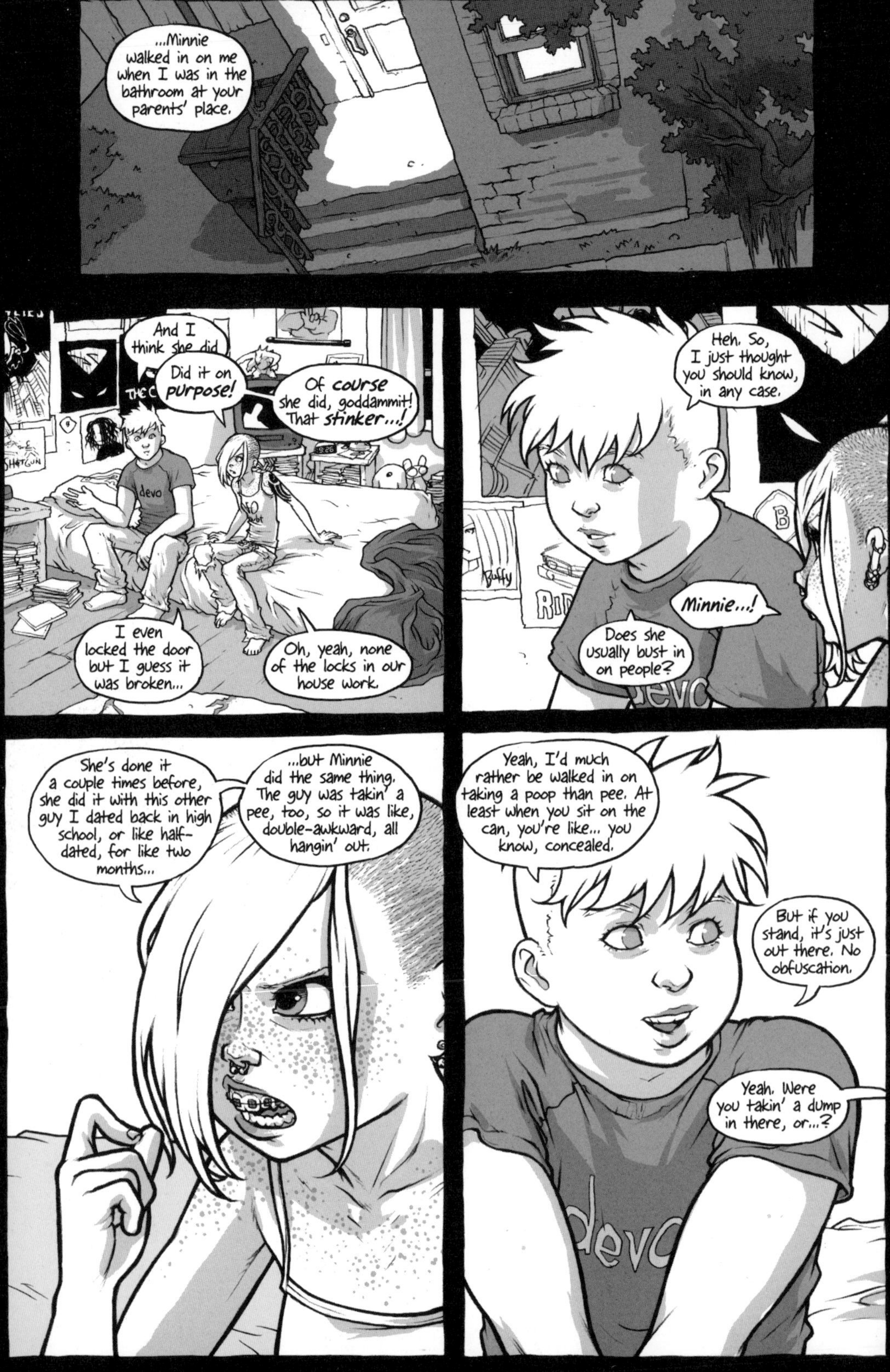
...Minnie walked in on me when I was in the bathroom at your parents' place.
And I think she did
Did it on purpose!
Of course she did, goddammit! That stinker...!
I even locked the door but I guess it was broken...
Oh, yeah, none of the locks in our house work.
Heh. So, I just thought you should know, in any case.
Minnie...!
Does she usually bust in on people?
She's done it a couple times before, she did it with this other guy I dated back in high school, or like half-dated, for like two months...
...but Minnie did the same thing. The guy was takin' a pee, too, so it was like, double-awkward, all hangin' out.
Yeah, I'd much rather be walked in on taking a poop than pee. At least when you sit on the can, you're like... you know, concealed.
But if you stand, it's just out there. No obfuscation.
Yeah. Were you takin' a dump in there, or...?

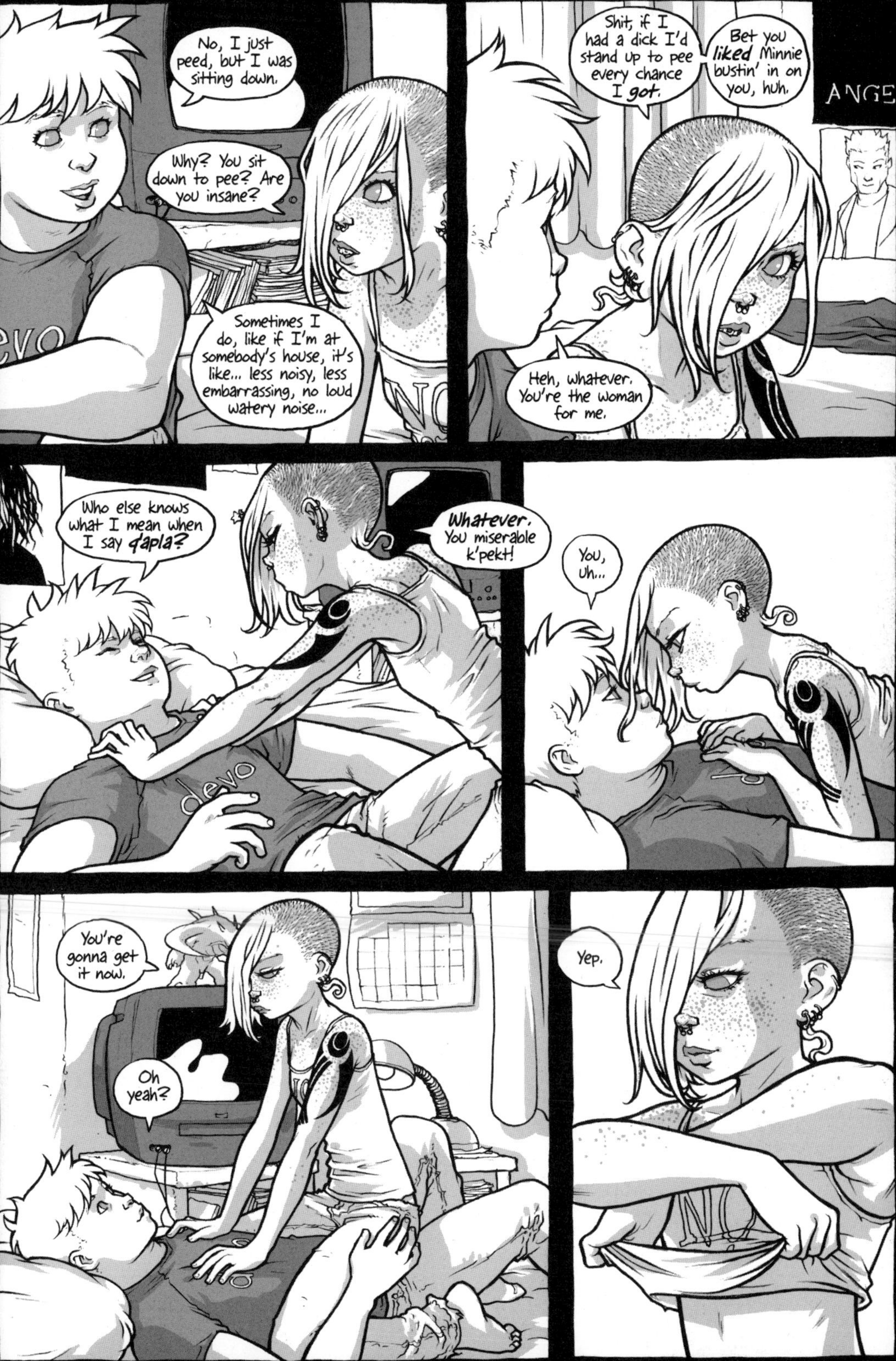
No, I just peed, but I was sitting down.
Why? You sit down to pee? Are you insane?
Sometimes I do, like if I'm at somebody's house, it's like... less noisy, less embarrassing, no loud watery noise...
Shit, if I had a dick I'd stand up to pee every chance I **got**.
Bet you **liked** Minnie bustin' in on you, huh.
ANGE
Heh, whatever. You're the woman for me.
Who else knows what I mean when I say **q'apla?**
Whatever. You miserable k'pekt!
You, uh...
You're gonna get it now.
Oh yeah?
Yep.

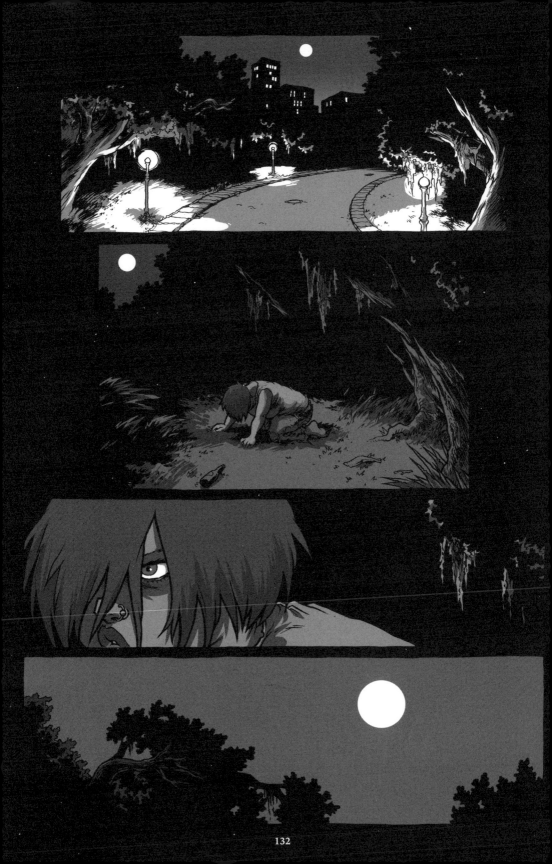

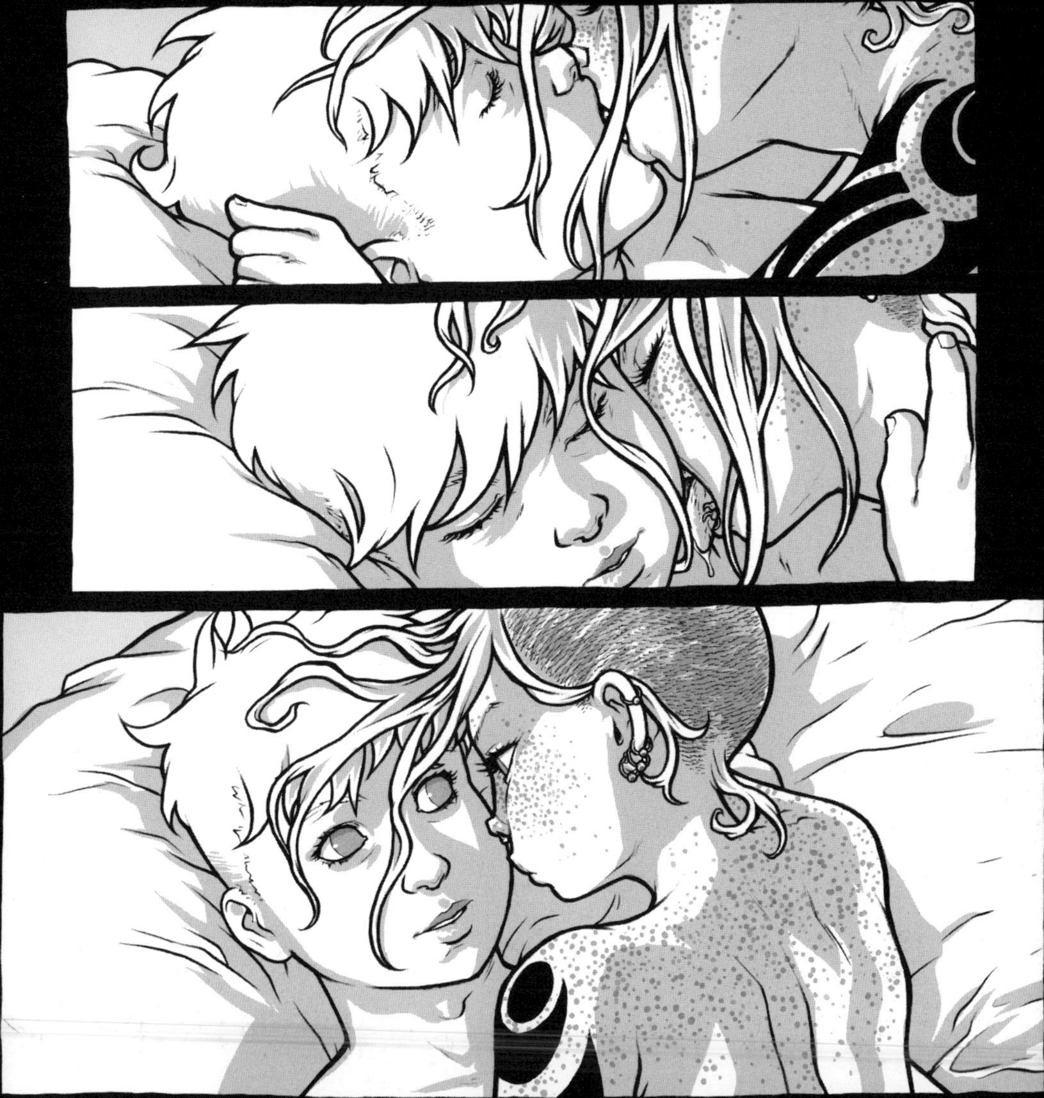

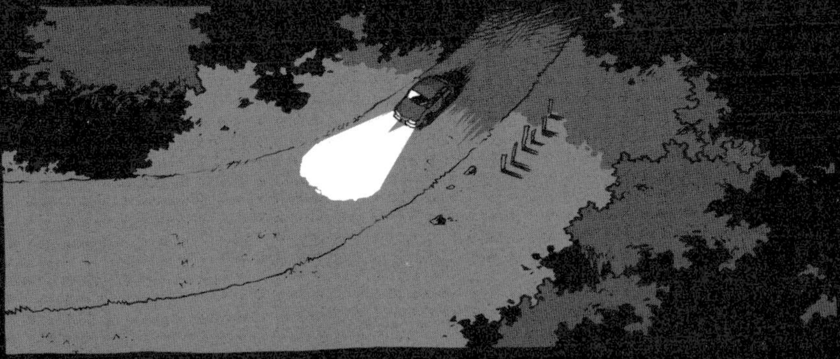

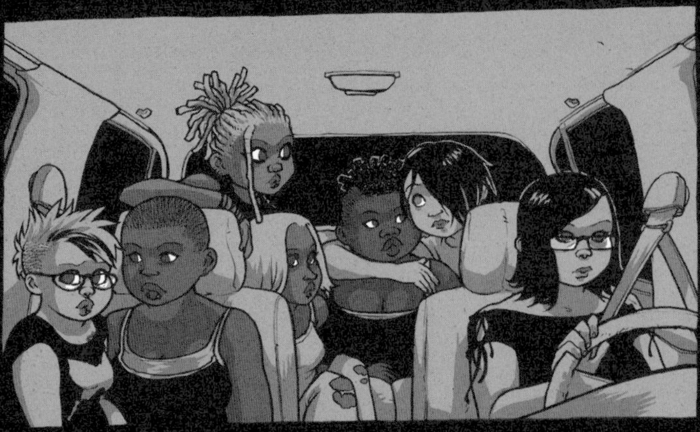

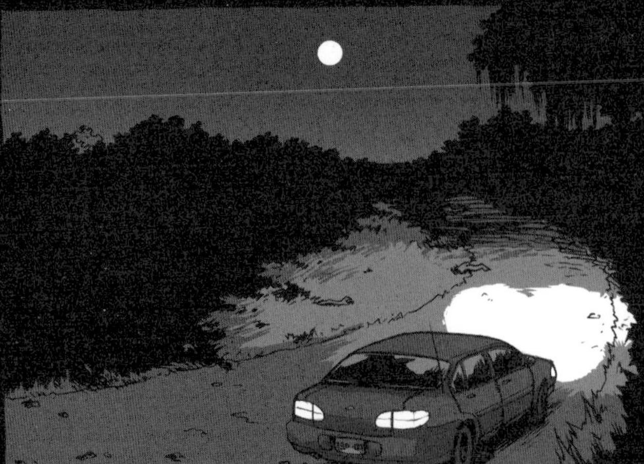

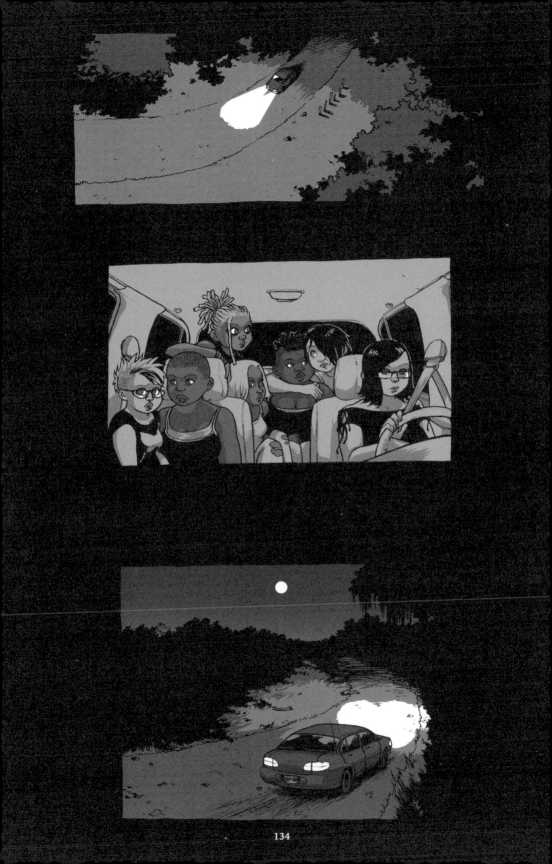

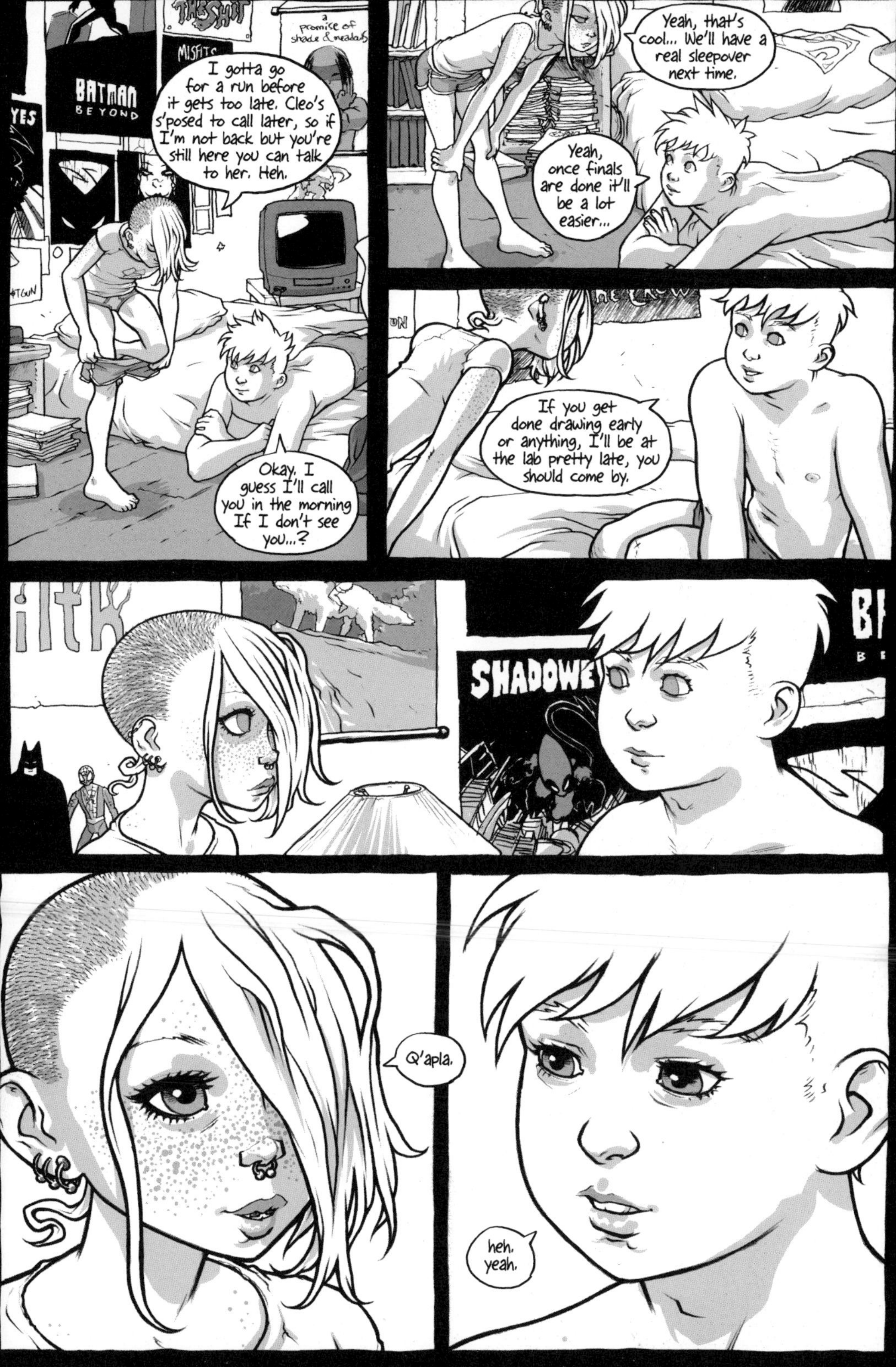

a promise of shade & meadows
MISFITS
BATMAN BEYOND
YES
I gotta go for a run before it gets too late. Cleo's s'posed to call later, so if I'm not back but you're still here you can talk to her. Heh.
Okay, I guess I'll call you in the morning If I don't see you...?
Yeah, that's cool... We'll have a real sleepover next time.
Yeah, once finals are done it'll be a lot easier...
If you get done drawing early or anything, I'll be at the lab pretty late, you should come by.
SHADOWE
Q'apla.
heh. yeah.

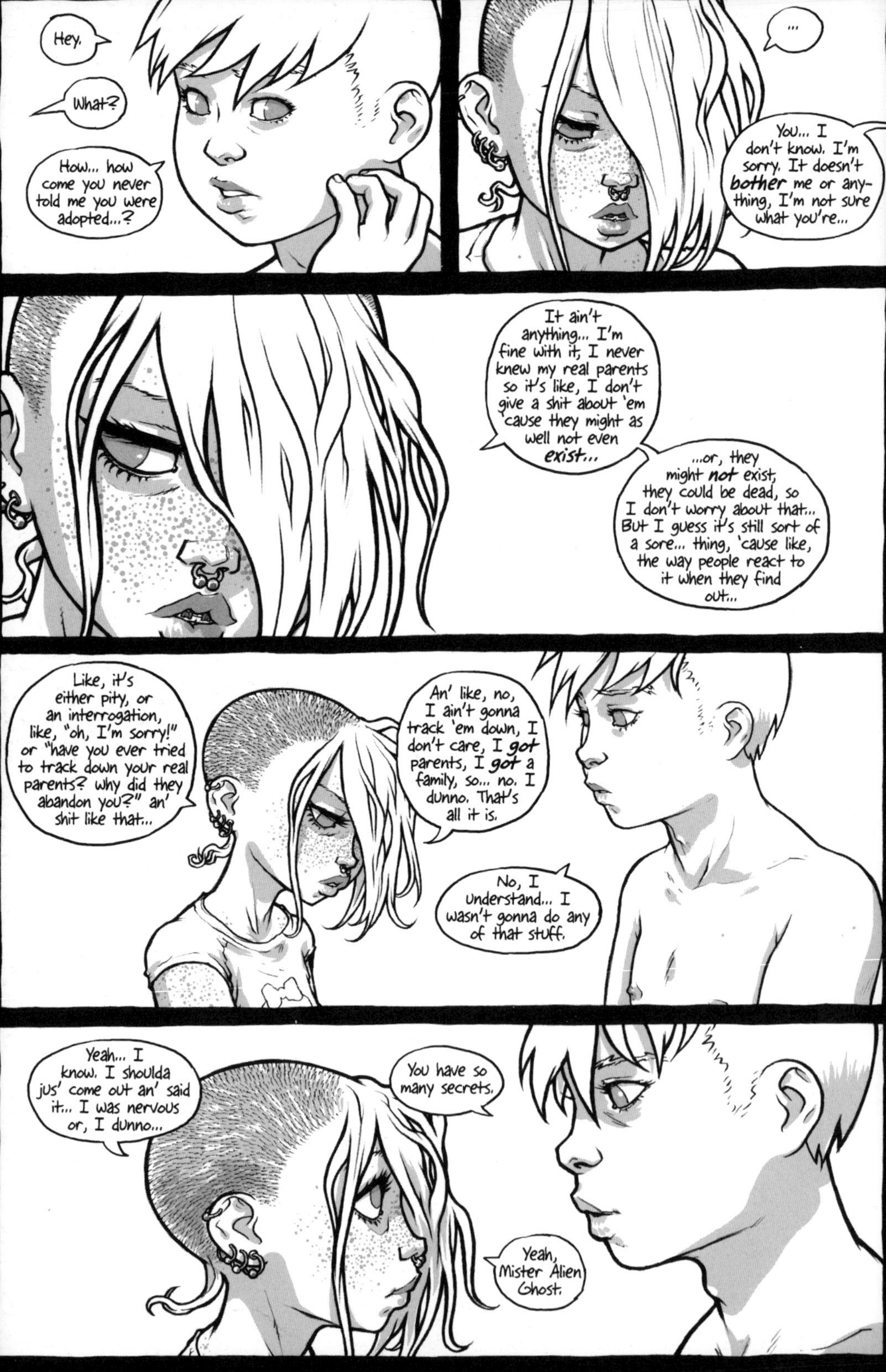
Hey.
What?
How... how come you never told me you were adopted...?
...
You... I don't know. I'm sorry. It doesn't **bother** me or anything, I'm not sure what you're...
It ain't anything... I'm fine with it, I never knew my real parents so it's like, I don't give a shit about 'em 'cause they might as well not even **exist...**
...or, they might **not** exist, they could be dead, so I don't worry about that... But I guess it's still sort of a sore... thing, 'cause like, the way people react to it when they find out...
Like, it's either pity, or an interrogation, like, "oh, I'm sorry!" or "have you ever tried to track down your real parents? why did they abandon you?" an' shit like that...
An' like, no, I ain't gonna track 'em down, I don't care, I **got** parents, I **got** a family, so... no. I dunno. That's all it is.
No, I understand... I wasn't gonna do any of that stuff.
Yeah... I know. I shoulda jus' come out an' said it... I was nervous or, I dunno...
You have so many secrets.
Yeah, Mister Alien Ghost.

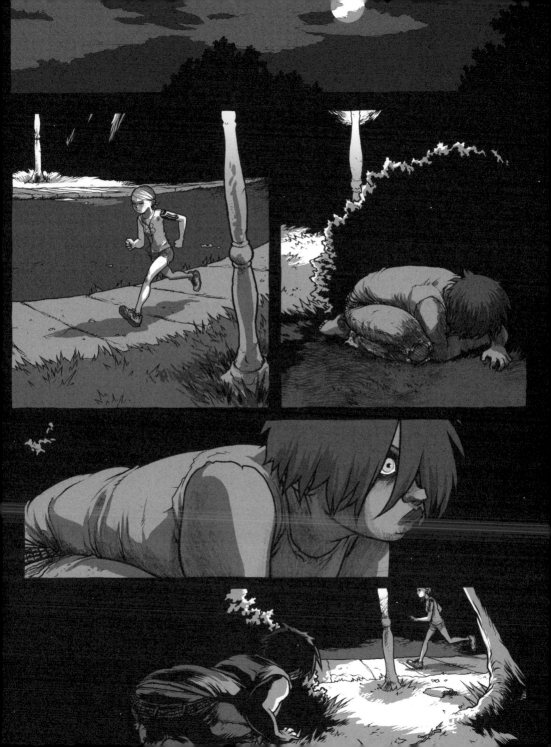

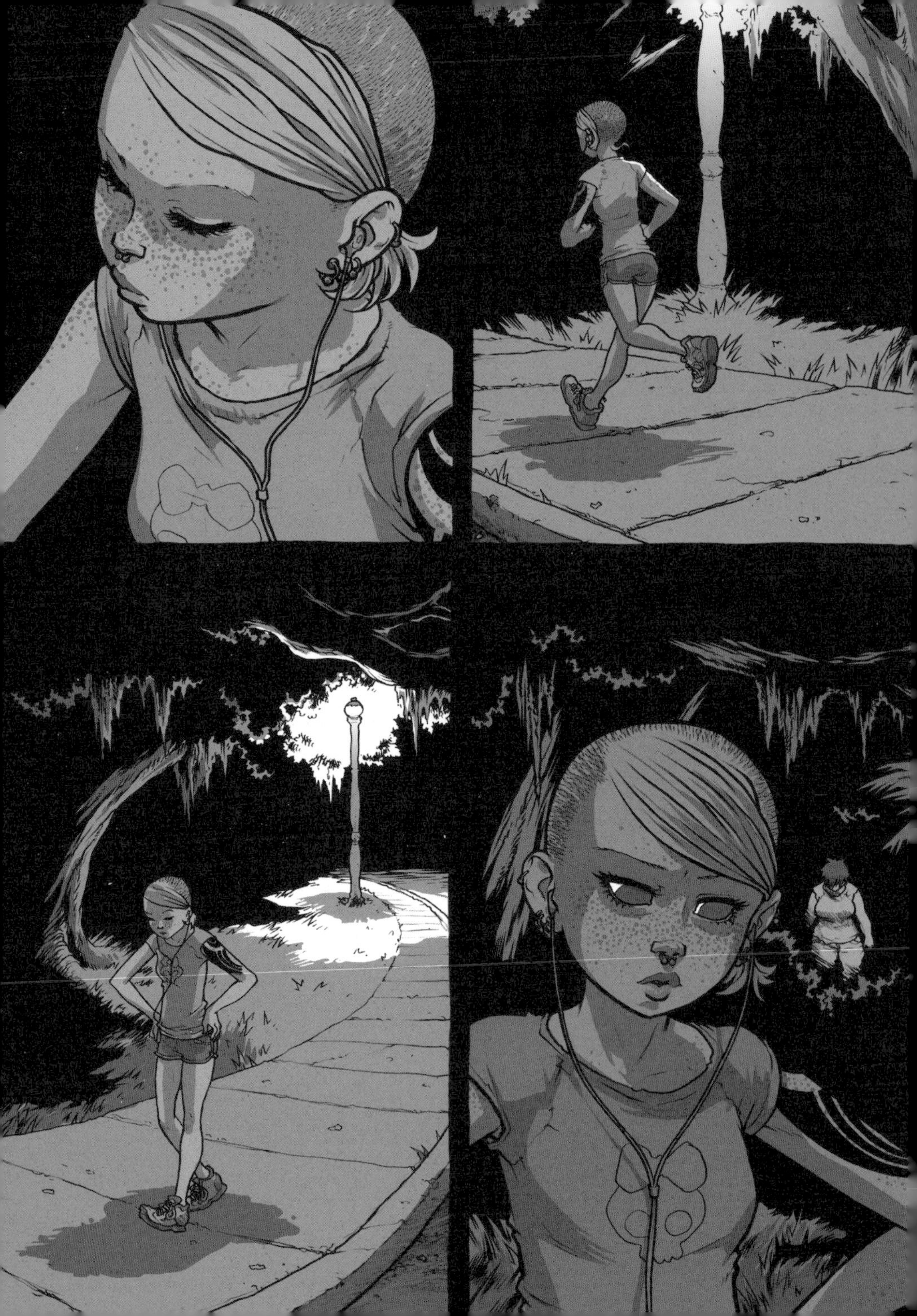

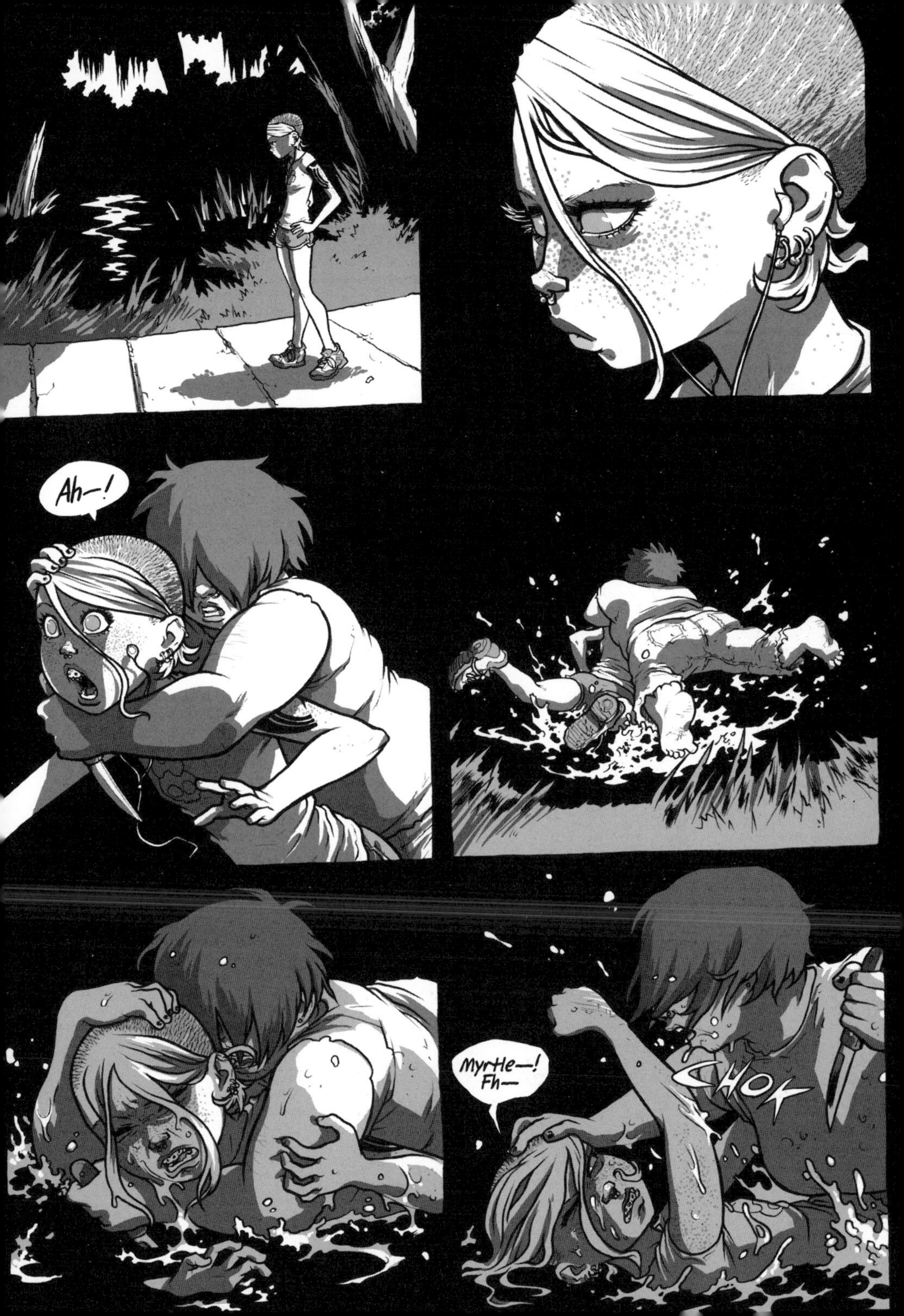
Ah—!
Myrtle—!
Fh—
CHOK

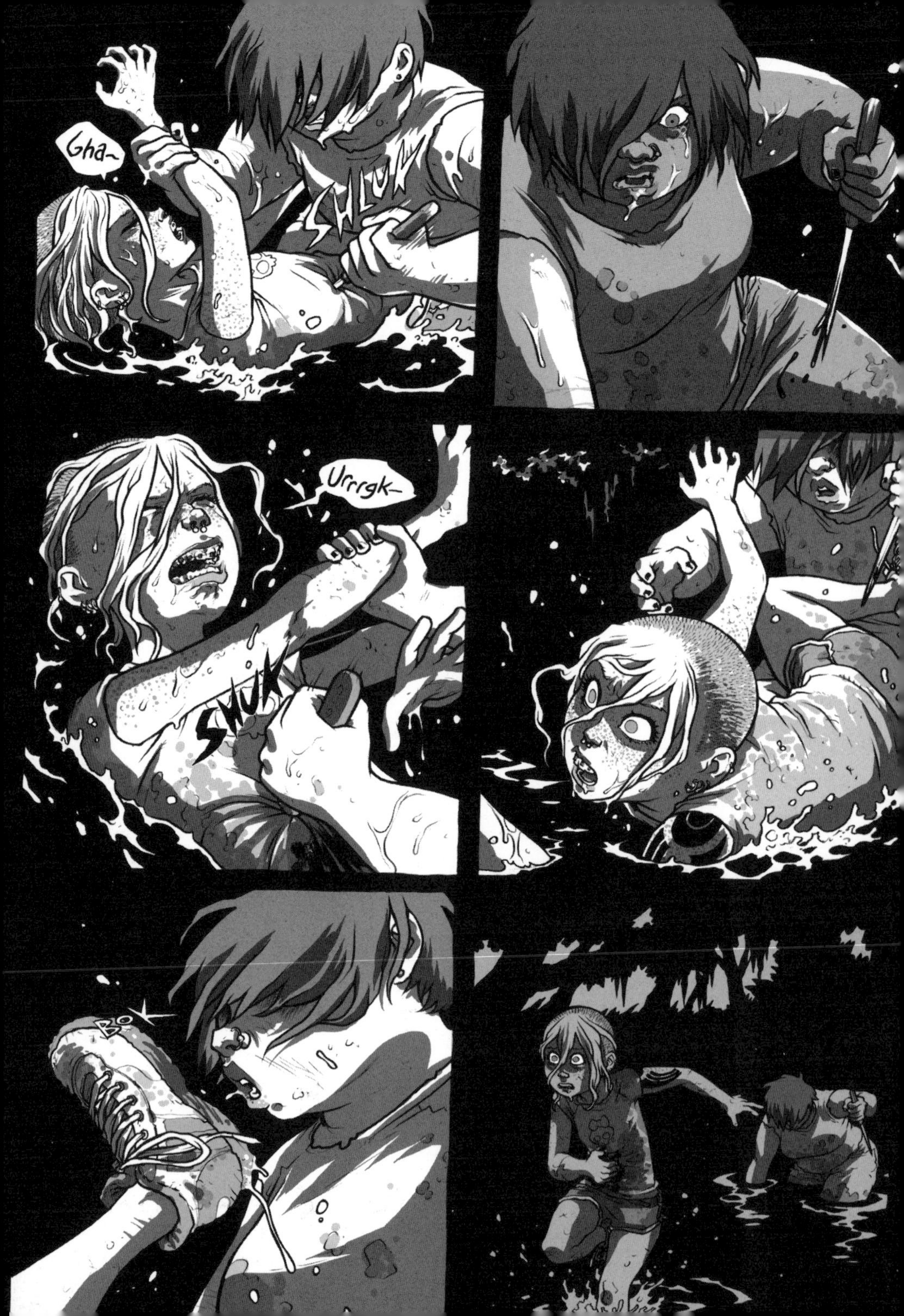
Gha~
SHLUK
Urrrgk~
SHUK
BOK

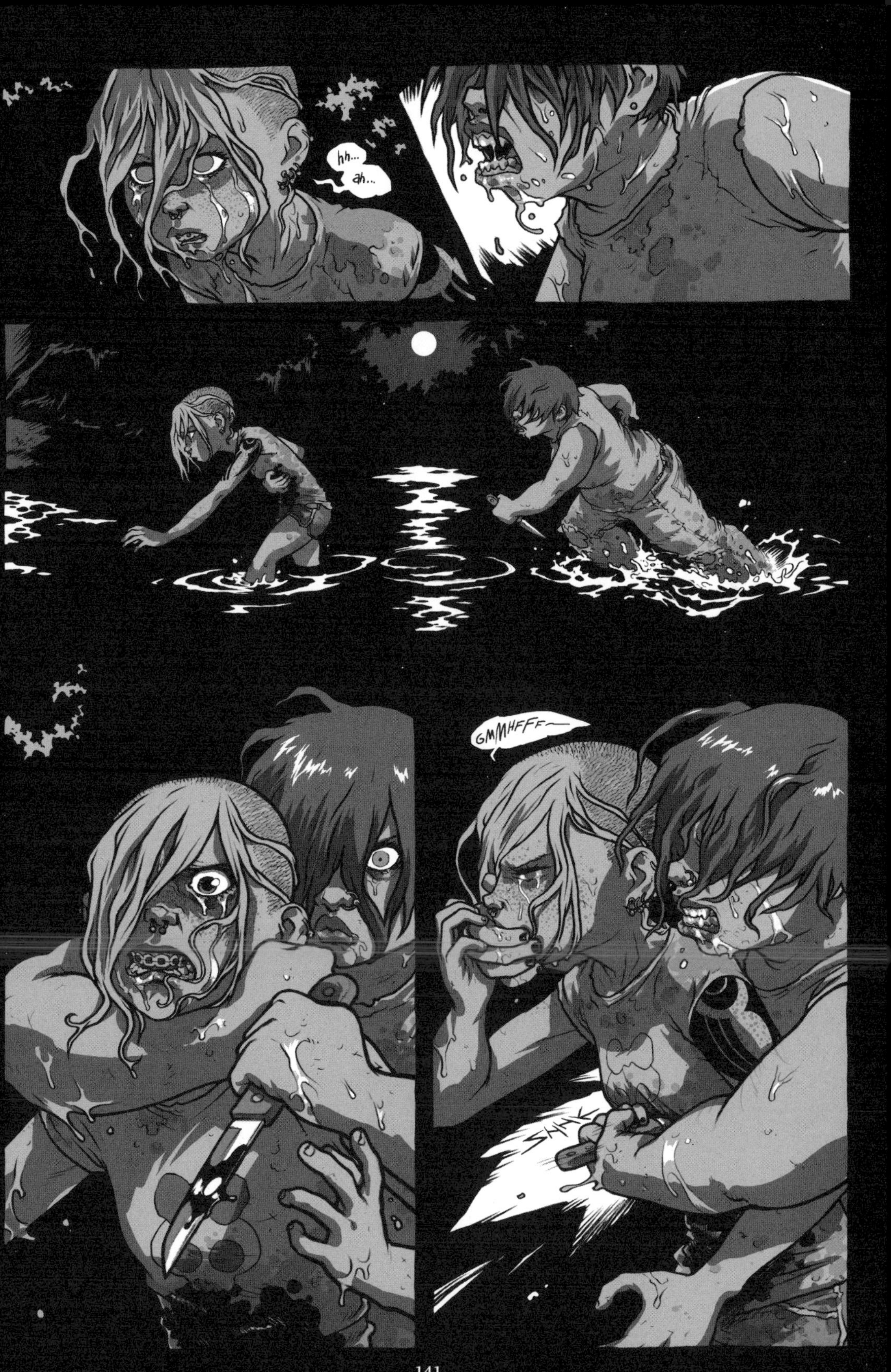
hh...
ah...
GMMHFFF~
SHAK

WHO'S WHO IN WET MOON

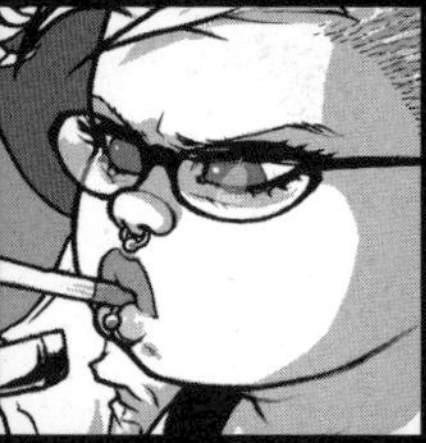
cleo lovedrop
(18)

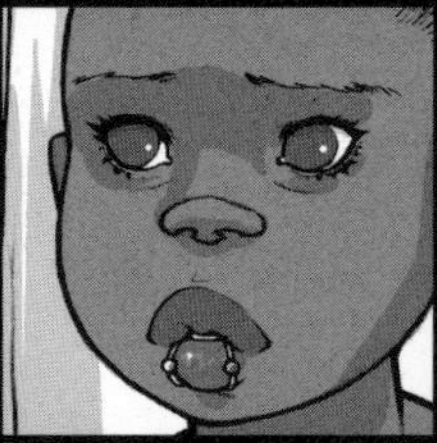
mara zuzanny
(18)

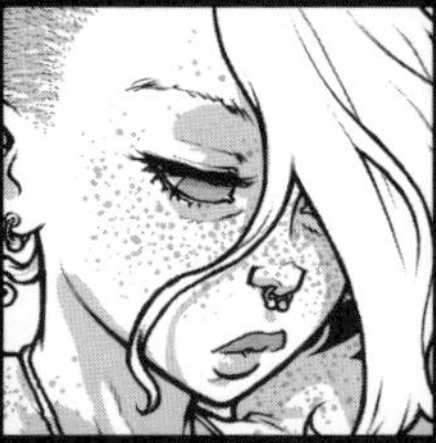
trilby bernarde
(18)

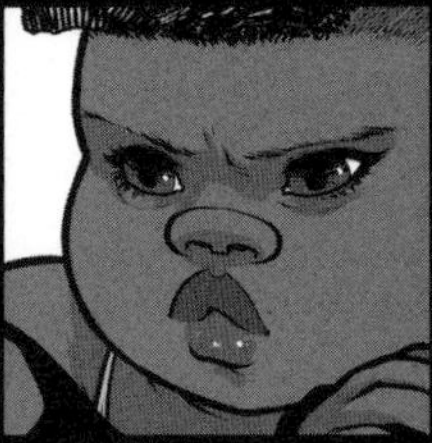
audrey richter
(19)

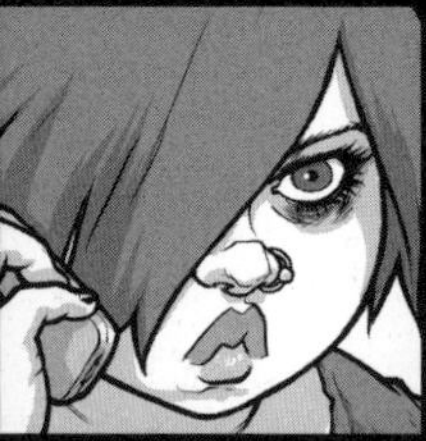
myrtle turenne
(19)

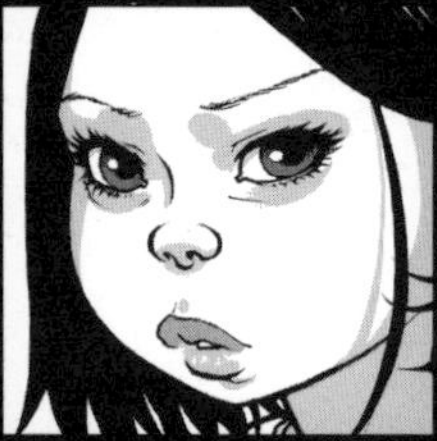
penny lovedrop
(23)

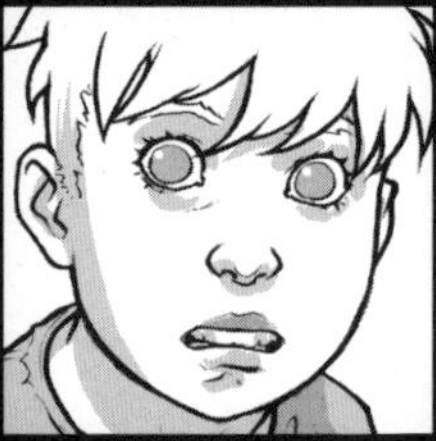
martin samson
(21)

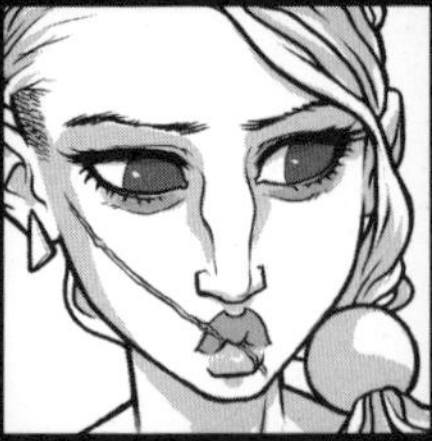
natalie ringtree
(21)

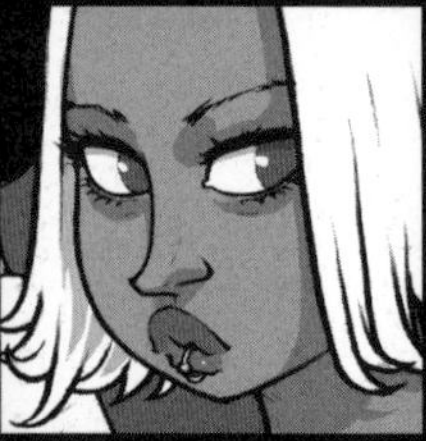
zia morlón
(19)

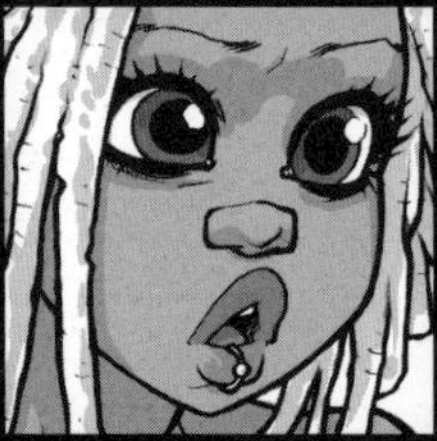
malady mayapple
(20)

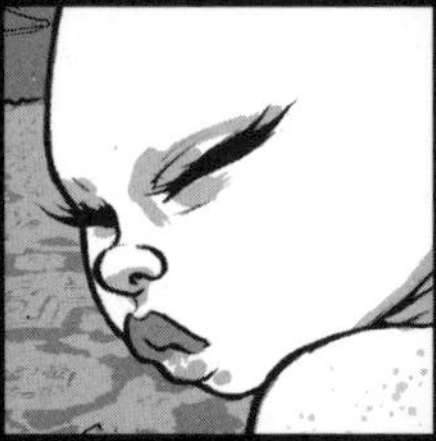
fern
(20)

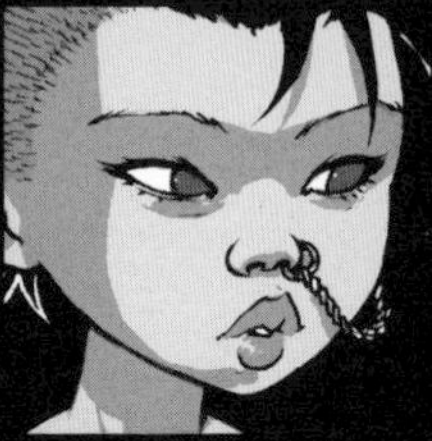
kinzoku
(19)

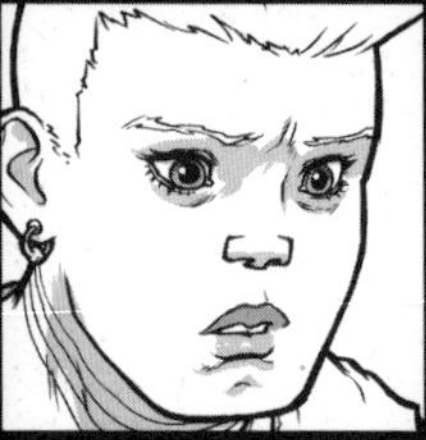
beth mckenzie
(17)

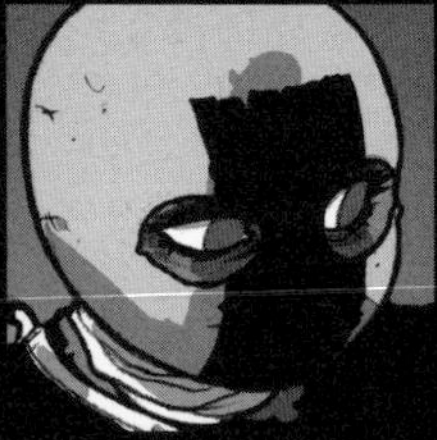
unknown
(?)

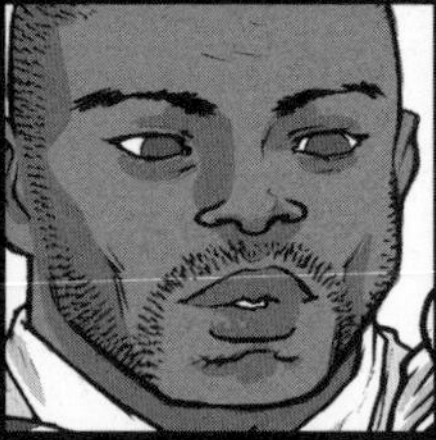
david wolfe
(37)

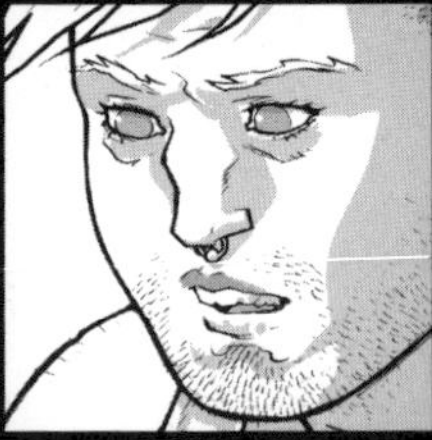
slicer
(26)

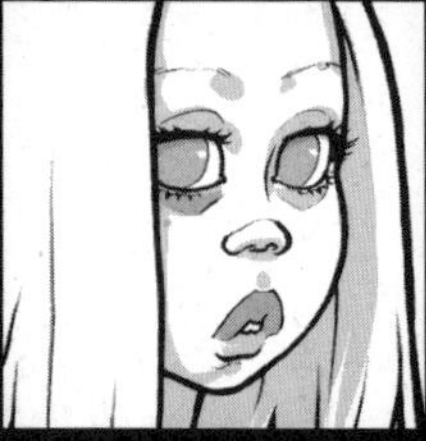
fall swanhilde
(15)

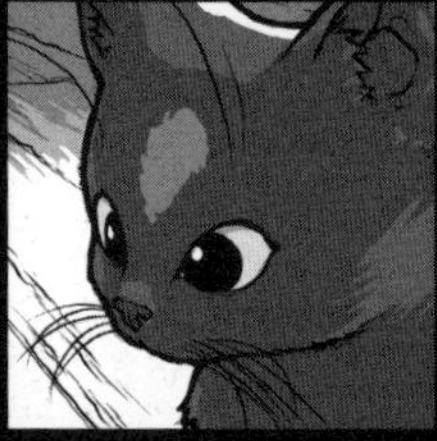
meiko
(5)

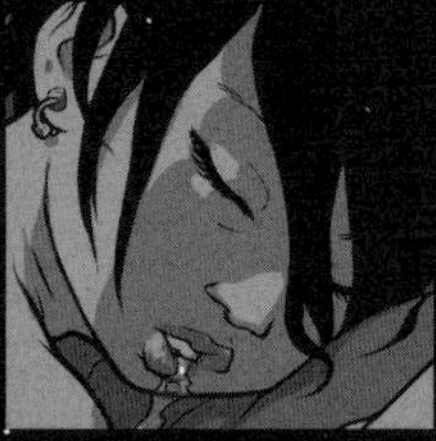
glen neuhoff
(20)

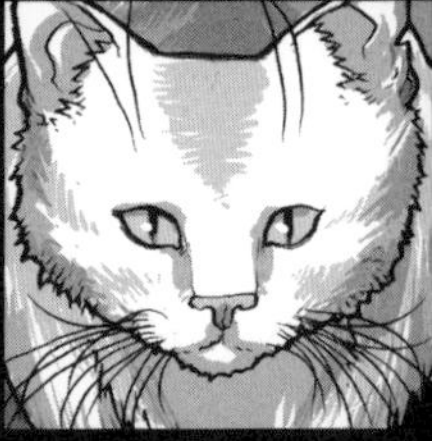
?
(?)

DAVID WOLFE

AGE: 37

SIGN: Taurus (April 24th)

HEIGHT: 6ft 2in

HAIR DYE: None

MAJOR: Majored in Law 18 years ago

HOMETOWN: Kansas City, Missouri

MUSIC: Nine Inch Nails, Coil, Rammstein

READING: Applied Thermal Engineering, NYU Law Review, American Journal of Primatology

MOVIES/TV: Bill Nye, any crime documentary series he can get his hands on, The Sopranos, Star Trek: The Next Generation and Deep Space Nine

LIKES: Antique lamps, pie, oatmeal, pottery, history, cherry tomatoes, paragliding, Madagascar, beer, and telescopes

DISLIKES: Halloween, birch trees, peanut butter, concerts, snakes, and carpeting

FUN FACTS:

- Wolfe's squirrel monkey sidekick, Booheith, is officially recognized by the FBI. The two met while Wolfe was investigating a murder case at a zoo in Oregon.

- Wolfe is acquainted with Trent Reznor.

UNKNOWN

AGE: Unknown but presumably between 20-25
SIGN: Unknown
HEIGHT: 5ft 8in
HAIR DYE: Unknown
MAJOR: Unknown
HOMETOWN: Unknown but presumably Wet Moon
MUSIC: Unknown
READING: Unknown
MOVIES/TV: Unknown
LIKES: Crimefighting, helping girls in trouble
DISLIKES: Unknown
FUN FACTS:
- Unknown's weapon of choice is a well-worn bokken.
- She has been operating in Wet Moon for only three months.

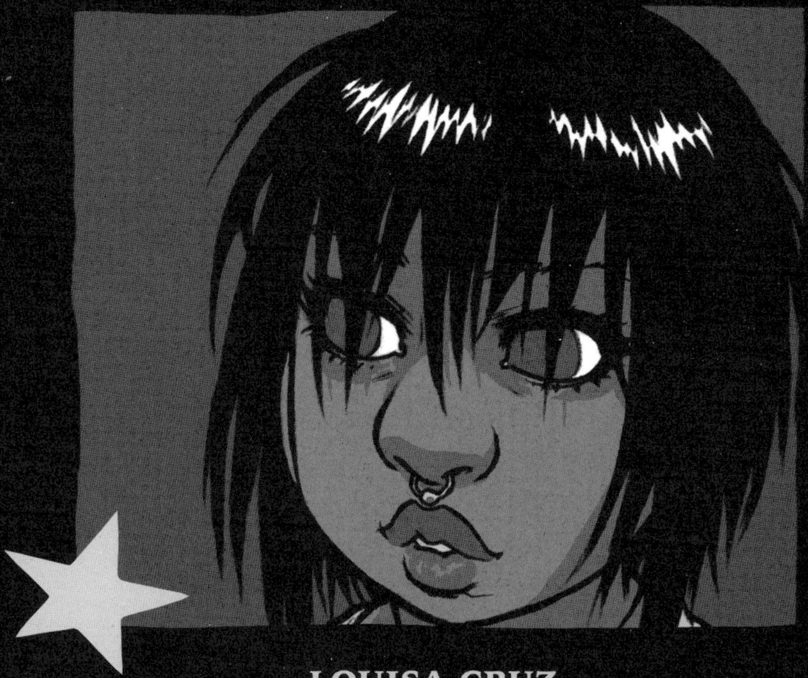

LOUISA CRUZ

AGE: 19
SIGN: Libra (October 3rd)
HEIGHT: 5ft 6in
HAIR DYE: None
MAJOR: None
HOMETOWN: Wet Moon, Florida
MUSIC: Cascada, S Club 7, Le Tigre, Madonna, Shakira, Beyoncé, Republica, Christina Aguilera
READING: Twilight, American Gods, Sherman Alexie, Monsoon Summer, A Great and Terrible Beauty
MOVIES/TV: American Idol, America's Next Top Model, Gossip Girl, The Fast and the Furious, Blue Crush, Pirates of the Caribbean
LIKES: Surfing, starfish, tennis, cloudy days with no rain, evening gowns, rambunctious puppies, the color combination of pale blue and beige, and drag shows
DISLIKES: Jellyfish, whales, curry, high heels, heavy metal music, and onions
FUN FACTS:
- Louisa is a prize-winning tennis player and surfer, and also plays on a local lacrosse team just for fun.
- She can bench press almost 200 pounds.

WHERE ALL STARS FAIL TO BURN

PLAYLIST

BELLA MORTE — **BURN THE SKY**
THE BIRTHDAY MASSACRE — **RED STARS**
NIGHTWISH — **FOR THE HEART I ONCE HAD**
FLATLINERZ — **RUN**
INDIA.ARIE — **WINGS OF FORGIVENESS**
BOOK OF LOVE — **YOU LOOK THROUGH ME**
KATE BUSH — **THIS WOMAN'S WORK**
ULTRAVOX — **HYMN**
CANNIBAL CORPSE — **MAKE THEM SUFFER**
MACHINES OF LOVING GRACE — **GOLGOTHA TENEMENT BLUES**
DEPECHE MODE — **THE DARKEST STAR**
IN THIS MOMENT — **INTO THE LIGHT**
WITHIN TEMPTATION — **FINAL DESTINATION**

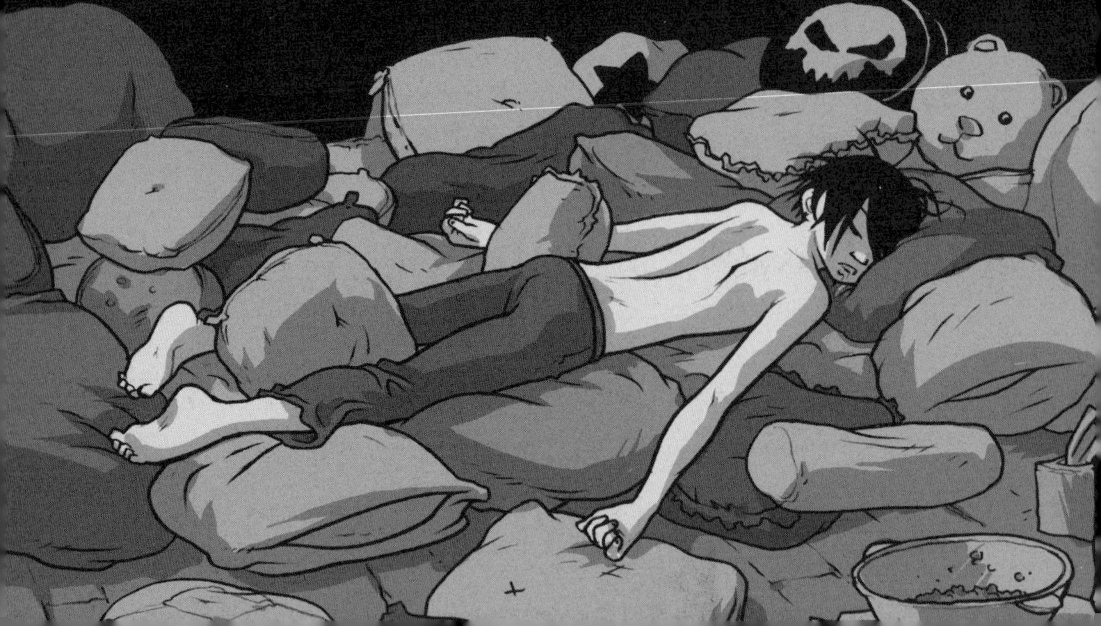

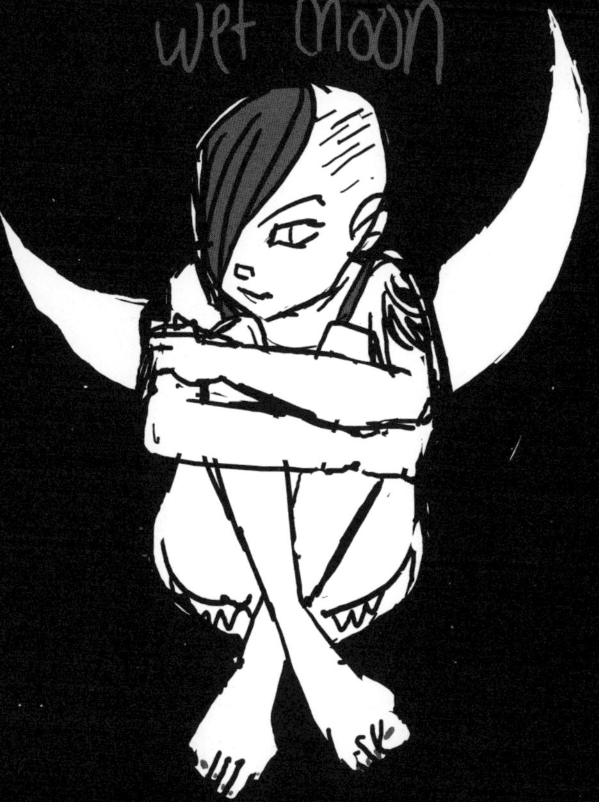
wet moon

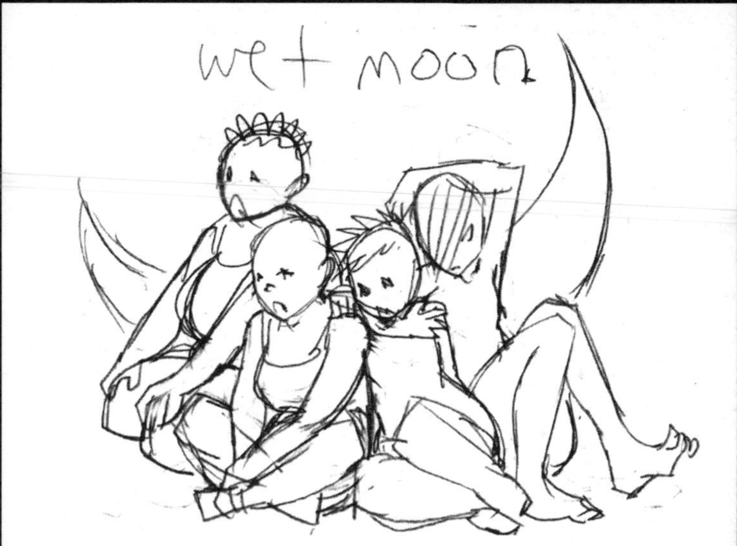
wet moon

SKETCHES FOR A POSSIBLE WET MOON T-SHIRT.

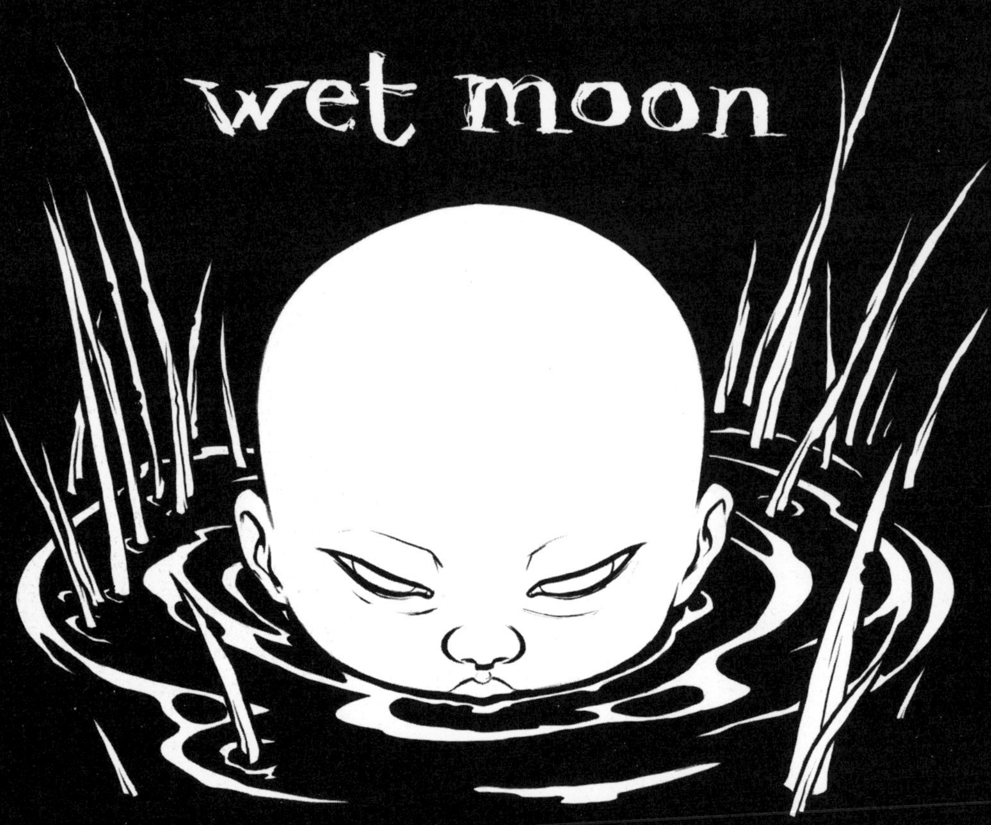
wet moon

DESIGN FOR A T-SHIRT THAT DEBUTED AT
SAN DIEGO COMIC-CON IN 2009.

CREATOR COMMENTARY

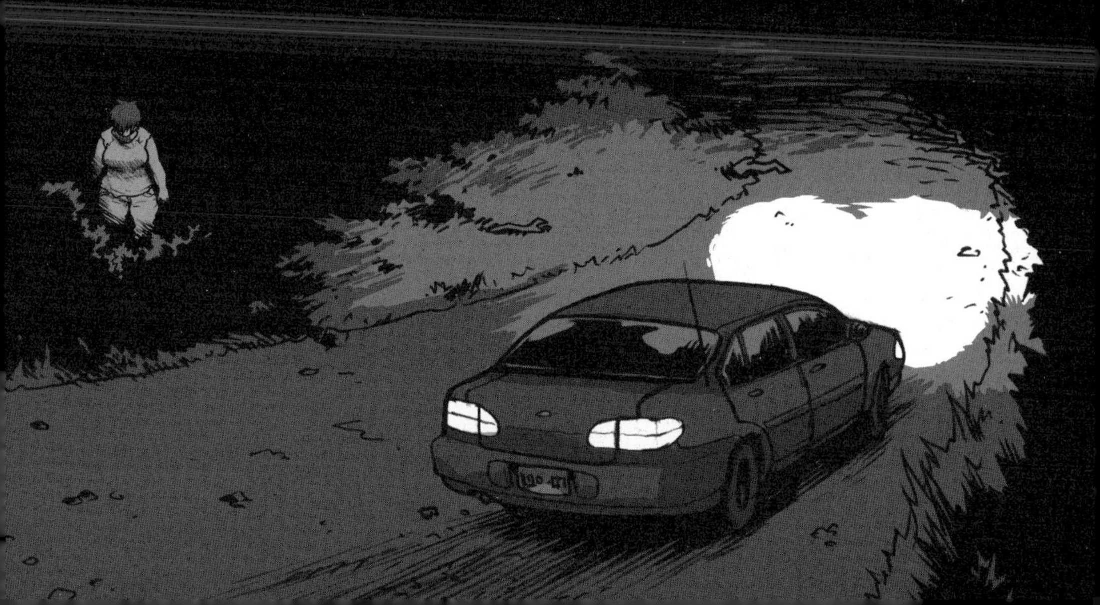

PAGE 13: I looked at so much softball reference, it was difficult! Drawing Beth's underhand pitch was particularly hard for me for some reason.

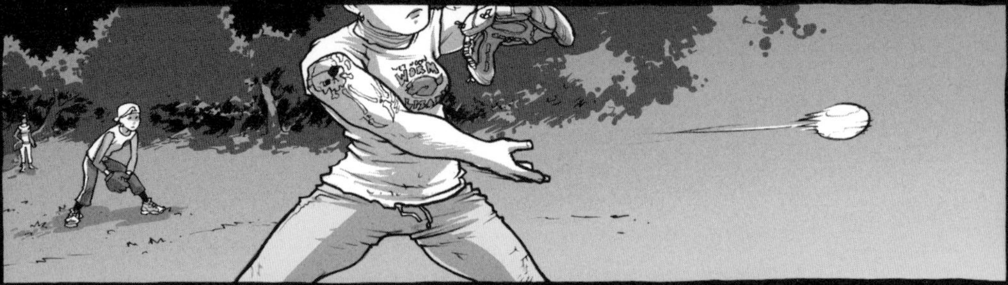
WET MOON
WORM
LIZARDS

PAGE 17, PANEL 4: I had been planning on a side story about the Worm Lizards but it fell by the wayside. Maybe some day! The girl on the far left is Galaxy and the girl next to Trilby is Nisha.

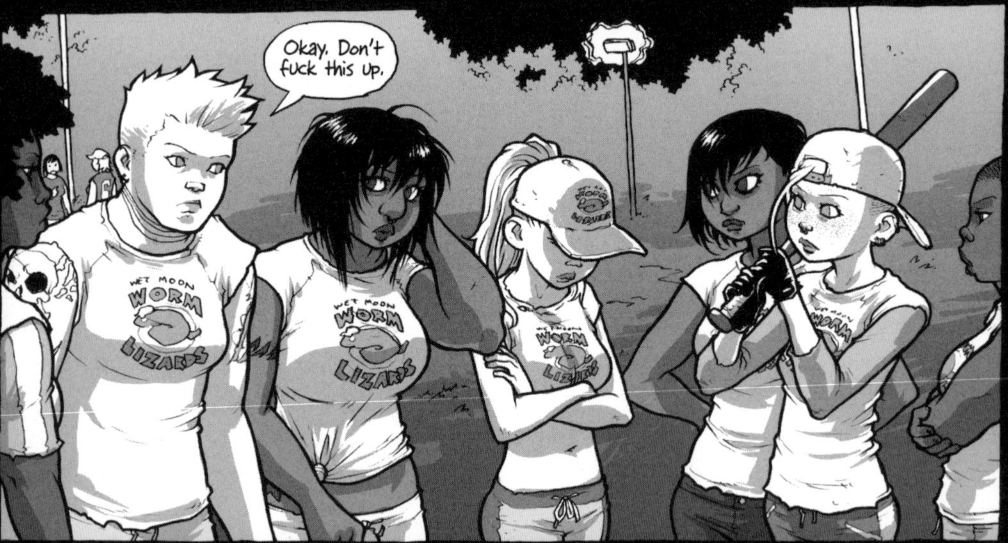
Okay. Don't fuck this up.
WET MOON
WORM
LIZARDS

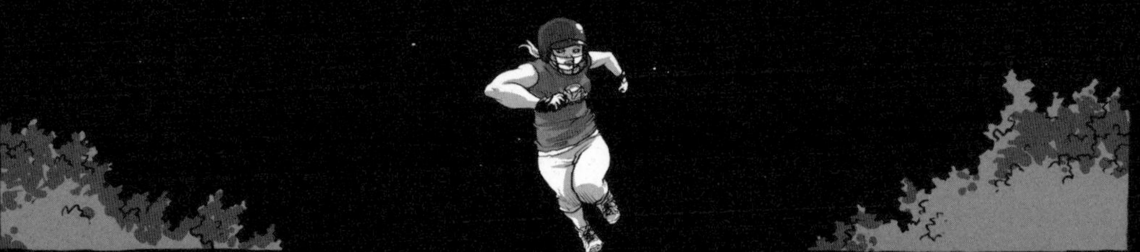

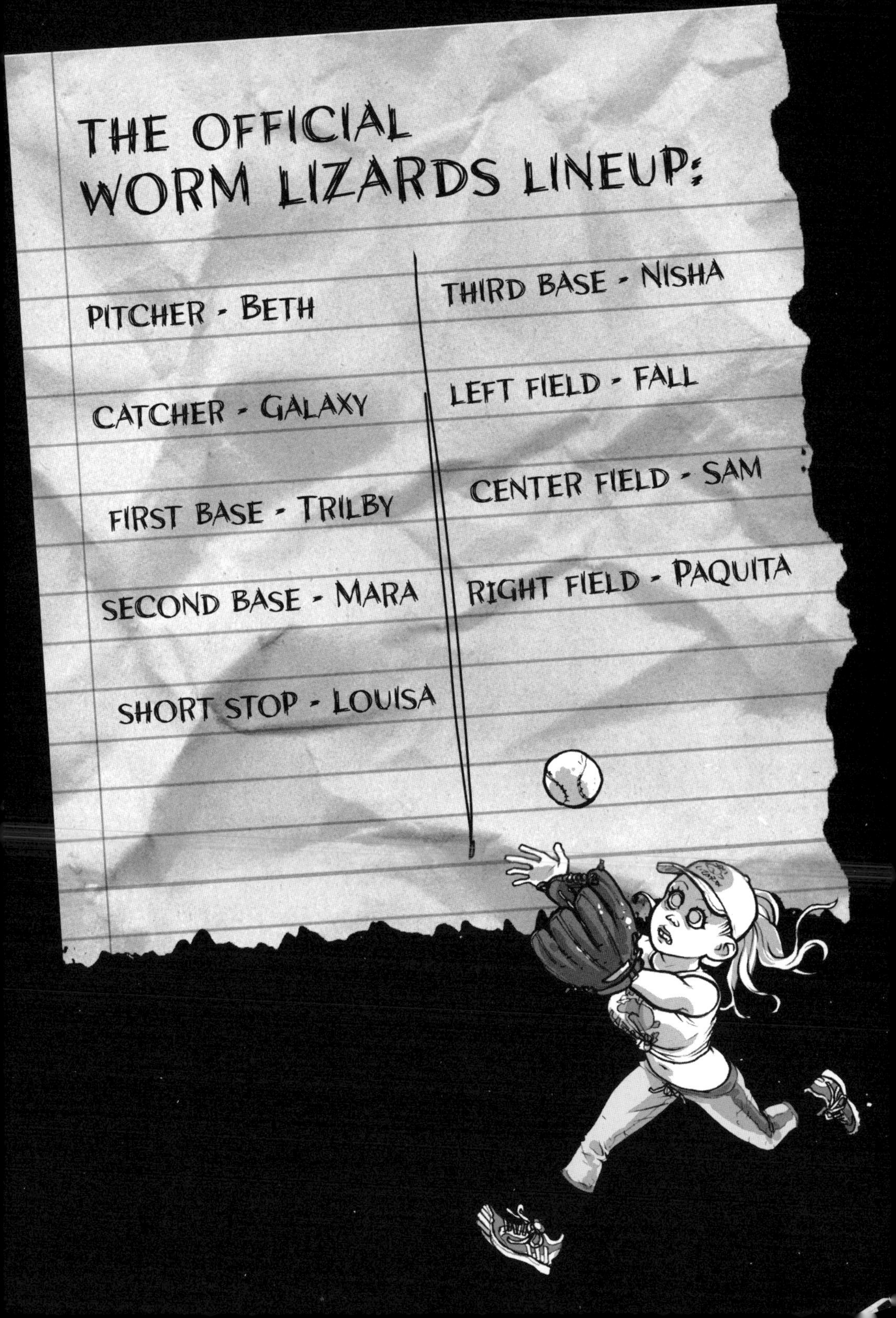
THE OFFICIAL WORM LIZARDS LINEUP:
PITCHER - BETH
CATCHER - GALAXY
FIRST BASE - TRILBY
SECOND BASE - MARA
SHORT STOP - LOUISA
THIRD BASE - NISHA
LEFT FIELD - FALL
CENTER FIELD - SAM
RIGHT FIELD - PAQUITA

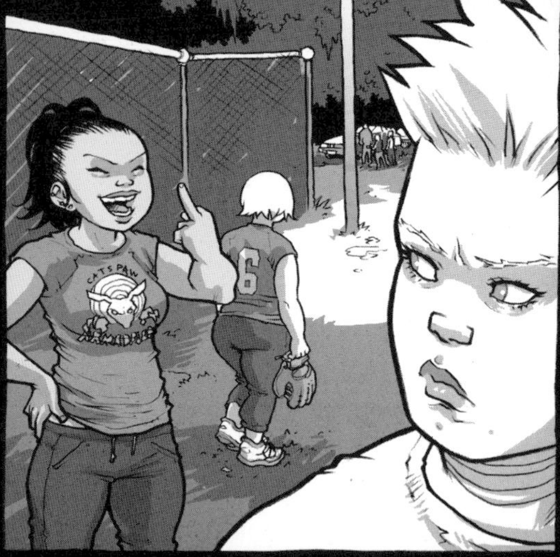
CATSPAW

PAGE 18: Catspaw is the next city over from Wet Moon, it's like the evil mirror universe city.

PAGE 19, PANEL 2: The girl Galaxy is talking to is named Paquita.

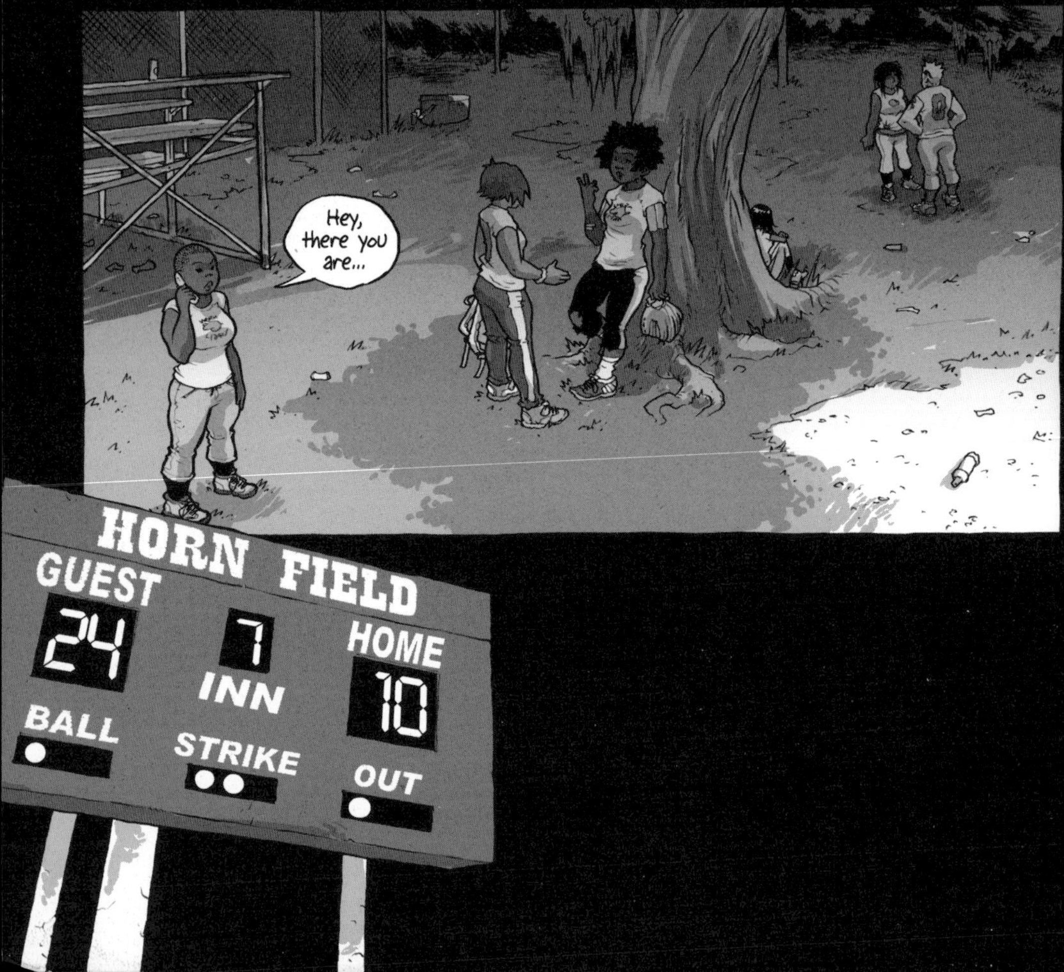
Hey, there you are...
HORN FIELD
GUEST
24
7
INN
HOME
10
BALL
STRIKE
OUT

PAGE 70: I think this single page encapsulates everything that Wet Moon is: A girl lying around in her underwear, Agent Wolfe and his monkey sidekick, Spanish moss, the college campus, and two punky lesbians talking about their feelings.

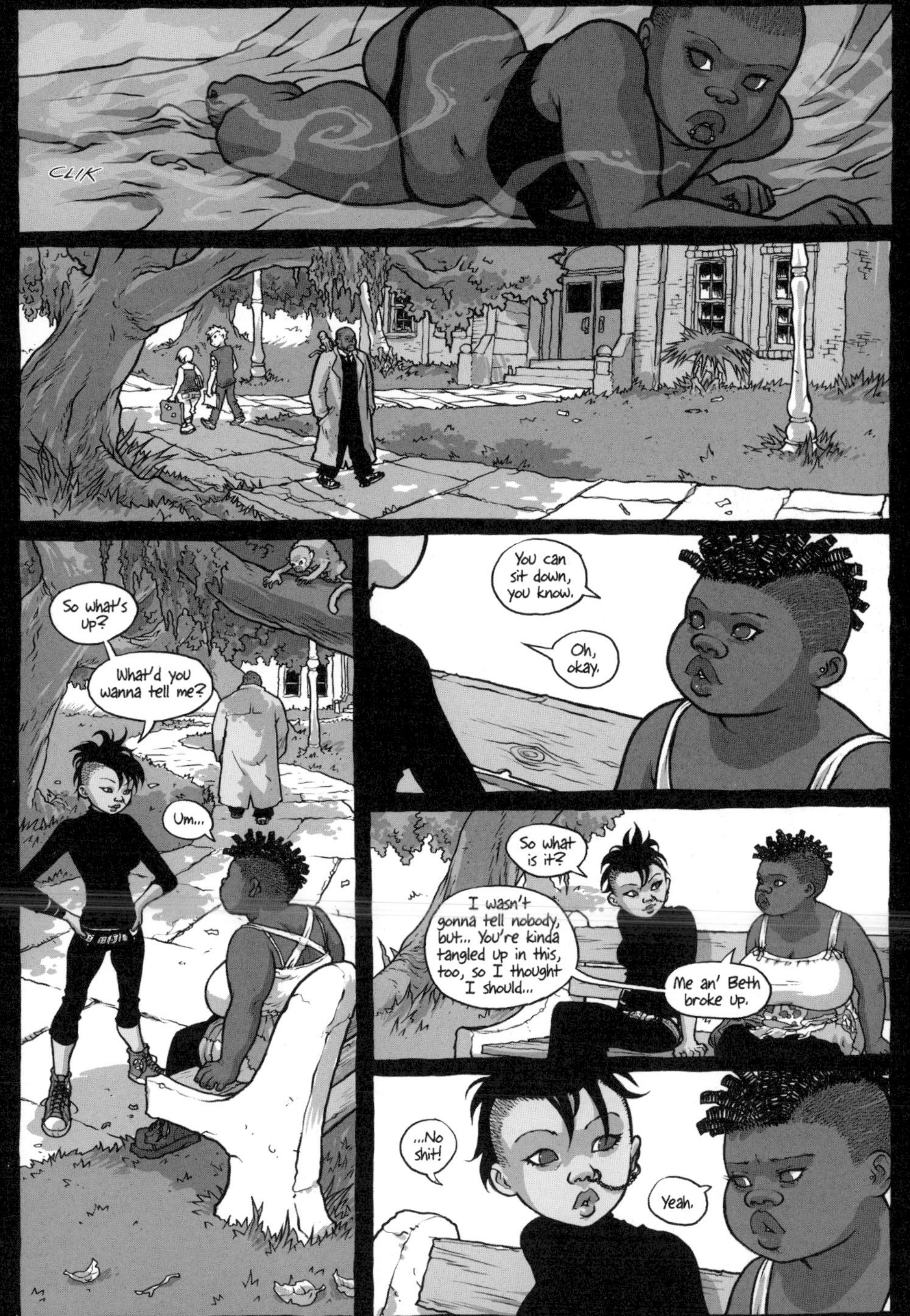
CLIK
So what's up?
What'd you wanna tell me?
Um...
You can sit down, you know.
Oh, okay.
So what is it?
I wasn't gonna tell nobody, but... You're kinda tangled up in this, too, so I thought I should...
Me an' Beth broke up.
...No shit!
Yeah.

PAGE 74: I always intended for Mara's tattoo to remain secret forever, but I'll reveal it here! It's a tattoo of the Tzimisce clan dragon symbol from Vampire: The Masquerade.

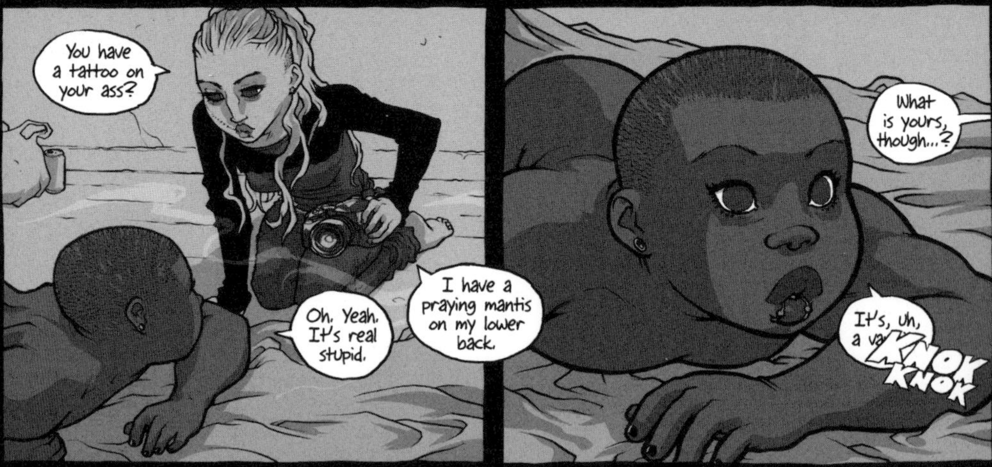

You have a tattoo on your ass?
Oh. Yeah. It's real stupid.
I have a praying mantis on my lower back.
What is yours, though...?
It's, uh, a va
KNOK KNOK

PAGE 80: Confession. I've never read *Harry Potter*. I've seen a couple of the movies, at least!

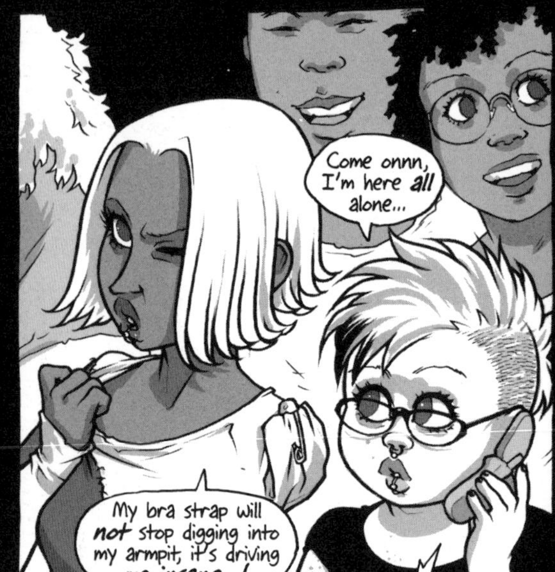

Come onnn, I'm here ***all*** alone...
My bra strap will ***not*** stop digging into my armpit, it's driving me ***insane***...!
Aren't you enveloped by Harry Potter nerds?
Yeah, but I'm not ***with*** them.

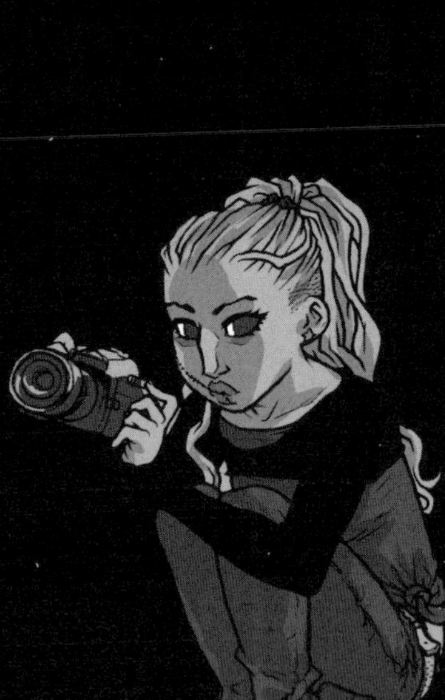

PAGES 94-95: At the time, I was really into the pupilless look for the characters' eyes, with pupils only showing up in panels that are a particularly emotional moment or "big" moment, but looking back on it I'm not sure it works.

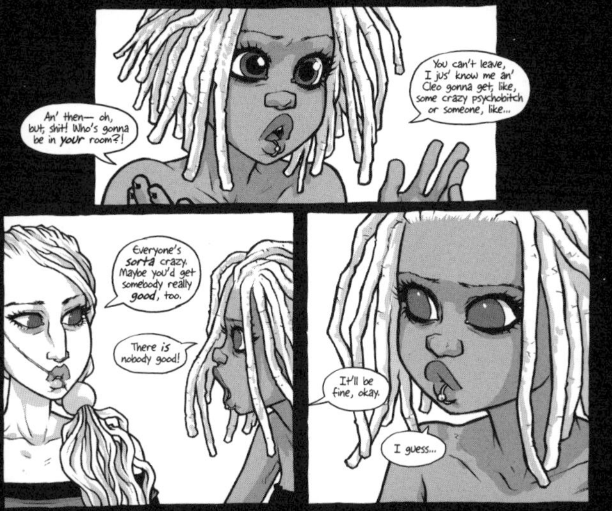
An' then— oh, but, shit! Who's gonna be in your room?!
You can't leave, I jus' know me an' Cleo gonna get, like, some crazy psychobitch or someone, like...
Everyone's sorta crazy. Maybe you'd get somebody really good, too.
There is nobody good!
It'll be fine, okay.
I guess...

PAGES 139-142: I had been planning this moment for years before getting to it in this book, but I almost called it off when I started actually drawing it. It was almost too much for me, but I made myself see it through. Even after all these years, I'm still not sure whether it was a good idea or not.

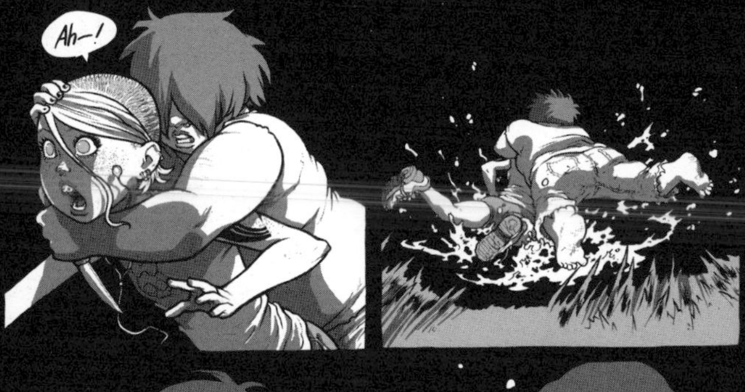
Ah—!
Myrtle—! Fh—
CHOK

SOPHIE CAMPBELL likes cats, Gamera, tea, *Final Fantasy 7*, and ice cream. She hates frogs, snakes, dogs, and traveling. She currently resides in Rochester, New York.

FOLLOW SOPHIE AT:

—*twitter.com/mooncalfe1*—*mooncalfe.tumblr.com*—
—*mooncalfe-art.tumblr.com*—*shadoweyescomic.tumblr.com*—
—*cantlookbackcomic.tumblr.com*—

MORE WET MOON

Wet Moon, Book 1:
Feeble Wanderings

ISBN 978-1-62010-304-3

OUT NOW!

Wet Moon, Book 2:
Unseen Feet

ISBN 978-1-62010-328-9

OUT NOW!

Wet Moon, Book 3:
Further Realms of Fright

ISBN 978-1-62010-329-6

OUT NOW!

Wet Moon, Book 4:
Drowned in Evil

ISBN 978-1-62010-330-2

OUT NOW!

Wet Moon, Book 6:
Yesterday's Gone

ISBN 978-1-62010-332-6

New Edition Available
SPRING 2018!

Wet Moon, Book 7:

COMING SOON!

ONI
PRESS
www.onipress.com